Detroit
Reprints
in
Music

Frederick Freedman, General Editor
Case Western Reserve University

LIFE
OF
ROBERT SCHUMANN

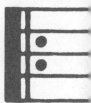

BY
JOSEPH WILHELM VON WASIELEWSKI

TRANSLATED BY
A. L. ALGER

WITH
NEW INTRODUCTION
BY
LEON PLANTINGA

Detroit Reprints in Music
INFORMATION COORDINATORS
1975

Copyright © 1975 by Information Coordinators, Inc.
Library of Congress Catalog Card Number 74-75897
International Standard Book Number 911772-71-5

Printed and bound in the United States of America
Designed by Vincent Kibildis
Published by
Information Coordinators, Inc.
1435-37 Randolph Street
Detroit, Michigan 48226

Introduction

J. W. von Wasielewski's *Life of Robert Schumann* has always occupied a special place in the literature on this composer. Wasielewski was an estimable musician and music historian who came into personal contact with Schumann during two rather widely-spaced periods: first as a young student at the Leipzig Conservatory in 1844-1845 when Schumann was a teacher there, and later during 1851-1852 as concertmaster of the Civic Orchestra of Düsseldorf when Schumann was its conductor. It was during this latter period that Wasielewski began to collect materials with a view to producing a biography; the work appeared promptly in 1858, only two years after Schumann's death.

Wasielewski worked with the thoroughness of a seasoned scholar. He tirelessly sought out Schumann's companions from earlier years, prodded their memories for bits of unknown information, and collected from them an impressive store of letters and other pertinent documents. (In fascinating asides the author tells us what became of Schumann's student friends of the late 1820s: Töpken, for example, was to be Doctor of Jurisprudence in Bremen, while Sörgel "went to Texas and has never been heard of since.") Church and municipal records were culled for factual data, and after the composer's death the biographer even managed to secure the report of a private autopsy. Only one essential source of information remained closed to him: Clara Schumann, for unknown reasons, steadfastly refused to co-operate in the venture.

The result of Wasielewski's ingenuity and zeal is one of the most reliable "eye-witness" biographies of a composer we have. Based much more upon documentary matter than the Griesinger or Dies biographies of Haydn, much more discriminating in the use of such evidence than Nissen's Mozart biography, and without a trace of the tendentiousness of Schindler's reminiscences of Beethoven, Wasielewski's account of the events of Schumann's life is a spare, discerning, and for the most part accurate narrative. Modern readers may be impatient with some details. As Wasielewski records Schumann's move from Heidelberg to Leipzig, from the study of law to the study of music, he reports earnestly on the state of the young man's heart (it is "full, glad, and hopeful"), without even telling us just when this momentous event occurred. But such reservations that we may have about Wasielewski's judgment are probably rooted more in the diversity of sensibility between his century and ours than in any question of substance—for even the information we are offered about Schumann's state of mind reflects not Wasielewski's inventiveness, but his study of the young composer's letters.

Subsequent biographies of Schumann up to the Second World War do not significantly alter this premiere portrait of Schumann's life, though through the efforts of Gustav Jansen, Martin Kreisig, Georg Eismann and others the store of documentary information about the composer and his life was steadily increasing. It had long been known that Schumann was a compulsive keeper of "books:" account books, correspondence books, and diaries. Many of these have been preserved; the largest collection is in the Robert Schumann-Haus in Zwickau. During the early 1940s Wolfgang Boetticher published tantalizing scraps from these sources in *Robert Schumann in seinen Schriften und Briefen*, and in his gargantuan *Robert Schumann: Einführung in Persönlichkeit und Werk*. But in these books Schumann's life and writings are pressed into the service of extraneous ideological causes, and the cause of accurate and objective biography is scarcely advanced.

Schumann's diaries and other personal documents are now at last appearing in a meticulous edition by VEB Deutscher Verlag in Leipzig. The first volume (containing the diaries up to 1838) promises rich dividends in new information. The testimony of Schumann's friend Emil Flechsig that the young law student-musician "never entered a lecture hall" seems amply borne out. And there are engaging discrepancies between the student life Schumann described to his mother (brewing coffee at five o'clock in the morning for a brisk early start at his work—see the letter below on pp. 56–57) and the late hours and fearful hangovers vividly chronicled in these early diaries. On the basis of this and other emerging evidence perhaps we can hope for an early appearance of the first modern, comprehensive, critical biography of Schumann.

The avowed aim of this book is to provide a clear and correct narrative of the events of Schumann's life. Any discussion of his music remains decidedly secondary; and it is here that the present-day reader is most likely to take issue with some of the author's judgments. Wasielewski prefers big pieces to small ones; in a sense he shared Schumann's own conviction that the ultimate goal of a composer must be the creation of original but structurally coherent large-scale works. Most of the piano compositions of the 1830s, including the sonatas, lack the formal cohesion Wasielewski demands; the songs are admired in passing, but as lyrical *Kleinigkeiten* and nothing more. It is only in his symphonies and chamber music (most particularly the piano quintet) that Schumann wins Wasielewski's unstinting praise. Many of us might feel that the biographer thus misses some of the best of Schumann. But at least his book is a work of integrity and candor; he is sure of his facts and of his opinions, and both he reports to us faithfully.

This translation by A. L. Alger first made Wasielewski's work available to English readers in 1871. One might cavil at certain peculiarities in the translator's procedures: sometimes German titles like *Neue Zeitschrift für Musik* and *Allgemeine musikalische Zeitung* are (needlessly) reduced to English equivalents, and sometimes not. There are occasional plain mistakes: the German musical term *Akkord*, for example, means "chord," not "accord." Yet, overall, the translation is an acceptable one, and it is useful to bring Wasielewski's worthy effort to the attention of the English-reading public once more in this form.

Leon Planting

Yale University
June 1974

VIII

LIFE

OF

ROBERT SCHUMANN.

BY

VON WASIELWSKI.

TRANSLATED BY

A. L. ALGER.

———•———

BOSTON:
OLIVER DITSON COMPANY.

NEW YORK: CHICAGO: PHILA: BOSTON:
C. H. Ditson & Co.   Lyon & Healy.   J. E. Ditson & Co.   John C. Haynes & Co.

STEREOTYPED BY C. J. PETERS & SON,
5 WASHINGTON ST., BOSTON.

PRINTED BY GEO. P. CARTER & CO.

CONTENTS.

I.

II.

INTRODUCTORY.

THESE pages do not pretend to give an exhaustive critical analysis nor a comprehensive æsthetic critique of ROBERT SCHUMANN'S
works, but simply his biography. I have confined myself to the
close inspection of such compositions as mark important and decisive moments in his development. Besides this, particular examination is made of that field of art in which Schumann labored.

It is in many respects desirable to determine the facts of Schumann's life. Already, all sorts of inexact and erroneous reports concerning his history have been spread abroad, both verbally and in
writing ; therefore an impartial statement, founded on carefully-sifted
oral and documental accounts, seems necessary, and at once, in order
that any errors unconsciously committed by me may be corrected by
contemporaries. I have abstained from all controversy in this account : the facts speak for themselves. A history of the artistic development of this significant character seems of the rarest historico-
musical interest ; for it gives a picture of an artist's life, with its
struggles and labors, repeated in its outlines in other characters of
the present time, as it stands in close connection and reciprocal action
with the modern aims and intellectual emotions of music. And
Robert Schumann was so rare a nature, that his creative powers,
especially at the outset, can be fully understood and correctly judged
only by a knowledge of his life and its manifold conditions.

Our tone-poet himself says, " It is impertinent to judge a whole
life by a single action ; since the moment which threatens to over-
throw a system may often be explained and justified." And farther
on, " With some timidity, I express my opinion of works, with
whose forerunners I am unacquainted. I would gladly know somewhat of a composer's school, his youthful views, his exemplars, ay,
even of his actions the circumstances of his life, — in a word, some-

7

what of the whole man and artist as he has hitherto proved himself." *   All this is applicable to no one better than to himself.

Robert Schumann does not belong to those masters whose artistic
creations form a row of pictures in constantly ascending scale, which
afford throughout immediate and easily admissible delight : the
productions of his mind never became objective, and never broke
loose, or freed themselves from his individual self so far that the
knowledge of their origin essential to the intrinsic meaning was
lost.   He belonged to those, who, in many cases, enter into daily
events, and create tone pictures from them.   Such creations, often
leaving behind an indissoluble breach, can only be understood when
one looks behind and beyond them for the motives of their origin,
and for the peculiar circumstances under which they were conceived
and depicted.   For this reason, a great deal is heard, on the one
side, of the obscurity of Schumann's compositions; and, on the
other, complaints, with an accent of reproach, of their purpose :
while a nature stands before them, showing itself *exactly* as it is,
and as the peculiar relations of its organization with the impressions made by life have shaped it.   Objective artistic work points
back to the subjective quality of the creating artist ; and the purpose
of these pages is to show this intelligibly.   They may serve to illustrate how Schumann's method in art and in life, and the numerous
monuments thereof, could not have been created otherwise than as
they appear to the unprejudiced and dispassionate observer.   *His-
toric truth*, so far as man is able to render it, is thus the accent which
must be most distinctly sounded.

Let me say, as excuse and cause for this work, that, being from
October, 1850, to May, 1851, as well as from October, 1851, to June,
1852, in almost daily never-to-be-forgotten intercourse with Robert
Schumann in Düsseldorf, and specially called upon by the accounts
of his early life and works, received from his own lips, in the course
of conversation in the summer of 1853, I resolved to write down
these records of the master's artist-life.†   This resolve was confirmed, when, on my writing to him, he readily sent me material for
its execution.   This material was in a book; which contained, be-

---

* See R. Schumann's collected works (Leipsic, Geo. Wigand), vol. i., p. 87.
† So far as I know, Fr. Brendel was the first to make a comprehensive study
of Schumann and his works. See New Journal for Music, pages 22, 63, 89,
113, 121, 145, 149, and Fr. Brendel's History of Music, vol. ii.

sides a brief summary of musical composition in his own hand, most valuable accounts of the master's youth and life up to 1834 A series of pages also explained many plans, some of which had been carried out, others left unfinished. The more I reflected on my plan, the farther I advanced in it, the clearer it became to me that it would be impossible to say any thing worthy of notice concerning a certain portion of Schumann's leading works to those who had not heard all that is connected with them. My task, although successful in a certain degree, from that circumstance, is nowhere entirely satisfactory ; but it is not in vain, since it has taught me to know the right.

When, in the beginning of August, 1856, the mournful news of Schumann's death spread through Germany, I returned to my idea of undertaking his biography ; which had also received incitement from occurrences and events communicated to me. I at once began to collect the requisite materials, addressing inquiries to every source known and accessible to me. To my great content, I can say that they resulted most favorably. My two visits to Zwickau were productive of interesting information from eye-witnesses, not only concerning his childhood, but I also found the desired opportunity for informing myself in regard to a later period of his life, from acquaintances of the master, and thus gradually completed the picture of this glorious spirit which I had conceived in my mind.

Besides this, letters of the most valuable description were sent me, at my request, describing Schumann's early residence in Leipsic and Heidelberg, by the Messrs. ROSEN of Detmold, Councillor SEMMEL of Gera, and Dr. JUR. TÖPKEN of Bremen, and from many other sources.

I finally made a most considerable collection of Schumann's letters, soon almost reaching the number of two hundred. I know very well, that this is by no means even the major portion of the letters written by him ; but my plan never ought or could extend to a complete collection of Schumann's letters. I therefore contented myself with my acquisitions, which suffice to explain certain passages in his career, or to unveil his rich soul-life. I have incorporated the larger half with this text, wherever it was feasible, some being added in an appendix,* under the heading " Letters for 1833 –

* This appendix has lately been increased by a number of hitherto unpublished letters.

1853." They are unchanged, and in the original words, wherever regard for living persons or unimportant tenor does not render the suppression of passages necessary or desirable. Such passages are marked.

Messrs. STEPHEN HELLER of Paris, ADOLPH HENSELT of St. Petersburg, and Dr. F. LISZT, musical director at the royal chapel in Weimar, regretted that they were unable to comply with my request for some Schumann letters, since all in their possession had been lost.

I think it would be wrong to omit saying, that I applied to Mrs. CLARA SCHUMANN, who lives on the memories of her husband in the most dignified manner, begging her to aid me in my work; to which she replied, that reverence for her husband would prevent her assisting me with her insufficient materials.

By the beginning of the year, I had so far advanced towards the completion of my arrangement that I was able to begin my task.

I here offer to the musical world whatever remarkable facts I have been able to learn concerning Robert Schumann; which I have endeavored to frame, in the persuasion that *nothing essential* has been omitted.

Allow me here to express my hearty thanks to all those who so kindly and speedily assisted me to reach the goal I strived for.

                                        VON WASIELEWSKI.
DRESDEN, Nov. 1857.

I.

ROBERT SCHUMANN'S CHILDHOOD, YOUTH, AND STUDENT LIFE.

ZWICKAU, LEIPSIC, HEIDELBERG.

1810 — 1830.

R OBERT SCHUMANN, as far as we can discover, sprang from a family by no means musical.

His father, Friedrich August Gottlob Schumann,[*] was the eldest son of a poor pastor, Friedrich Gottlob Schumann, in the village of Entschütz, near Gera, afterwards archdeacon of Weida. He was, at an early age, intended for a merchant, and, in his eleventh or twelfth year,[†] was sent to his grandmother's house, in the town of Eisenberg, that he might attend the Latin School there; which he left at the age of fifteen, and was apprenticed to a merchant in Nonneburg. After this, he passed several years, full of difficulties, trials, and distresses, called forth by his mistaken choice of a profession.

August Schumann was highly gifted in a literary way, as he showed by many early attempts at poetry. His parents, not appreciating his talent, persuaded him to devote himself to trade: however, innate inclination urged him unceasingly on

---

[*] The following communications concerning him are taken from the biography written by C. E. Richter, published, in 1826, by the brothers Schumann, in Zwickau.

[†] *Pierer's Universal Dictionary of Biography* says Aug. Schumann was born in 1773. The biography quoted above gives no date.

to the study of scientific and æsthetic works. Prominent
among them were the writings of Young and Milton; which
interested him, and, according to his own confession, "at
times almost drove him mad."

No wonder, when his chosen vocation grew more and more
repulsive, and *nothing occurred to force him*, at least to declare
his preference for literature. However, poor as he was, this
desire, and its final realization, were only purchased by long
and severe mental struggles and material deprivations. The
result was a feeble constitution, which he never entirely outgrew, and which cut his thread of life in the strength of man-
hood.

August Schumann soon forsook his mercantile life in Leipsic,
where, after many changes of condition in various places, he
had obtained a situation in a mercantile establishment. When
so near the fount of knowledge, the eager and assiduous youth
could no longer repress his desires. He was registered at the
Leipsic University as *studiosus humaniorum*, sure that, after
sufficient study, he could earn his living by literature. He
therefore wrote to Heinse* of Zeitz, sending one of his articles for examination. The latter decidedly dissuaded him
from his plan. In no wise deterred by this, he steadfastly
followed his chosen path. For a long time his labor was vain.
Extreme poverty forced him to return to his parent's house.
Here he composed a romance: "Knightly Scenes and Monk-
ish Tales," which he sent to Heinse, begging his advice. This
step won as little recognition of his efforts as the first; but the
result was, that Heinse asked him to enter his bookstore as
assistant. He accepted the more gladly, that he thus not only
could earn his living, but become familiar with the most recent
literary productions. Another event made his stay in Zeitz
important. Fate led him to a maiden, the daughter of his
host, who afterwards became his wife. The engagement was

---

* Not to be confounded with the well-known author, Wilhelm Heinse.
This one was a bookseller, and also engaged in literature. — See *Pierer's
Universal Dictionary of Biography.*

allowed, on the condition that Schumann should leave the book-trade and set up for himself, since Heinse's long-established business offered no inducements from a lucrative point of view. Although this condition at once reduced him to naked prose, nothing was now necessary to enable him to gratify his heart's desire but submission to the demands of his future father-in-law. But whence should he obtain means for an establishment of his own? Here, too, his fertile mind discovered an expedient. He left Heinse at once, and returned home, in order to earn the requisite amount by literary labor. How well and how soon he succeeded is shown by the fact, that, after a year and a half of arduous and assiduous toil, he received for different works almost 1,000 thalers, — at that time a handsome sum. Among these writings, " The Merchant's Compendium," in four volumes, well known in the mercantile world, is deserving of mention.

In the year 1795 he went into partnership with a merchant of Nonneburg, and soon after married the faithful chosen one of his heart. After the lapse of four years, he again gave up the business he had acquired, to devote himself for the rest of his life to book-selling. In his newly-established sphere of action, Schumann displayed an untiring and ceaseless industry in different directions; which even cast in shadow his earlier efforts, but which gradually increased his means: he wrote sixteen works, some on literary, others on business topics, which he published himself. The gradual increase of his business rendered his removal to a more favorably situated city desirable : he therefore decided, in 1808, to remove to the Saxon mountain mining town of Zwickau. Here he entered into a partnership with one of his brothers; which lasted till 1840, under the name, well known in literary circles, of the " Brothers Schumann."

His business soon began to flourish. At this time he prepared a pocket edition of the classics of all nations; which gave the signal for many other undertakings of the same kind. He then established a journal, the " Mountain Mine Messenger " (1808–1812), which was followed by the " Leaves of Memory "

2

(1813–1826). In 1813, he published two large compilations. One was " The Saxon Cyclopædia " (Staats-Post und Zeitungs Lexikon), continued and completed by A. Schiffner (in all thirteen volumes and five supplements). The other was called " Portraits of Contemporaneous Celebrities," text annexed. *

One of Schumann's last efforts as publisher was a German translation of Walter Scott and Byron. The poems of the latter author filled him with such enthusiasm, that he translated " Beppo " and " Childe Harold " himself.

From this concise account, which contains none but essential facts, it is evident that our tone-master's father was a man who, spite of manifold changes and reverses, by untiring industry and a happy use of his talents, won results which inspired universal respect. Although his efforts in the realm of poetry were only of relative worth, we cannot deny that they gained some notice through the literary requirements of certain circles : they also testify to quite uncommon endowments and rare effort on the part of a practical business man ; while the above-mentioned compilations earned him an honorable and enduring name in the literary world.

August Schumann would be unanimously described as honest and reliable ; as one who, despite many weaknesses, possessed the love and affection of all who were brought into intimate relations with him. In person, he was slight but well-formed : his features, as shown by a still-existing portrait, taken at the age of thirty-eight, were benevolent and noble in expression, but decidedly indicate a quiet, reserved, and earnest disposition. This disposition, whose characteristic signs may have been stamped upon his countenance by the conflicts of his life, seems to have been retained even in later years.

As already mentioned, August Schumann married, in 1795, Johanna Christiana Schnabel, † eldest daughter of Abraham

---

* Robert Schumann, then but fourteen years old, assisted in the preparation of this text.

† The date of Schumann's mother's birth has not been handed down to us. All search in church registers was vain.

Gottlob Schnabel, chief surgeon of Zeitz. The official notice in the church books reads as follows: "August Schumann, merchant proprietor of Nonneburg, lawful son of the Right Reverend Johann Friedrich Schumann, arch-deacon of Weida, and Johanna Christiana Schnabel, the lawful eldest daughter of Abraham Gottlob Schnabel, chief surgeon of Zeitz, had their banns published on the 19th, 20th, and 21st Sundays after Trinity (i.e. on the 11th, 18th, and 25th of October), 1795, and then received the holy rite of matrimony at Geusznitz." *

Johanna Schumann, endowed with innate intelligence, yet educated under the influence of provincial, narrowing circumstances, showed no special culture; although she was attractive in appearance, and gifted with a certain talent for display. In later years she fell into an exaggerated state of romance and sentimentalism, united with sudden and violent passion, and an inclination to singularity, to which conjugal differences may have contributed.

Five children were the result of this marriage; of whom Robert, born on the 8th of June, 1810, at half-past nine in the evening, † at Zwickau, in the fifth house on the market-place, was the youngest. Before him came three brothers, Edward, Carl, and Julius; also a sister, Emilie. It is noteworthy that the latter died in the beginning of her twentieth year, in consequence of an incurable melancholy, which gave unmistakable signs of quiet madness. His brothers also all died before he did.

Robert's early years were principally passed in the society of women. Besides his mother, there was his God-mother, the wife of Burgomaster Ruppius of Zwickau, a very dear friend of the whole Schumann family; who took a great interest in him, and in whose house he often spent whole days and nights. We may feel assured, that being the youngest, and so-called "handsome child," he was accustomed to a great deal of petting

* A village near Zeitz.

† According to the parish register of St. Mary's Church, Zwickau. It also says that Robert was christened on the fourteenth of the same month.

and attention; since his father, occupied with business, could never or rarely bestow any thought upon his son's early education. As he advanced in years, it was still the same; for, as his talents developed, Robert became the spoilt darling, not only of the whole family, but of all who knew him. He scarcely ever had a wish ungratified,— a doubtful good; which in most cases produces evil results, and probably induced that extreme irritability and susceptibility, ay, that obstinacy when his will was opposed, which characterized Schumann's riper years.

Robert's later life proved him to be more highly endowed by nature than any of his brothers and sisters. We are led to suppose that he inherited with increased power the mental and physical constitution of his father, who, at the time of his birth, was very feeble; but he also seemed to possess some share of his mother's nature.

In the beginning of his sixth year, Robert was sent to Archdeacon Döhner's * school. This was a popular private school, which then supplied the place of a grammar-school in Zwickau. Here he was first brought into contact with a number of children of his own age; and as men early unconsciously display a love for certain qualities, so Robert soon chose a select few from among his companions for closer intercourse.† The first symptoms of one of his characteristic attributes now began to appear. This was ambition; which, as often shown in his future life, was always of the most rare and noble kind. Even then, although naïvely and unconsciously, it was plainly revealed as a characteristic feature of the child's mind. It made Robert the life of every game; and in their favorite, "Soldiers," he was always captain. The others yielded to his rule without a struggle; because they all loved him as a generous, good-na-

---

Formerly on the school committee, and a member of the consistory.

† Among these, Schumann himself names as his oldest friend Emil Herzog, a physician in Zwickau, who became known through a history of that town. Nor must we omit to mention, that he first suggested the erection of a memorial to Robert Schumann in his native town.

tured, friendly fellow. So Schumann, from his youth up, was the personification of command, unconsciously exemplifying that old sentence, "Ever striving to be first, and to outrun the rest," which afterwards became his watchword in struggle.

His progress at school was followed by no remarkable results: he was as good a scholar as a hundred others, without in any way distinguishing himself. Far more glimpses of his active mind must have been disclosed in his direct intercourse with his mother; for she, as eye-witnesses testify, often made the rather high-flown remark, "Robert is my star of hope.' But he was so far advanced, that he now began to receive instruction in music, in addition to his school-lessons.* He received this, and also piano-lessons, from a professor at the Zwickau high school, who has since died, at a ripe old age, Baccalaureus Kuntzsch. This man, from the lowest stratum of society (his father was a poor peasant of the village of Wilschdorf, near Dresden), had gradually risen, by steadfast industry and many deprivations, to a sphere of action commanding the respect of all: he is described to us as a formally polite man, old-fashioned in his habits, and pedantic even in trifles. Besides his duties at the school, he employed his leisure hours in the study of music, and profited so much by the practice, that he was soon competent to take a situation as organist, and to give music-lessons. If we look back to the past, to a time when the modern school of piano-forte playing was in its infancy, we can easily conceive of the execution and method of a self-made man, entirely cut off from the musical world, and living in a place† then very insignificant. And in truth his practical and theoretical abilities were by no means fitted to develop successfully a nature so musical, so richly gifted, and therefore all the more exposed to error. Robert owed to

* In spite of all inquiry, the date of these lessons cannot be fully established. We find a note among the manuscripts of Robert's music-teacher stating that he was taking lessons in September, 1817; which confirms the statement that his musical education began in his seventh year.

† Zwickau has since increased in size and importance through its coal mines.   2

his teacher a knowledge of the most indispensable qualities of piano-playing, and of his own innate genius; wherefore he, even to the last years of his life, preserved him in friendly remembrance. The following note confirms this statement: —

GODESBERG (near Bonn), July 1, 1852.

DEAREST TEACHER AND FRIEND, — Would I could congratulate you in person on this day of joy* for all who know you! Would I could speak in the full notes of the choir the emotion which fills my heart! But, alas! the distance suffices to prevent my first wish; and I did not hear of the jubilee until later than my friend Dr. Klitzch intended, as I was absent from Düsseldorf, and his letter was sent after me.

So let one of your scholars, who faithfully cherishes the memory of your kindness, offer you a wreath,† wherewith my wife — who sends most respectful greetings — and I would fain have crowned you, but which, alas! we can only place upon your venerable brow in spirit. Think, with your old love and sympathy,

Of your truly grateful

ROBERT SCHUMANN.

In spite of inadequate guidance and tuition, music soon kindled the boy's soul: its magic, as it were, burst the bonds of his spirit, and at the same time exercised such an influence over the excitable young nature, that Robert made attempts at composition unaided, and ignorant of the principles of thorough bass. The earliest of these, consisting of little dances, were written during his seventh or eighth year. His gift for extemporizing was manifested at the same time. A supplement, issued in 1850, to No. 52, for 1848, of " The Universal Journal of Music," contains a valuable biographical sketch of Robert Schumann, which is founded on fact; among other things, we read that, " It has been related that Schumann, as a child, possessed rare taste and talent for portraying feelings and characteristic traits in melody, — ay, he could sketch the different dispositions of his intimate friends by certain figures and

* Kuntzsch celebrated the fiftieth anniversary of his installation as teacher.

† It was a laurel crown.

passages on the piano so exactly and comically that every one burst into loud laughter at the similitude of the portrait."

Reading attracted him as much as music ; and he found rich and ample opportunity to satisfy this taste in his father's book-store. As in music, attempts at authorship soon followed. He wrote robber-plays; which were produced on a little stage built for the purpose (with admission fee indeed) with the aid of his father, his eldest brother Julius, and such of his comrades as were qualified. His father, as is shown by his assisting in the representation of these poetical efforts, rejoiced in Robert's tastes, and favored them as far as his time allowed, hoping that his favorite son would tread that path which he had so often himself essayed. This hope was afterwards clouded by Robert's rapidly-increasing love for music, which now received fresh food.

Robert heard at this time, in Carlsbad, whither his father took him, Ignatz Moscheles, the famous pianist,* and received, as all did, the impression of his wonderful art. We can see how powerfully and strongly it worked upon Schumann's young mind, by the fact that he preserved to the latest years of his life an undiminished remembrance of this event, and often spoke of it with real enthusiasm. It is also confirmed by a letter from Schumann to Moscheles, dated November 20, 1851 ; in which he writes, " The dedication of your sonata † afforded me joy and delight. I esteem it as an encouragement of my own efforts, in which you will henceforth take a friendly interest. When I, a total stranger to you, long preserved as a sacred relic a concert programme which you had touched, more than thirty years ago, in Carlsbad, how little did I dream that I should ever be thus honored by so illustrious a master ! Accept my most heartfelt thanks ! "

We can readily believe that Robert returned stirred to the quick by this example of early and complete mastership, and

* He gave two concerts in Carlsbad in the summer of 1819, on the 4th and 17th of August.

† Moscheles' sonata for piano and violoncello, op. 121.

applied himself to music with redoubled ardor. He had now won a guiding star, which supplied the place of proper direction and instruction in his musical studies, and spurred him on in emulation. The soul of the enthusiastic youth was soon filled with bold hopes and plans; but, ere they could be realized, many a temptation, many a battle, must be fought.

In the mean time, Robert had made such progress at school, that at Easter, 1820, he was fitted to enter the fourth class * at the Zwickau Academy. He now entered this public school, and upon a broader field of action; which, in comparison with the private school he had hitherto attended, demanded incessant industry. Nevertheless, amid all these events, he remained true to his love of music and literature : although, if a decided inclination in that direction was now first manifested, it was the natural result of his peculiar musical talent, and the impulse given by Moscheles' skill; which was made more powerful by being the first important one of his life.

As the doors of the temple of art opened wider and wider to the tender boy, whose hopeful eyes gazed into its entrance-halls, a barrier was erected between him and his childish playmates; but he soon won other friends, who sympathized with his ardent love for the beautiful, and, urged on by him, joined in and aided his work. Among them was a boy of his own age, whom Robert visited constantly, almost daily, in his father's house, that they might practise together: he was the son of a musician named Piltzing, leader of a regimental band stationed at Zwickau with the staff of Prince Frederic of Saxony, in 1821. Young Piltzing became a pupil of Kuntzsch † with Robert, as soon as his father was settled in his new home. They thus became acquainted, and made a musical alliance.

* According to Schumann's own account, he remained at the Zwickau Academy till Easter, 1828, and was two years in the fourth class, one in the third, three in the second, and two in the first.

† Who at this time gave a public performance of Schneider's " Day of Judgment," in St. Mary's Church; on which occasion, Schumann played the piano accompaniment. Schumann mentions this fact in the second volume of his writings, page 125.

Their love for music, to which both were devoted, led them to play with four hands works of Haydn and Mozart, then some of Beethoven's symphonies, as well as the then new original compositions *à quatre mains*, by Weber, Hummel, and Czerny. The greatest ecstasy was caused by the arrival of a grand piano in Schumann's house, of the celebrated Steck make, from Vienna. By this, it is evident that old Schumann rather aided than hindered his son's taste for music. Without any appreciation for music, he justly valued his son's endowments, and in indirect ways assisted to develop them. So by degrees he procured a rich collection of the current piano-music, which, being a bookseller, he had many opportunities to increase; and in these treasures Robert could fully indulge his budding inclination for art.

The simple musical life in Schumann's home was soon enlarged by an accidental discovery. Robert found, as if by chance, in his father's shop, the overture to Rhigini's " Tigranes," with all the orchestral parts complete, which had probably been sent by some mistake. This discovery at once excited the bold idea of performing the piece. All the disposable orchestral strength of the boy's acquaintance was summoned; and soon a little company was formed, which, though wholly incompetent, was devoted to music. This orchestra consisted of two violins, two flutes, a clarionet, and two horns. Robert, who directed all with the requisite fervor and zeal, undertook to supply the missing instruments, principally the bass, on the piano, to the best of his ability. This attempt of course filled the little band with joy and satisfaction; and Robert's father assisted them by a present of the necessary music-racks. From time to time they undertook other orchestral works, not too difficult of execution ; which Robert directed. He also set to music, most certainly inspired by these meetings, the one hundred and fiftieth psalm for a chorus, with orchestral accompaniment, which was performed with the help of such comrades as could sing. This composition occurred in his eleventh or twelfth year. These very select soirées (only the father was present in a corner, pretending to take no notice of the boys' doings) were generally closed by a fantasy, ex-temporized by Robert on his instrument; which impressed his associates in no slight degree.

Meanwhile Robert found opportunity to display his musical abilities beyond the home circle, in a friendly family of Zwick-au, the family of a merchant, long since dead, Carus * by name, and at evening entertainments given by the pupils of the academy, which consisted of various performances. He occasionally consented to play a solo at them, or sometimes accompanied on the piano such chorus pieces as were sung, among others Anselm Weber's music to Schiller's poem "The Message to the Forge." We see what progress he had made, by the fact that he played Moscheles' "Alexander Variations" and Herz's Variations of "I was a Youth," &c.† This per-formance so enraged his music-teacher, who ordinarily took no interest whatever in the musical proceedings at Schumann's home, that he declared he would no longer continue his instruc-tions. Robert might take care of himself.

In reality, this event was no disadvantage to the artistic youth; for, since he never claimed his teacher's advice, and always followed out his own ideas in musical matters, the former declared that his lessons were useless, and it mattered little whether they were continued or not.

August Schumann, who had hitherto watched his son's pro-ceedings in silence, but rendered more attentive by this fever for production, ‡ became more and more convinced that Robert

* Schumann wrote a few lines in memory of him in a leading periodical; in which he says, " It was in his house where the names of Mozart, Haydn, and Beethoven were spoken daily and enthusiastically, — in his house that I first saw these masters' works, especially their quartettes, but seldom heard in that little town, often playing the piano parts myself,—in Carus' house, so well known to almost every native artist, where artists were always hospi-tably welcomed, where all was joy, serenity, and music."—See *Neue Zeit-schrift*, f. *Musik*, vol. xviii., p. 27.

† Schumann subsequently recited the monologue in the first act of Goethe's Faust at one of these entertainments.

‡ Schumann's note-book says, that fragments of operas and overtures were composed at this time.

was intended by Providence for a musician. This opinion was most violently opposed by his wife. Destitute of all interest in music, she was as incapable of appreciating her son's gifts as of disregarding the petty prejudices which then prevailed in certain circles against any artistic profession. She thought only of the deprivations and discomforts felt by Mozart and other masters, and emphatically pointed out to her darling the hardships of such a calling. Future statements will show how firmly and immovably she held to this opinion after long years.

Nevertheless, Robert's father took a decisive step in the matter. He addressed a letter to Carl Maria von Weber, requesting him to undertake his son's musical direction and formation.* The master readily acceded to this wish; but the scheme was never carried out: so Robert thenceforth received only "the usual grammar-school education, besides pursuing his musical studies with perfect devotion, and composing according to his ability," as he himself expresses it. An important event, which should not be overlooked, was connected with this autodidactic beginning; namely, that he was given over to his own tuition at an age when neither taste nor judgment were firmly established. He had no one to guide or advise him, and, without knowing it, depended in all his musical undertakings upon his own judgment or upon chance.

Not only was he deprived of the guiding and pruning hand of a master or judge of musical matters, but he was at the same time exposed to the dangers of vanity, which has destroyed so many talented youths.

Robert had no rivals in his native town, either among his seniors or juniors: his skill and dexterity at the piano were even then considerable. As we have seen, he had already appeared as a pianist in public, always exciting not only deep attention, but enthusiasm. What wonder, then, if the admira-

* Unfortunately the correspondence in question no longer exists. It was probably among those papers which were destroyed, by a lamentable mistake, after Weber's death.

tion, faith, and confidence awarded him on such occasions by the little town produced and confirmed the belief that he was on the right road, and no longer required to study under the direction of another, especially as his former teacher had not given him a very high opinion of the necessity of a pruning and polishing hand? And in fact, as will be shown, Schumann in later life made many experiments contrary to the advice of competent judges, for which he atoned by the loss of the free use of his right hand, and was also debarred longer than desirable from an earnest and methodical study of the theoretical part of his art. It is, and will ever be, wonderful that Schumann won such fame as a composer: this fact furnishes a strong proof of his rich productive powers.

We have now viewed Robert Schumann's career from childhood up. As he grew older, a great change took place in him, having a marked influence upon mind and body; for while Robert as a child had always showed the most overflowing spirits, and always seized every opportunity to tease and play tricks upon his playmates, his sister, and his mother's servants, his whole being entirely changed during his fourteenth year. Every thing henceforth indicated a more reserved and inward life. The maturing youth was more reflective, more silent, and showed that love for reverie which hinders communion with men rather than with spirits.

This outward passiveness, which, as we know, never left Schumann throughout his life, produced a certain constraint and lack of freedom in intercourse with his comrades. Nevertheless, his mind received harmonious impressions from all external objects, and assimilated them suitably, repulsing such influences as would have enriched and developed him in many ways, but which would, at the same time, have destroyed his independence of thought. He was reserved in his manner when displeased, and to all appearance equally passive when deeply interested. Seldom was more than a transient glance at the opposing forces in his mind granted: so that he often appeared indifferent, indolent, and inattentive.

Even his dearest friends felt the truth of this. The chief of these were at this time his sister-in-law Theresa, wife of his eldest brother, Edward,* to whom he was for many years united by most intimate relations, and two of his schoolmates, Röller and Flechsig.† Both these youths, of whom Schumann designates Emil Flechsig as his truest and dearest friend, attracted him by their mutual love for learning; and in their society the stores of his father's establishment were passed in review, Sonnenberg and Schulze being chosen as their favorite authors, and becoming the criterion for choice and criticism. After Schumann's death, Röller wrote to his friend Flechsig in regard to their intercourse: " Although often in his (Schumann's) society, one could tell but little of his inner nature. He was not so clear and open that all his thoughts could be discovered and laid bare."

Amid the alternating influences of his school education, the musical studies which we have described, and his literary pursuits (his preference being for love poems) his sixteenth year came on. The conflicts of his soul now began to transform the maturing boy into a quiet, dreamy youth. It seemed the first important epoch in his life.

Two very different events stirred Robert's soul with a force hitherto unknown, and waked him to a higher knowledge of himself, — the death of his father, Aug. 10, 1826, ‡ and his first though apparently but slight experience of the tender passion. How agitated must his young heart have been by the contradictory feelings of joy and sorrow! And these events influenced him so strongly, that, after a long season of rest, he eagerly resumed his musical and poetical labors ; which fit of enthusiasm was soon succeeded by others. He received still

* After her husband's death, in 1839, she married Counsellor Fleischer, a well-known bookseller of Leipsic.

† The latter now fills the office of sub-deacon in St. Mary's Church, Zwickau; while the former is a game-keeper in Augustusburg, Saxony.

‡ According to the parish register. He succumbed to a disease of long standing in the prime of life, while busied with the translation of Byron's works.

further incitation from a musical amateur, who spent the summer of 1827 in Zwickau, and by means of her charming singing exercised great attractive power over Robert. She was a relative of the Carus family, wife of Dr. Carus, then living at Colditz in Saxony, afterwards Professor of Medicine at the universities of Leipsic and Dorpat. According to his own statement, he now enjoyed perfect musical revels with her, which resulted in various productions in the kingdom of song. To this period belong a number of Byronic, Schultzian, and original poems set to music.* A knowledge of Jean Paul's writings was requisite to bring Robert to this pitch of exaltation. The Jean-Paul fever literally attacked him in all its transcendentalism; and any one who was ever in a similar situation will understand what this means.

One would think, that, after so many spontaneous efforts of his creative genius, his mother could with prudent counsel have easily devised some plan for the future suited to his taste and ability. Nevertheless, and although Robert had declared his preference for music by a public appearance as pianist,† she could not be convinced that he was destined for art. She was confirmed by Robert's guardian, Rudel, a merchant of Zwickau, in her opinion, that her son's duty was to study some profession after graduating from the grammar school. She would only consent to recognize his musical work as amateur amusement, and in this light had no objection to its continuation, but thought her tender, anxious, maternal love best proved by urging him to choose such a profession as she deemed would secure his future. Robert, still bound by a thousand ties of childish submission and affection, for a time obeyed her wishes. Accordingly he went to Leipsic, in March, 1828, to prepare for a long stay there, and

---

* We find a piano concerto in E-minor, marked in Schumann's note-book as begun at this time.

† In Schneeberg, a village near Zwickau. He played a composition by Kalkbrenner, according to the testimony of a reliable witness, Günther, a music teacher still living in Dresden.

to effect his matriculation at the university as a student of law; which occurred on the 29th March.* Here he founo his friend Emil Flechsig, who had left the grammar school be fore he did, and was now a divinity student; with him he agreed to live, together with Moritz Semmel,† a law student brother of his sister-in-law Theresa. Through the latter, he soon made the acquaintance of Gisbert Rosen, ‡ also a stu dent of law. They felt a strong mutual attraction, on account of their unbounded admiration for Jean Paul, who so easily arouses the young to long for lofty, enthusiastic friendship. Both felt desirous of closer communion; but Rosen was obliged to leave the Leipsic university for Heidelberg at Easter, 1828. Schumann therefore invited his new-found friend to go to Heidelberg by way of Zwickau, and to pass some time with him at his home. Rosen accepted this invitation, and spent a couple of weeks in Schumann's native town, after an excursion from Teplitz to Prague, where he visited his mother. The welcome guest remained until Robert's graduation, who then accompanied him on his journey to Heidelberg as far as Munich.

A family gathering was on the eve of celebration in the Schumann house, on the occasion of the marriage of the second son, Julius Schumann. This afforded Robert fresh opportunity to prove his poetic talent by an epithalamium, which he wrote in a very short time, one evening, in the presence of his friend Rosen, spite of his anxiety in regard to his graduation. Moreover, this wedding, which took place April 15, 1828, was accompanied by a singular event, distressing to all the participants, which made a lasting impression on Robert. The ceremony was to take place at a village three hours' journey from Zwickau; but the priest who was to officiate was struck dead by apoplexy, while proceeding from the parson-

---

* According to the matriculation tables, in the hands of the university questor at Leipsic.
† Counsellor at Gera.
‡ Chief Justice of Detmold.

age to the church with the bridal pair.   After this unfortunate occurrence, the bride's father, Superintendent Lorenz, took upon himself the bestowal of the ecclesiastic blessing.

The graduation was at last happily passed ; and so brilliantly did Robert succeed, that he left the school with the highest honors.   The great joy which this caused his family was in a measure subdued by his signal failure in the recital of a poem on " Tasso's Death," composed by himself, at the public enter-tainment given by the graduating class.   From his earliest youth he showed creative power, but a lack of ability to pro-duce his works properly.

The two young friends soon started on their journey : they first went to Bayreuth by the stage-coach, which passed through Zwickau nightly.   Here the Jean-Paul enthusiasts could not refrain from lingering a day, that they might visit all the spots made famous by the poet, especially his grave, the " Phan-tasy," and the " Hermitage."   Old Rollwenzel, who lived close by, was not forgotten, but was eagerly questioned.

From Bayreuth they went by Nuremberg to Augsburg, where they again paused.   Here, too, they had a special pur-pose, this time concerning not the dead, but living.   Schumann had a letter of introduction to deliver to Dr. von Kurrer of Augsburg, not unknown to fame in his day as a chemist, whose wife was from Zwickau.   This occasioned the stay of the two travellers for several days in the former's hospita-ble home.   Schumann was all the more pleased with this tem-porary sojourn, that he was deeply smitten with his amiable host's pretty blue-eyed daughter, whose charms for some time absorbed him, though nothing came of it; since Clara, for such was her name, already had an ardent admirer, whom she after-wards married.   The latter, however, instead of being angry, revenged himself most generously on Schumann, — who, when young, was a dangerous rival,— by giving him an introduction to H. Heine (then in Munich), to which von Kurrer added an-other, to the artist Clemens Zimmermann.

The young men hastened to deliver these letters as soon as

they reached Munich. Especially did they burn with desire to become personally acquainted with H. Heine, then at the height of his fame, and whose " Pictures of Travel " and " Book of Songs" had just burst upon the world. He lived in a lovely garden-room, whose walls were richly adorned with pictures by most of the artists then resident in Munich. The gifted poet fully realized the ideal portrait which his strange visitors had formed from his writings : any thing that was wanting was soon supplied by Heine's sarcastic, pungent style of conversation. Schumann lingered several hours with Heine ; while Rosen soon left, wishing to visit a countryman. The three met again in the Leuchtenberger gallery, where the two friends were afforded rich and ample opportunity for admiration and delight at Heine's witty fancy, whose freaks seemed inexhaustible.

The visit to Zimmermann, although very different from that to Heine, was no less satisfactory. The young people met with a cordial welcome, increased by Schumann's performance at the piano; and they had the great pleasure of seeing the cartoons for the master's pictures in the Glypthothek, as well as the paintings themselves.

After visiting every thing noteworthy in the Bavarian capital, the friends parted May 2. Rosen's path led through Augsburg to Heidelberg ; and he was not uncharged with a tender message from Schumann to his fair one : the latter went to Regensburg, and thence to his native city, to take a long leave of it. His departure thence soon after occurred, as is shown by a letter to his friend Rosen. It reads as follows : —

LEIPSIC, June 5, 1828.

MY DEAR ROSEN, — To-day is the 19th of June, so long is it since I began this letter. Ah! were I but with you in Heidelberg! Leipsic is an infamous den, where no one can enjoy his life. Money makes rapid progress, more than I can in the lecture-rooms, — a remark which is ingeniously taken from life, my own into the bargain. Here I sit without a penny, silent, comparing the present with those hours so lately flown, which I passed so cordially and merrily with you; and I dream over your picture and the comical fate which brings men together from such opposite paths only to snatch them apart again. Perhaps even now you're sitting among the ruins of the old mountain castle, smiling gayly and happily at the blossoms of June; while I stand amid the ruins of my blasted air-castles, and gaze, weeping, out into the black horizon of present and future. Heavens! This letter is growing horribly serious, and by Jove! it shall not: melancholy faces like yours must be brightened; and I'll keep my mournful gravity for myself.

My journey to Regensburg was confoundedly stupid; and I sighed for you in that most catholic of regions. I never like to describe a journey, especially such a one as would revive unpleasant memories better left to slumber. It suffices to say, that I thought most affectionately of you; that the lovely Clara's image floated before me, both sleeping and waking; and that I was heartily glad to see my dear native town of Zwickau once more. All were astonished that I would only remain three hours; for no one in Zwickau had ever heard, much less seen, any thing of Nuremberg, Augsburg, or Munich. All wished to be told something; but I was inexorable, seated myself after a three hours' visit in the corner of the stage-coach, and — wept bitterly, and thought of all that had been torn from my heart, and even now lay crushed before me, and mused on the lazy Utopian life which I had led for weeks, and alas! still lead. You are far from right if you think I'm wild. By no means: I am better than ever, but feel quite miserable here; and student life seems so vile to me that I cannot mingle in it. I am not indisposed to unfold to you my ideas on the subject of student life; but they're not worth the postage, which already will cost you eight groschen, six pfenniger.

Agreeable Rosen, how wags the world with you? The weather to-day is glorious: yesterday I went to the Rosenthal, and drank a cup of coffee! To-day I'm astonishingly merry, if that fact is interesting to you, for the simple reason that I have no money; and it's an old fashion to be jollier then than when you have plenty. Agreeable Rosen, I ask you again, how do you do? It's a pity to have to pay eight groschen to learn. But it can't be helped: the world pulls the ass's skin over both ears alike, and just proportions result. And yet every line, every letter, from you warms my heart; and I will be glad to pay if I can only get letters from you.

. . . Semmel sends cordial greetings: he doesn't trouble himself about the students, and laughs sarcastically at their vague, obscure ideas of nationality and Germanity; and the inflamed students are greatly offended thereat. Alas! what an ideal I formed of a student, and how frivolous most of them are! Now I am leisurely reading over my sober beginning; and the genius of Friendship conjures up my stay in Augsburg, and yours in Zwickau and Gera,* before my longing eyes. Alas, that every happy moment should slay itself!

On my return through Bayreuth, thanks to old Rollwenzel's kindness, I was enabled to visit Jean Paul's widow, and from her obtained his portrait. If the whole world read Jean Paul, it would be decidedly better, but more unhappy. He has often reduced me to the verge of despair; † but the rainbow of peace always floats softly above the tears, and the heart is wonderfully exalted and transfigured.

With this letter, two go to Augsburg, to the doctor (von Kurrer) and to Clara; and you cannot expect, that, after such exhaustive effusions, I should gush any more. Clara's picture. . . . . May you be happy! Every angel be with you; and may the genius of joyful tears ever accompany you ! Hold dear the friend who was with you but for a few fleeting moments, but who conceived a deep, true, and hearty affection for you, because he found you to be a human, tender, and yet strong youth. Never forget those lovely hours which we passed together, and remain as human, as good, as you now are. Answer soon.   Yours,

R. SCH.

The whole tone of this letter shows how deep an impression Jean Paul's mind had made upon both friends, especially Schumann. The superabundant sensibility which finds vent in strained utterances, and is never satisfied, caused him to grasp at such an expression as "the genius of joyful tears ever accompany you ; " and it is evident, that, as music plays so significant a part in Jean Paul's works, so every overflow of sensibility seeks to find expression in music. This Jean-Paulism is a distinguishing characteristic of Schumann's feelings and creations, to which other elements were afterwards added.

In explanation of the student matters mentioned in this letter, be it said, that, on his arrival in Leipsic, Schumann joined a society to which his friend Moritz Semmel already belonged. But both soon after gave up their membership, when this association began to pursue other tendencies, and went over to the regenerate association "Marcomanscia."

* A visit was made to some relatives there, on the occasion of Rosen's visit to Zwickau.

† Schumann's father made a similar confession in regard to Young's and Milton's writings.

This club, however, had no deeper importance to Schumann than that it afforded opportunity to meet his friends in the coffee-house or on the fencing-ground.

The want of money, mentioned above, from which we shall see that Schumann often suffered, was relieved by a supply from his guardian, not unaccompanied by fatherly admonitions to remain faithful to the profession he had chosen. Schumann's answer was as follows : —

LEIPSIC, JULY 4, 1828.

DEAR SIR, — Receive my most sincere thanks for the money sent me. . . . . Be assured that I shall turn the money to the best account, and incur no unnecessary expense.

I have decided upon *law* as my profession, and will work at it industriously, however cold and dry the beginning may be.

Accept my cordial good wishes for your health and welfare, and rest assured that I am, with the utmost respect, dear sir,

Yours truly and gratefully,
ROBERT SCHUMANN.

A letter soon after written by Schumann shows to his friend Rosen how ill he succeeded in subduing his distaste for the law. It also gives us further information concerning his life in Leipsic. It reads as follows : —

MY DEAR ROSEN, — It must be a confoundedly queer sort of pleasure to read my Sanscrit: so I'm taking great pains to write handsomely to-day, that I may be the exception which proves the rule; for poets and pianists generally write just such shocking hands as I do. Now the real letter begins; and the *captatio benevolentiæ* is ended.

O my dear Rosen! those happy hours which we spent together! for with our separation began my glory, — in other words, my student life. But how have I found it? No more roses in my life, no other Rosen among men. I sometimes flee to Jean Paul, or to my piano, which the Teutomanes * here can't bear. Enthusiasts or castle-builders bear the same relation to matter-of-fact men as bees. When they're lying, they harm no one; but, if you touch them when on a flower, they sting! Although I can't sting, I strike out with hands and feet, and knock all these ideas of nationality, &c., into a cocked hat. Gotte,† Semmel, and

---

* By this, Schumann means those students to whom he referred in his letter to Rosen.

† A native of Brunswick.

Flechsig are the only ones with whom I'm on intimate terms. The others are insignificant; and I care little about them, with the exception of Schütz and Günther, if they weren't so one-sided.

I shall certainly come to Heidelberg, but unfortunately not until Easter, 1829, alas! If you were only to be there then, that I might roam about in that blooming paradise with you. The pretty little pictures, for which I thank you heartily, give wings to my dreams. I have not yet been to any lectures, and have worked entirely alone; that is, played on my piano, written letters, and Jean-Pauliads. I have not yet become intimate in any family, and fly, I know not why, from miserable mankind; go out seldom, and am sometimes heart-sick at the pettinesses and miseries of this selfish world. Ah, what would a world without men be? A boundless churchyard; a dreamless sleep of death; a flowerless, springless nature; a lifeless peep-show, without a puppet. And yet what is this world of men? A vast cemetery, filled with faded dreams; a garden of cypresses and weeping willows; a dull peep-show, with sobbing dolls. O God! that is it. Yes. Whether we shall meet again, the gods alone know; but the world is not so large that men can be parted forever, especially friends. The meeting is never so remote as the parting; and we will not weep. . . . (illegible). For Fate's giant fists may silence men's tongues, but not their hearts; which love the warmer and esteem the dearer for distance, because they regard each other as invisible, dead, or super-terrestrial.

I am exhausted by much letter-writing: so do not frown if I close. It can't give you any pleasure to listen to my babbling. Your Leipsic acquaintances, who, without exception, love and esteem you, send a thousand greetings.

Farewell, beloved friend! May your life have no more clouds than are necessary for a fine sunset, and no more rain than is needed for a lunar rainbow! When you sit at evening amid the castle ruins, and gaze enchantedly at the blossoming vale and starry heaven, forget me not, your absent friend, who is crushed and unhappy, and wish me all that I wish you from afar. May your gentle, humane spirit flit lightly over the fairs of life, and you yourself remain what you are and were, —human, human. Farewell. Your SCHUMANN.

This letter, with its peculiarly Jean-Paul expressions, gives so clear and undisguised a glimpse of Schumann's mind, that it needs no further comment. The germs of his future eventful life, which was even as happy as unhappy, are revealed therein. We can easily recognize the mature Schumann, with his lofty

3

mental endowments, his sensitive and impressionable, but sometimes apathetically melancholy nature. He has not revealed his soul so unreservedly in any other of the letters lying before us.

Schumann's early life in Leipsic proved to be quite other than what these two letters to Rosen paint it. A gradual withdrawal from his loved solitude added to its charms. He soon renewed his acquaintance with Agnes Carus, who had so excited his musical interest in 1827 by her singing,* and whose husband had since been appointed professor in the Leipsic University. A prolonged intimacy in this gifted woman's house not only exercised a salutary influence over Schumann's shy nature, but afforded him opportunity to become acquainted with many interesting people, among whom he himself mentions Marschner, afterwards an opera-master. More important, however, than the friendships formed in Carus's house was that of Friedrich Wieck, whose merry, active temperament henceforth exercised considerable attractive power over Schumann. But Wieck's eldest daughter, Clara, † then in her ninth year, who had already attained to a high degree of musical culture, was also an artistic centre of gravity to Schumann. His natural desire to emulate so gifted a nature necessarily produced a desire to share the instruction to which she owed her early development. His wish was granted. Schumann, with his mother's consent, requested Wieck to give him lessons ; which he accordingly received, although but in limited number. His playing even then revealed considerable skill and facility, though it was without pretensions to such requisites of a perfect execution as correct tone-formation, purity, correctness, ease, and a fine symmetrical interpretation. Under Wieck's instruction, he was, for the first time in his life, obliged to study a rational system of music, clearly requiring technical knowledge, of which he for a time availed himself, readily recognizing its merit. Although Schumann now proved him-

---

* Compare page 26.   † See appendix A.

self to be a susceptible and docile pupil, he as yet displayed no interest in the study of harmony, which is so invaluable to a pianist. He had no liking for it, and thoughtlessly considered such a knowledge of the harmonic system as useless, believing it quite enough to be able to extemporize harmonies on the piano by ear. This erroneous idea, to which he clung somewhat obstinately, is a characteristic mark of his musical nature; and all the remonstrances of his experienced teacher were vain. He remained true to it for some time, but only until he became sensible of his total ignorance in such matters; which period his later attempts at composition clearly mark. Then first did he arrive at a knowledge of the indispensableness of theoretical study.

His new instruction lasted, with many interruptions, until February, 1829, when Friedrich Wieck felt compelled, from want of time, to give it up. But the connection must, under any circumstances, have soon been severed, as Schumann left Leipsic for a long time, and entered the Heidelberg University.

The more intimate acquaintances formed by Schumann in Leipsic were far better suited to increase his ardent love of music than to quench it. As homogeneous or even kindred spirits feel a mutual attraction, there gradually came to be no one in the circle of his friends who did not take an active interest in his musical struggles, — who did not, working like himself, essay the art to which he belonged body and soul. The chief of these persons were Julius Knorr,* Täglichsbeck, professor and musical director at Brandenburg; and Glock, mayor of Ostheim in Meiningen, — all fellow-students of Schumann Mid many vicissitudes, he gave himself up to the fertilizing influence of the tone-works of different masters, in company with one or more of these friends; when he was always to be found in his place at the piano, generally in his shirt-sleeves, with a cigar in his mouth, while Täglichsbeck played the violin, and Glock the violoncello.

* He died June 17, 1861, in Leipsic.

At this time Schumann was as deeply and powerfully impressed by the genius of Franz Schubert as he had shortly
before been by Jean Paul. He eagerly played this master's
two and four-hand piano compositions; and his death * filled
him with most profound grief, — ay, even moved him to tears
of heartfelt sorrow. His enthusiasm for the hero of German
song, to whom, as his writings prove, he remained true to the
end, soon spread to his musical friends.

They were not to be deterred from perfecting their knowledge of Franz Schubert's works, and resolved, in their ardor,
to practise one of them together until they reached the highest
pitch of perfection. Their choice fell on the trio in B-flat
major, op. 99, whose beauties had caused them great ecstasy.
It was studied until the performance was worthy of the work.
Schumann then arranged a musical party, at which this trio
was played. Besides student-friends of the performers, Friedrich Wieck was there in the seat of honor.

This evening suggested to them the idea of weekly gather-
ings at Schumann's rooms with another student, Sörgel,† to
play the viola; when various pieces of chamber-music, from
Beethoven to Prince Louis Ferdinand, or *vice versâ*, were performed in turn. In the intervals, they conversed on musical
matters, especially of the old master Bach and his " Well-tempered Clavichord," even then a source of ardent study to Schumann, and always laid upon his piano. Although Schumann
found in chamber-music frequent occasion to increase and complete his knowledge of perhaps the most pleasurable department of music, he was also stimulated to fresh creative efforts.
He wrote various compositions at this time, — eight Polonaises
for four hands, clearly imitations of Schubert's works of the
same class; ten or twelve songs, to words by Justinus Kerner
(also music to Goethe's " Fisher ") ; ‡ variations for four hands,

* Schubert died Nov. 19, 1828, at Vienna.

† He went to Texas, and has never been heard of since.

‡ Schumann sent these songs to Widebein, then a well-known song composer of Brunswick, whose lyrics charmed him, requesting his opinion

on a theme by Prince Louis Ferdinand; and lastly, a quartette in E-minor, for piano and stringed instruments. It is very evident that such unreserved devotion to music, even when confined to a delightful survey of its boundaries, left but little time for the study of law. It did indeed fare ill, although Schumann sometimes made a feeble attempt * to attend the legal lectures; but it remained an attempt: and all his good intentions did not suffice to turn his wavering mind from the art to which it involuntarily inclined, as the magician's rod tremblingly points out hidden treasure. However, he took some interest in the *humanioribus*, and specially enjoyed the discourses by the philosopher Krug, who induced him to study the writings of Kant, Fichte, and Schelling.

Schumann, as already shown by his letters, had determined to enter the Heidelberg University at Easter, 1829. He held to this resolve, although renewed intercourse with his friend Rosen, who was about to return home, was out of the question. This news from his Heidelberg friend prompted the following letter from Schumann : —

LEIPSIC, Nov. 7, 1828.

It has been my rapturous and inspiring hope for a whole year, to visit Heidelberg at Easter. The joyous horizons of a life of delight lay stretched before me, — the great tun and all the little tuns, the light-hearted people, Switzerland, Italy, France, the whole life there, — which I painted in glowing, Titianesque colors. It is enough for me to know, that from your, henceforth my room, I can behold the Neckar with its vine-trellises. Be the chamber what it may, I ask no more. Your flowers, if not faded before Easter, shall be, like my friendship, perennial. If you have any really noble men among your Heidelberg acquaintance, I should not dislike to take your place in their affections; for at Easter there'll be no one in Heidelberg who knows me, or whom I know. Alas!

Widebein answered. The eighth volume of the New Journal of Music, page 106, contains a letter from the editors, and one sent by Schumann, the names being disguised by the heading: "From an old master to a young musician;" which is evidently Widebein's reply.

* Schumann afterwards laughingly confessed, when asked about his legal studies, that he went as far as the door of the lecture-room, paused, turned, and slowly went away.

into what hands will fate confide my heart? I'm getting on better than ever, if I only weren't such a poor, miserable Job in money matters For the last six months, I've led an irregular, disorderly life, although not a dissipated one; but I thought too seldom of that line from the Ideals, "Industry that never tires." The glorious great concer*s* make me perfectly happy! It is growing dark: so you may bless your stars if I cease. Write soon, and much more than I do to you. Next time more and better! Farewell, my dear, good Rosen. Think of the hours when we were so happy with the same affection as I do; and still be, both in memory and in future, my friend, as I am ever yours,

R. Sch.

P.S. Do you know a poet, Grabbe, author of the "Duke of Gothia?" and can you tell me any thing about him? He is said to have spent some time in your native town. An answer will greatly oblige me.

Meanwhile, circumstances altered so unexpectedly, that the friends were permitted to meet once more, in Heidelberg. Rosen remained longer at the University than he had intended; and this event caused most joyful communications. Before leaving Leipsic for an indefinite time, Schumann visited his relatives in Zwickau and Schneeberg. From the latter town he wrote to Rosen, —

SCHNEEBERG, Last of April, 1829.

Mr Good Rosen, — My Heidelberg air-castles have been very near bursting: my brother Julius was taken dangerously ill shortly after his wife's confinement. My mother implored me not to leave her if he died, since she would then be entirely alone. But his disease has now abated, and I can write to you with joyful confidence; three weeks from to-day I shall hang upon your neck.

It was fearfully hard for me to leave Leipsic at the last. A lovely, cheerful, pious, womanly spirit had enchained my own. It cost many a struggle: but now all is over; and I stand up strong, stifling my tears, and gaze hopefully and courageously forward to my Heidelberg life of flowers.

I believe I have not written you that our friend Semmel will fly to Heidelberg after his examination. That will indeed be life. At Michaelmas we go to Switzerland; and who knows where else? May the fine triplet never fade!

Day before yesterday, there was a very brilliant concert in Zwickau,

* The Gewandhaus Concerts in Leipsic.

where eight hundred to a thousand people were assembled: of course I had a finger in the pie. There's no end to the gayeties and festivities. First, there was a *bal paré* at the colonel's (von Trosky *); Saturday *a thé dansant* at Dr. Hempel's; Sunday, a school-ball, where I got uncommonly tipsy; Monday, a quartette at Carus's house (Matthäi †) from Leipsic; Tuesday, a Gewandhaus concert and supper-party; Wednesday, *a déjeûner a la fourchette;* and this evening there's to be a farewell ball here: ‡ and the whole thing hasn't cost me a penny, to say nothing of other forgotten breakfasts and suppers devoured by me.

I will write you from Frankfort, where I intend to spend a few days, the date of my arrival. I shall certainly leave Leipsic on Monday, May 11. I'm sorry to say I can't bring much money, because I have a great many debts to pay in Leipsic. Perhaps you can help me for a time: if not, I shall discover some remedy. At any rate, I shall be with you by the 18th. It has snowed here all day. I hope I sha'n't have to travel to Heidelberg on runners. With you I suppose every thing is green and rosy by this time: it glistens before my eyes. Farewell, my beloved friend. Re-union outweighs every long parting; and so shall it be with us. Bloom on as brightly as the spring which smiles upon me; and may your gentle spirit know naught but this, and never a winter!   Your brother,

                                                            R. SCH.

I pity your eyes; for I can't read this letter myself.

Schumann started on his journey May 11, as he wrote his friend, by the coach from Leipsic to Heidelberg. A happy chance gave him as travelling companion Willibald Alexis (Dr. W. Häring). They became acquainted, and were so mutually pleased, that Schumann could not refuse to accompany the clever writer for a short distance down the Rhine, before hastening to his friend's arms.

He reached Heidelberg towards the end of May; and, when he had provided a good piano, the most delightful life dawned upon the friends.

The charm was enhanced when Moritz Semmel, who had

---

* Schumann visited and played at Col. von Trosky's house while at school.

† Matthäi was then a conductor in Leipsic.

‡ That is in Schneeberg, while the other entertainments took place in Zwickau.

won the degree of bacc. juris. joined them, prepared to spend some time in Heidelberg. The "life of flowers," of which Schumann had dreamed for a whole year, came to pass; for, almost daily, short excursions were made in a one-horse carriage into the delightful suburbs. They also took longer trips to Baden-Baden, Worms, Spires, and Mannheim; and it is noteworthy, that these parties never went off without what is called a "dumb piano," upon which Schumann busily practised finger-exercises during the conversation on the way. For music was his chief employment, indeed, his chief study, in Heidelberg; while law, for which not even the learned Thibaut could inspire him with interest, was, as it were, excommunicated. He did, indeed, attend the latter's pandect lectures, but more from curiosity and on Thibaut's account than from any desire for juridical knowledge. He lacked the first requisites, such as college or law books, and never conversed on legal subjects without evident reluctance. An event relating to this is worthy of mention here, since it plainly reveals the nature of the son of the Muses. They were coming from one of Thibaut's lectures, in which he had spoken of "pubertas," and specially explained the reasons why a woman should attain majority and the possession of property earlier than a man. "A youth of eighteen years," Thibaut happened to say, "is an unlicked cub, — a creature who never knows what to do with his hands and feet. If he enters into society, nothing more awkward can be imagined. He is sure to have his hands behind him, and to seek out some table or chair in a corner where he may fly for shelter. On the other hand, a maiden of eighteen is not only the most graceful creature imaginable, but also a very intelligent person; who sits, knitting in hand, in the midst of company, ready and able to join in the conversation. There, gentlemen, you have the simple reason why women earlier attain majority than men."

"It's all very fine," said Schumann afterwards, "for Thibaut to spice his statements thus: in fact, he must; for his learning is dry and stupid enough. But, spite of all his embellishments,

I can't take any fancy to it. I don't understand it. *Vice versâ*, there's many a man who don't understand the language of music! but you," meaning his friends, "know somewhat of it: so I'll tell you a little about it." With these words, he seated himself at his piano, took up Weber's "Invitation to the Dance," and played it. "Now she speaks," he said; "that's the prattle of love. Now he speaks," he continued; "that's the man's earnest voice. Now they both speak at once," interpreted he, going on with his music; "and I clearly hear what the two lovers say. Isn't all that much better than any thing jurisprudence can utter?"

Schumann, as you see, never concealed his deeply-rooted dislike to the study of law, to which no one could have objected, had it not been allied to an almost unwarrantable neglect of his own special branch of it. He agreed with the saying, "Sufficient unto the day is the evil thereof," never accounted for his actions, never thought of the consequences. Moritz Semmel considered it his duty, as a friend and near relation, to warn him, that, if he really meant to pursue the law, it was high time for him to strive to reach the goal; but if this profession, as was apparent, were repulsive to him, he ought openly to follow the promptings of his heart, and become a musician. This earnest, urgent warning seemed the more necessary, that the property left him by his father was by no means sufficient for him to live upon its income. A speedy consumption of the capital was the more clearly to be foreseen, that Schumann while at home had often had desires, which, if not impossible, were hard of refusal. In spite of this serious and well-meant admonition, in spite of his predilection and evident vocation for art, he could not yet decide to devote himself solely to music, in which he lived and breathed. Affection for his mother prompted him to persevere a little longer in the study of law.

Summer was over; and Schumann and his friends were about to spend the remaining holidays, until the beginning of the winter term, in a journey to Upper Italy, which they had planned while in Leipsic. They had prepared for this journey

by an assiduous study of the Italian language; and Schuma in
soon became so familiar with it, that he translated some of Pe-
trarch's sonnets into German, in the same metre, and, as Gisbert Rosen assures us, with wonderful fidelity, and in the true,
poetic strain of the original. He wrote to his mother and
guardian, requesting sixty or seventy ducats for his travelling
expenses. The guardian was ill-pleased: he thought Schumann should postpone the trip until the end of his collegiate
course, and told him that the conditions of the will would hardly allow him to give the desired sum for such a purpose.

To this Schumann replied as follows:—

HEIDELBERG, Aug. 6, 1829.

Dear Sir,—I gladly acknowledge the receipt of the long-expected bill
of exchange for one hundred thalers on Emmanuel Müller of Frankfort-
on-the-Main. You will see, most honored Mr. Rudel, by the following
calculation of my expenses, that I can hardly get along with it until November.

(This account of his half-yearly expenses in Heidelberg follows, amounting to four hundred and thirty-one florins.)

Had I thought that living would be so frightfully dear in Heidelberg.
as you will perceive by my dinner-bill, I should have changed my mind
in Frankfort, and returned to Leipsic. You may ask, "How can the
other students afford it?" to which I would answer, that at Heidelberg
three-fourths are foreigners, who are all rich, and able to spend plenty of
money.

I hope, honored Mr. Rudel, that you will not consider it an insolent
protest against your kind advice, if I reply to some parts of your second
letter.* All the foreign students who come to Heidelberg are attracted,
not only by the celebrated professors, but also by the fine situation, the
good living, and the proximity to Switzerland and Italy. You and my
mother know that I planned this *journey* when I left Leipsic. Among
many reasons, besides the common one that travel perfects a man's practical and theoretical knowledge, and those which I wrote to my mother,
who has probably told them to you, I will only mention the financial
one, that I should take this journey sooner or later: so that it's all the
same whether I spend the money now or in the future. If your duty as

* In regard to the journey.

my guardian forbids so irregular a proceeding, you can still gratify your wishes as a *private individual:* I mean, that you can consent, or at least not forbid, that I should borrow from my brothers, paying them when able. I could obtain any sum I chose here, by paying ten or twelve per cent interest; to which means I shall have recourse, if it comes to the worst, — that is, if I can get no money from home.

I must also undeceive you, if you think I should lose any of the lectures: the holidays are not meant for the study of books, but for the study of one great book, the world; or, in other words, they are specially designed for travelling. The Heidelberg vacation begins Aug. 21, and ends the last of October; so that my journey will begin and end with it. I therefore hope that you will not withhold your kind consent. The snail's pace of Saxon justice is too well known for me to doubt that it will debate and deliberate over pronouncing me of age long after I really am so legally. It would have been very kind of you to have rid me of some of my tormentors.

For the rest, I am well and strong, although as poor as any beggar, or more so. As much as I wish the former for you, honored Mr. Rudel, so little do I wish the latter. With these heartfelt wishes for your happiness, and with the prayer that you will misinterpret none of my remarks, I commend myself to your favor, and close this tedious letter as,

Dear sir, yours most truly and obediently,

R. Sch.

This letter produced the desired result; and his journey, which extended to Venice, was permitted. It was not, as he hoped, taken in the society of his friends Rosen and Semmel, but alone. It passed happily in undisturbed enjoyment, except for some financial distress, as the three following letters prove. The first, which betrays the presumptuous student, is to his sister-in-law, Theresa; the other two are addressed to his friend Gisbert Rosen, who had been left behind in Heidelberg.

BRESCIA, Sept. 16, 1829.

I have just seen a picturesque Italian girl, who looked rather like you: so I thought of you, and write to you, my dear Theresa! Would I could paint it all distinctly for you, — the deep blue Italian sky; the fresh living green of the earth; the apricot, lemon, and mulberry trees; the hemp and tobacco fields; the whole [illegible] full of beautiful butterflies and gentle zephyrs; the distant, steadfast, honest, German, expressive, and angular Alps; and then the handsome, great, passionately languishing eyes of the Italian women, almost like yours when you're pleased with any thing; and then the whole strange, affecting, *living* life, which *ex-cites*, but never *is* excited; and then myself, when I almost forget my dear Germany, so firmly rooted in my breast, for this lyric Italy, and when I gaze in regular German sentimental style at the setting sun, or at my native mountains, red with the sun's last kiss, which glow, die and then stand there cold as giant corpses, — oh! would I could paint all this for you; you would have to pay as much postage again, my letter would be so thick and voluminous.

Yesterday I left Milan in splendid weather, where I lingered for a week, although I only meant to spend two days there. The reasons were many: first and best, because, on the whole, I liked it. Second, on a great many accounts: for example, the cathedral, the *palazzo reale*, *escalier conduisant au Belvedere* at *Hotel Reichmann*, also a lovely English girl, who *seemed* to have fallen in love with my playing rather than with me; for English girls love with the head, — that is, they love Brutus or Lord Byron or Mozart and Raphael, rather than mere outward beauty, like Adonis or Apollo, if the mind is not equally beautiful. The Italians reverse the situation, and love only with the heart. The Germans unite both, or love a knight, a minstrel, or a rich man, who will marry them at once. But *sans comparaison*, I beg, don't take this in any personal sense. Count S. of Innspruck was a third reason: although he is fourteen years older than I, we became quite intimate; we always had a deal to say, to tell, and to talk about, and were mutually much pleased. He gave me a purely refreshing proof that the world holds something more than blackguards and fools, although he was deaf, slightly deformed, and made horrible faces, not at mankind, but at men.

Were not the Italian language perpetual music (the count calls it a long-sustained chord in A-minor), I should hear nothing sensible. You can form as little idea of the ardor with which it is played as of the negligence and lack of elegance and precision: of course there are exceptions, as at *la Scala* in Milan, where I quite forgot Dr. Carus and Madame H. of Chemnitz over Signora Lalande * and Tamburini. I will send you a favorite aria of the Lalande and some other little songs.

I'm getting on very well with my Italian: which is a good thing; for it's an every-day affair to cheat strangers. I give myself out for a Prussian, which helps me much, since that is the favorite nation. Of course, it's hard to deny one's fatherland; but it's a good trick, harms no one, and helps me. Yesterday, I had quite an adventure. It's the fashion here for ladies to go to the coffee-houses. I was sitting quietly at my ta-

---

* The singer Signora Meric-Lalande. She left the stage, after a glorious career, in 1836.

ple, drinking chocolate, when a lady approached with majestic tread, accompanied by an elegant, shallow-brained butterfly signor. The tables were all occupied; and they took seats close by me. I could not construe this to mean that I must rise, since my cup was almost full, so sat still. I soon saw that the signora looked often and inquiringly towards me, as if anxious for me to go, since both seemed desirous to begin a *discorso innamorato.* In the course of their conversation, I heard the gentleman say, though in an undertone, "*Guesto signore*" (he meant me), "*è certamente dalle campagne;*" that is, "This gentleman is surely from the country." At first, I pretended not to understand Italian; but it grew still better. When I arose, and was about to go, the signor broke off his talk with the lady, and said mockingly, "*Addio, signore!*" I did not wish to answer in the lady's presence, so asked the *cameriere* if he would tell that gentleman that the *dalle campagne* had something to say to him. He replied, if I wished to speak to him, I might come to him. The anecdote of Frederic the Great occurred to me as I went towards him, and said, with a quiet smile, "*Ah, mio signore, sa a parlare spagnolo;*" (that is, "Can you speak Spanish?") "*perché io non ben so l'italiano,*" ("because I don't know Italian well.") He replied hesitatingly, "*Nô.*" "*Veritamente,*" I continued, "*me ne dispiace, perciocchè altrimente potrebbe leger il Don Quixote nell' originale; ma io son Cavaliére e me piacerebbe a revederci;*" (that is, "Really, I'm sorry; for otherwise you could have read Don Quixote in the original; but I am a gentleman, and should be glad to meet you again.") With a puzzled, "*Bene, signore,*" he turned towards his lady, and thus dismissed me. However, I have seen and heard nothing more of him. Perhaps I shall lie dead upon the scene of action to-morrow, killed by an ill-mannered Jew, as I afterwards learned him to be. But the worst is, that I fear he did not understand my, or Frederic the Great's, wit, since the Italian people's ignorance both of their own and foreign literature is beyond description.

God grant I've written this plainly, so that you may understand the crazy affair aright. Day after to-morrow I go to Verona, then to Vicenza, Padua, and Venice. I am eternally grateful to Edward for sending me so much money: still I cannot deny that I shall have to be very economical; as, on closer inspection of my funds, I always return to the accursed thought, that I sha'n't have enough, and shall have to pawn or sell my watch. Would heaven would shower down a few ducats! and all my tears and letters to guardians and brothers would forever cease!

How goes it with you? and do you ever think of the distant, lonely wanderer, who has now nothing left but his heart, with which he can speak, weep, and smile? Alas! a mantle like Dr. Faust's would be splendid. I should like to steal in at your window now, unseen and unwatched, and then to fly back to Italy, and weave past, present, and future in *one* wreath. Had men as many cheerful moments in their hours of sorrow as they have mournful ones in their hours of joy, they would surely be happier than I am just now.

But I am very happy, believe me; and I owe it all to my good Edward and to that other lofty spirit, whose veil is now removed; for they gave and granted me this pleasure. Addio, my dear sister, in gayety and in grief, I am ever yours,   R. Sch.

Clasp your Helen close when you kiss her; for you kiss her for me Remember me kindly to mother, Edward, Julius, Carl, Emilie, Rosalie,* and all your friends in Gera, and don't forget Malchen and *Erttel.*

Schumann to Rosen.

VENICE, Sept. 21, 1829.

I can't get a decent sheet of paper here, so tear a leaf from my pocket-book. I'm well, even happy. I fell in love in Milan, and staid there a whole week. My purse is empty; and I shall have to sell my watch, and borrow from Currer in Augsburg. I have written often, but always torn the letter up. I can give you no idea of Venice, although I can of other cities when we walk on Castle Hill. We've had wretched weather; but my mental sky was all the more clear and bright. O Rosen! why didn't you come to Venice with me, or why did I come without you? Please hire me new lodgings, do you hear? just what I like: you know my taste pretty well. Don't delay a moment. Alas! my heart is heavy, and my spirit is on the *escalier conduisant au Belvedere, in Hotel Reichmann.* She gave me a cypress-leaf when we parted there. She was an English girl, right haughty and kindly, loving and hating, hard, and yet so tender when I played, — accursed reminiscences! From Augsburg again.† Farewell, friend.   Your   R. Sch.

To the Same.

MILAN, Oct. 4, 1829.

As I forgot to prepay the letter I wrote you from Venice, I fear you never received it, my beloved Rosen. On the whole, I should be glad; since it was written in rather a melancholy mood, caused by many things which I will not now detail. For several weeks I have been (and am ever more and more so) so poor and so rich, so weak and so strong,

---

* Emilie and Rosalie were Schumann's sisters-in-law.
† This letter was never written.

so decrepit and so full of life, that I — . . . To-day, too, I can hardly hold my pen: so in all brevity this. I was ill in Venice: it was a kind of sea-sickness, with vomiting, head-ache, &c., — a living death. I could not get rid of the cursed memory of the cypress-trees in Milan. A doctor took a Napoleon from me; and a scamp of a tradesman cheated me out of half a one: total, two Napoleons. After short consideration, I resolved to return to Milan. Alas! I repeat, I ought not to have travelled without you. I won't describe any thing to you. I'm much more successful in conver-sation, especially when there's a great deal of it. I shall be with you again by the end of October. Don't forget my request in regard to rooms. Do it to please me, Rosen. That's all for to-day. Farewell.

Your   R. Sch.

Soon after his return, Schumann wrote to his guardian as follows : —

Heidelberg, Nov. 28, 1829.

Dear Sir, — You will by this time have heard from my brothers of the happy completion of my *journey;* and it will give me great pleasure, six months hence, to tell you of all that I have seen and felt. As for the money that this journey cost me, I regret, to speak frankly, not a penny of it. I did indeed return to Heidelberg a beggar, and am there-fore all the more grateful to you for your kindness in sending me one hundred thalers, which I received Oct. 25. I should like, dear Mr. Rudel, to know how long it must last, and how much I may expect at Easter. I have very little left of the one hundred thalers. I spent most of it. . . .

It is better that I should be perfectly open with you. I therefore beg that you will be the same with me, honored Mr. Rudel. If you wish me to economize, I shall be glad to do so as far as possible.

I am well and happy, and live very quietly in my little room. I have a great many invitations, but visit very little. On the whole, I shall be heartily glad to return to Zwickau and Leipsic. I often feel homesick.

Hoping for speedy information on these points, and that you will send me a small sum of money at once, I commend myself to you and your honored family as, dear sir,   Most truly yours,   R. Sch.

In the winter of 1829 and 1830, Schumann devoted himself to music more entirely than ever, — "played piano much," says the note-book. It was indeed so, as his few intimate friends unanimously testify, chief among them being Rosen and Sem-mel, — the latter in the mean time had again left Heidelberg, —

and their fellow-student, Töpken,* whose love for music had brought him into closer relations with Schumann.

The latter says, in his valuable communication in regard to his acquaintance with Schumann, "My interest in him. was first aroused by hearing that he was a friend of music and *in specie* pianist. It was greatly increased by his playing. He performed for me the first movement of Hummel's A-minor concerto.† I was greatly impressed by his aplomb and consciously. artistic execution, and now saw with whom I was dealing. I gladly embraced every opportunity of meeting him, of playing four-hand pieces with him, and for musical intercourse. At least *one* evening in the week was always set aside for our meeting; and we soon began to study compositions for four hands, Schumann's favorites being Schubert's polonaises, which he preferred to any of his other works, as also his variations ‡ on a theme by Herold and others (op. 82). This practice was made most instructive and interesting to me by the hints and intimations which he threw out and illustrated practically about the conception and performance of each composition. The concerted playing was usually followed by free extemporizations from him, which enchanted all hearts. I confess that these direct musical effusions afforded me such satisfaction as I have *never* since felt, however great an artist I may have heard. Ideas flowed in an inexhaustible stream. From one ever-recurring thought, others would gush and well spontaneously; and, throughout all, his individual spirit attracted in its profoundity with all the magic of poetry, still clearly revealing the characteristics of his musical nature, both from its energetic, original side, and its fragrantly tender, reflective, dreamy side. Those evenings, which often became nights, and which bore us far up above the external world, will never be erased from my memory. Music was Schumann's real study while in Heidelberg. The earliest hours of day often found him at his instrument;

---

* Doctor of jurisprudence in Bremen.

† Schumann made a special study of it under F. Wieck.

‡ The Marien variations.

and, when he said to me, ' I played seven hours this morning. I shall play well to-night: we must meet,' then I was always sure that there was a treat in store for me. Nor was he content with his progress in technique, which often caused him great trouble : he longed to reach the goal more swiftly than was possible in the natural course of events. We meditated much on ways and means for abbreviating the process, and soon believed that we had really discovered one, and must use it. He afterwards acknowledged his mistake."

Schumann's skill as a pianist gradually became known throughout Heidelberg. He had already delighted wide circles, gotten up for the purpose, by his improvisations; and the musical people of the City of the Muses formally sued for the honor of his company. But, where the greatest advances were made, he often replied with indifference, not to say obstinacy. It once happened that he was invited to a brilliant soirée, given by an English family living in Heidelberg. They had specially reckoned on a musical contribution from him to the entertainment of the company. He accepted the invitation ; but, when the evening came for which it held good, he showed no desire to comply with it. His friend Töpken, who happened to be present, reminded him that he would be expected to keep his promise, and urged him to go. All remonstrance and persuasion were vain : he staid at home ; and his non-appearance, naturally offending that family, all intercourse with them was forever at an end.

In the mean time, Schumann found occasion to step before a larger audience as a pianist, at a musical club, mostly composed of students, — " *Museum*," — whose purpose was to practise fine instrumental music, particularly symphonies, at regular meetings, and then to bring them before the public at their leisure. Schumann was a member of this club; and its committee therefore felt authorized and induced to ask him to play a piano solo at one of the concerts. He readily consented, and chose Moscheles's brilliant variations on the Alexander March ; which, as has already been stated, he knew, and was conversant with.

while a mere child. He played it with great power, his friend
Töpken at his request turning the leaves for him, and remarked with heartfelt pleasure that his assistant trembled more
than he did.

The great success of this public performance was proved by
his immediately receiving invitations to Mannheim and May-
ence, to play at concerts there; which he, however, declined.
He decided to end his brief public career in Heidelberg with his
brilliant début. He also gave up playing in large companies,
and confined himself to his own immediate friends, and could
scarcely be persuaded to break through his retirement, even for
so attractive a house as that of the celebrated Thibaut, author
of the book, " On the Purity of the Tone Art." His meetings
with this witty scholar were but few, and without any direct
influence on his musical aims and development. Perhaps this
was caused by Thibaut's ascetic view of music; although he
once succeeded in completely converting the silent, thoughtful Schumann to his opinion. On one occasion, the conversation turned to Rossini's music ; and Thibaut said rather sarcastically, " That it seemed to him just as if some one said (in
the softest flute-like tone), I love (screaming) THEE ! " This
excited Schumann's heartiest laughter and delight.

Schumann likewise took no real share in student-life, which
played only a periodic and peculiar part with him. At first he
held aloof from it : his wealth of heart and mind could not
consort with such wild actions. He was afterwards induced to
join in them occasionally ; indeed, during his last winter term
at Heidelberg, these occasions were more numerous, and almost
threatened to draw him into the whirlpool of academic pleas-
ures. Yet there was something beneath all this. The often-
quoted note-book calls it " Chaotic social life," not student-life :
the latter had no other meaning to Schumann than the former.
He never joined in any but great movements, and then thoroughly.

However different Schumann's college-life may have been
from that of others, he was not averse to romantic adventures

now and then. The following anecdote may serve to illustrate this : —

Schumann once attended a masquerade during the carnival of 1830, in company with his friend Rosen, for the purpose of paying some attention to a pretty but otherwise insignificant girl. He knew that she would be present at the ball, and, as a pretext for approaching her, put a poem in his pocket. Fortune favored him: he met and recognized her; but, as he was about to take a carnival liberty, and hand her the poem, the girl's mother stepped threateningly between, " Keep your poems to yourself, Mask : my daughter does not understand poetry."

He was not satisfied with regular and uninterrupted study of the piano : he also did justice to his creative muse, when she urged him to action. He here experienced the daily need of theoretical knowledge, and was thus impelled to study the art of composition, that he might gain therefrom a base for his productions. We may rest assured that this self-tuition profited him but little, when we reflect that books on theory are generally intended rather for teachers than for scholars. We shall see the truth of this farther on.

Of the compositions occurring in 1829, those specially deserving mention are : hints for symphonies, shorter pieces for the piano, — several of which were afterwards published in the "Papillons," namely, numbers 1, 3, 4, 6, and 8, — and piano-studies, designed for the extension and perfection of his own execution.

The first half of 1830 was far more fertile. He then wrote : Hints for a piano concerto in F-major, Variations on the name of *Abegg*, and *Toccata* in D-major.

The Abegg variations, which appeared in November, 1831, as opus 1,* owe their origin to an acquaintance formed at a Mannheim ball with Meta Abegg, the lovely daughter of a man then high in office there. According to Schumann's own account, she was adored by one of his friends ; and therefore no deeper signification can be attached to the affair. Besides his

---

* It was his first published work.

desire to celebrate the fair one in music, as a delicate attention to his friend, the capacities for musical treatment of the name Abegg must have rendered its investiture in melody interesting to him. The theme is founded on the notes, a b♭ e g g, which produce the following pleasing and melodious figure : —

which continued regularly, but gradually sinking, in four-fold division, forms the first part of the theme. In the second part, an inversion of the above figure follows. The variations themselves, some of which were never published, although of unusual kind, are without any special musical importance. On the whole, they can only be considered as amateur productions of an extremely gifted nature ; and it would be wrong to demand more from Schumann's ignorance of theory at that time. Their most conspicuous fault seems to be, an insufficient mastery of the subject, — the greatest enemy to enjoyment.

The dedication of this work to the " Countess Pauline von Abegg " is, as has been already shown, a feigned one. Since Schumann had reasons for not dedicating his composition to her who had inspired it, he made use of this title, to show that the work was composed for some special occasion.

We will speak later of the *Toccata*, which underwent a total change before its publication.

Easter of 1830 drew near, and, with this spring festival, the time when Schumann was to leave Heidelberg after a year's residence there, to complete his legal studies in Leipsic, — a cruel dilemma, which must have caused a violent mental struggle : for how would he manage at home, how account for the studies which he had left unheeded, while his genius urged him with ever-increasing strength to the pursuit of art ? Added to this was his knowledge of his mother's decided aversion to an artistic career ! Is it not very explicable and natural, that, under such circumstances, he feared to return home, and sough⁴ to defer it ?   He himself hardly knew what the result would be.   The mental fermentation must be thorough; and this required respite : for, as the old proverb says, " Gain time, and you gain all."   He requested this respite in the following letter to his guardian : —

HEIDELBERG, March 26, 1830.

DEAR SIR, — You must not think that forgetfulness or neglect is the cause of my delay in thanking you for and acknowledging the due receipt of your kind letter with the hundred thalers, sent so long ago. It was partly to save the postage, partly because I could answer more easily and shortly through my brothers.

However expensive my life may have been for the last three months, my brothers must have told you that it has been pleasant and cheerful I'm as well as a fish in water, and happy besides.   You must also be aware that I am in debt, — the only thing which troubles me frequently. I have paid my tailor alone a hundred and forty florins for this winter term, to say nothing of all the other bills that I did not have to pay with the money allotted me by the court for purposes of study, when in Leipsic.   If you will reflect, you will find that my Leipsic expenses were much the same as these.   The worst is, that *every thing* is dearer, finer, and better here; because the student lords it here, and, for that very reason, is cheated.   How much you would oblige me, dear Mr. Rudel, by sending me as much money as possible and as soon as possible.   Believe me, a student never needs more than when he hasn't a penny in his pocket, especially in little university towns where he can borrow as much as he likes.   For two out of the past seven weeks I have been without a farthing, and can truly say, that I never had so many wants as during those seven weeks; for then the landlords charge double prices; and you have to pay double crown-thalers.

You will have learned through my relations that it is my greatest wish to be allowed to spend another half-year in this truly glorious Heidelberg; and my mother has answered this request with an unqualified " yes."   How glad I should be, my honored fatherly friend, if you, too, would give your consent; since a sojourn here is far more profitable and interesting than in stupid Leipsic: so let me close my letter with most humble prayers that you will very soon grant me mine, as far as in your will and power lies.   I beg you will remember me most kindly to your worthy, honored family, and sign myself with great respect,

Your most obliged and devoted,

R. SCH

In reply to this letter, his guardian at once consented to his prolonged stay in Heidelberg; and he could again, undisturbed, pursue his musical studies, whose energetic prosecution soon received important incitation from without. At Easter, 1830, Paganini visited Frankfort, that the wonders of his art might be heard there. Hardly did Schumann hear of the presence of this phenomenon in that city than he determined to hasten thither, to hear this admirable performer; and it is more than probable that he then first decided to devote himself solely to music.

Töpken was his companion on this excursion. "The trip itself," says the latter, "was as pleasant as profitable to us. A student's carriage, in the boldest sense of the word, whose guidance we undertook in turn, being equally experienced in riding and driving, brought us, after many adventures and in spite of all the freaks and irremediable defects of our Rosinante, safely to our journey's end." It is interesting to read an extract from Schumann's diary relative to this trip,* since it clearly reveals the deep impression made on our master by Paganini's playing. Its strength is shown by Schumann's elaboration of a number of Paganini's capriccios for the piano.

Two months later he found opportunity to hear the well-known violinist Ernst; yet we can hardly suppose that the latter, spite of his wonderful execution, could exercise any decisive influence upon Schumann's resolve.

A letter from him to his guardian is here inserted; which gives us another glance at the financial distresses of his Heidelberg life.

HEIDELBERG, June 21, 1830.

HONORED MR. RUDEL, — You will have learned from my letter of April 28, that all goes right well with me, and that I duly received the . . . . . thalers, sent me by you. But, since neither my mother nor brothers have given me the least answer, I must suppose that the three letters which I addressed on the 28th April to you, my mother, and Edward, have by some means gone astray. I beg you will kindly tell me whether you received that letter. I have sad news to announce, most worthy Mr. Rudel. In the first place, I have a tutor or repetitor, who costs me

* See letters for 1833–1852. No. 1.

eighty florins every six months; then I shall be arrested (don't be frightened!) in a week, if I do not pay within that time thirty florins for other college-dues. Arrest is a kind of threat here; and it will by no means be so dangerous. . . .

Hoping that you will remember me kindly to your family,

I remain your true and humble servant,

R. Sch.

A few weeks after sending this letter, at length appeared the important and decisive moment, when Schumann stepped forward, after mature consideration, to declare freely and openly, that henceforth he neither could nor would follow any other profession than that of music. This purpose must have long been active in his mind; for otherwise it would have been impossible for him to employ his time at the university in the manner described. But, as has already been said, he required time for his ideas to ripen, and to fortify himself against all the attacks against his plans which he feared from his mother's dislike to an artistic career. He first of all imparted his resolve to her alone, and enclosed in the following one to his guardian, his letter to her : —

HEIDELBERG, July 30, 1830.

MOST HONORED MR. RUDEL, — I was just about to post a letter to you, with the usual request, when the letter-carrier overtook me at the door, with your longed-for letter. Accept my heartfelt thanks for all your kindness and for the trouble you have taken for me, which I can never requite.

The weather here is splendid, but terribly hot; and my life has lost none of the charms which fill every letter to you. I am well as ever. I have to work hard, and often know not how I can be ready in time, since I am also studying English and French, and ought not wholly to neglect my piano.

My departure will be very late in September; when my legal lectures, which keep me somewhat cool amid the scorching heat, come to a late close.

Will you be kind enough to hand the enclosed to my mother at once, as it requires a speedy answer. My mother will talk the matter over with you.

With cordial regards to you and your whole household,

I remain your most humble servant,

R. Sch.

The letter enclosed in this to his mother reads as follows : —

HEIDELBERG, July 30, 1830.
5 o'clock.

GOOD-MORNING, MAMMA! — How can I describe to you my bliss at this moment! The alcohol burns and bubbles in the coffee-urn; and the heaven is pure and golden enough to kiss; and the very spirit of dawn, clear and cool, breathes around. Besides all this, your letter lies before me, in which is disclosed a treasure of sensibility, intellect, and virtue; my cigar is capital; . . . in short, the world is beautiful at times, that is man, if he would always rise early.

Sunshine and blue skies abound in my life here; but a guide is wanting, and that Rosen was. Two more of my best friends, the von H. . . . from Pomerania, brothers, also started for Italy a week ago; and so I'm often very lonely, — that is, sometimes downright glad and sad, just as it may happen. A young man can do without a sweetheart better than without a friend. I burn when I think of myself. My *whole life* has been a *twenty years' war* between poetry and prose, or, let us say, music and law. I've had as lofty an ideal in practical life as in art. This ideal was hard labor, and the hope of struggling in a great sphere of action; but what prospect is there, especially in Saxony, for a plebeian without influence or money, with no true love for legal petitions and petty controversies! In Leipsic I led an idle life, dreamed and loitered about, and did really nothing: *here,* I have been more industrious; but both there and here have become more and more attached to music. Now I stand at the parting of the roads, and shudder at the question, Whither? If I follow out my own bent, it points, and, as I believe, correctly, to music. But truly don't take it ill of me, for I only say it lovingly and lowly, I always felt as if you held me back from that path, doubtless from good motherly reasons, which I perfectly understood: we always called it "an uncertain future and a precarious livelihood." But what can I say further? There can be no more painful thought to a man than that he has prepared an unhappy, dead, and shallow future for himself. It is hard to follow a profession in every way opposed to early education and taste; and it requires patience, confidence, and rapid progress. My fancy is now but young, and would be cherished and ennobled by music. I am also certain that with industry, perseverance, and a good teacher, I could in six years rival any pianist, since piano-playing is pure mechanique and skill. Now and then I also have a fancy, perhaps a taste, for composition. . . . Now comes the question, one or the other; for only *one* thing can be done greatly and well in a lifetime; — and I can give but one answer: undertake a good and worthy object; firmness and calmness will complete it, and bring it to a perfect end. I am now more eager than ever in this struggle, dear mother, — sometimes rash and confident in my own strength and will, sometimes terrified, when I think of the great career which I have already set aside and must now again renounce. As for Thibaut, he has long urged me to follow art. A letter from you to him would give me great pleasure; and Thibaut would also like it much. He, however, left for Rome some time ago: so that I shall not see him again.

If I stick to law, I must incontestably remain here for another winter, that I may attend Thibaut's pandects; which every lawyer must hear. But, if I stick to music. I must unquestionably leave here, and return to Leipsic. Wieck, of L., to whom I would gladly confide myself, who knows me, and can judge of my powers, must polish me a little more: afterwards, I must spend a year in Vienna, and, if in any way possible, go to Moscheles. One more request, dear mother; which perhaps you will willingly grant. *Write yourself to Wieck at Leipsic, and ask him frankly what he thinks of me and my plan.* Beg him to answer *quickly* and decisively, that I may hasten my departure from Heidelberg, hard as it will be for me to leave this place, where I shall leave behind so many good men, glorious dreams, and a perfect paradise of nature. If you like, *enclose this letter in the one to Wieck.* The question *must in any case* be settled *by Michaelmas;* and then I will set to work at my appointed task, fresh and brave, without a tear.

You see that this is the most important letter that I ever did or shall write; therefore do not grant my wishes ungraciously, but answer soon. There is *no time* to lose.

Farewell, my dear mother. Fear not: heaven can only aid when man helps himself.

Your most loving son,
ROBERT SCHUMANN.

The consternation into which the contents of this letter cast Schumann's mother is clearly mirrored in the following lines, written by her to Fr. Wieck : —

ZWICKAU, Aug. 7, 1830.

HONORED SIR,* — According to the request of my son, Robert Schumann, I take the liberty of applying to you in regard to the future of this dear son. With trembling and deep anxiety, I seat myself to ask you how you like Robert's plan, which the enclosed letter will explain.

* This letter is, with the exception of the correction of a few orthographic and grammatic errors, an exact copy of the original manuscript.

It is not in accordance with my views; and I freely confess that I have great fears for Robert's future. *Much* labor is needed to become a *distinguished* musician, or even to earn a living by music; because there are too many great artists before him: and, were his talent ever so marked, it is, and ever will be, uncertain whether he would gain applause, or earn a secure future. . . .

He has now studied for almost *three* years, and had many, very many, wants. Now, when I thought him almost at the goal, I see him take another step, which puts him back to the beginning, — see, when the time has come for him to prove himself, that his little fortune is gone, and that he is still dependent. Whether he will succeed. . . . alas! I cannot tell you how sad, how cast down, I feel when I think of Robert's future. He is a good soul. Nature gave him intellectual endowments such as others must struggle to attain, and he is not disagreeable in appearance. He has enough money to pursue his studies without distress, enough of which still remains to support him respectably until he is able to provide for himself; and now he would choose a profession which should have been begun ten years earlier. If you, honored sir, are yourself a father, you will feel that I am right, and that my distress is not groundless. My other three sons are greatly displeased, and absolutely insist that I shall not consent: but I would not force him, if his own feelings do not lead him; for it is no honor to begin again as a scholar, after three wasted years, and spend his few thalers upon an *uncertainty*.

ALL rests on your decision, — *the peace of a* LOVING MOTHER, THE WHOLE HAPPINESS FOR LIFE of a young and inexperienced man, who lives but in a higher sphere, and will have nothing to do with practical life. I know that you love music. Do not let your feelings plead for Robert, but consider his years, his fortune, his powers, and his future. I beg, I conjure you, as a husband, a father, and a friend of my son, act like an upright man, and tell me your opinion frankly, — what he has to fear, or to hope.

Excuse the distraction of my letter: I am so overcome by all that has passed that I am soul-sick; and never was a letter so hard for me to write as this. May you be happy! And send an answer soon to your

Humble servant,

C. SCHUMANN, née SCHNABEL.

Wieck's decision was favorable to Schumann: he had recognized his former pupil's great gift for music, and believed it his duty, in spite of all the disadvantages of a musical career, to advise its unconditional prosecution, since important talents were in question, which even under disadvantageous circumstances gave great promise.

Schumann's fate was thus decided, his future course marked out; for, after reading Fr. Wieck's opinion, his mother withdrew all further opposition to her son's wishes, and sent him Wieck's letter, to ratify her consent.

This happy issue surpassed his wildest hopes; and, intoxicated with joy at such a reply, he wrote to Wieck: —

HEIDELBERG, Aug. 21, 1830.

MOST HONORED OF TEACHERS, — It was long ere my ideas grew calm and smooth. Do not ask me how your letter stirred me. Now I am better: my first feeling was one of courage and resolve. The Atlas was crushed; and a child of the sun stood pointing to the East. Bow before nature; for else your genius will be forever lost — the path to knowledge leads over icy Alps: the path of art has its cliffs; but they are Indian, covered with flowers, hopes, and dreams — so it seemed when I read your and my mother's letter. — Now I'm much calmer. . . . I cleave to art. I will cleave to it, I can, and must. I bid farewell without a tear to a profession which I could not like, hardly respect; but it is not without fear that I look along the rugged path which leads to my ideal. Believe me, I am modest, have many reasons to be so; but I am also brave, patient, trustful, and plastic. I confide myself wholly to you: I give myself up to you. Take me as I am, and above all things bear with me. No blame shall depress me: no praise shall make me idle. Whole pailsful of very, very cold theory can do me no harm; and I will work at it without a murmur. I have gone over your five "buts" calmly and carefully, and examined myself strictly as to whether I can fulfil them. Head and heart reply at once, "Oh, of course!"

Most honored one, take my hand and lead me: I will follow where you will, and never tear the bandage from my eyes, lest they should be dazzled by the light. Would that you could see my soul: it is still therein; and all around the breeze of morn breathes clear and calm.

Trust me: I will deserve the name of your scholar. Alas! why is man so blessed at times in this world, most honored one? I know.

May you indeed fare well! in three weeks you will have me, and then —   Yours most truly,
ROBERT SCHUMANN.

With this exuberant letter went, on the same day, one to his guardian.

HEIDELBERG, Aug. 21, 1830.

MOST WORTHY MR. RUDEL, — My relations must have told you of my resolve and of my life-plan. Believe me, I was born for music, and will remain true to it. However well I know and esteem your views of life, and however long I have considered them, I am still sure that I can remove all your doubts.

My mind is firmly and fixedly made up to this. I will devote myself for six months exclusively to music under Wieck, in Leipsic. Rely on Wieck, most honored Mr. Rudel, and await his opinion. If he says, that I can *in three years from these six months* attain the highest pitch of art, then let me go in peace; for I shall not fail. But if Wieck entertains the slightest doubt (after these six months), then there is nothing lost to law; and I shall be ready and willing to pass my examination in a year: in which case I shall have studied no more than four years.

Most cordially esteemed Mr. Rudel, you will see by this the necessity of my leaving Heidelberg at once, since a residence here can only harm me.

Therefore be so kind as to send me a considerable sum at your earliest convenience, that I may pay my travelling and other expenses. From a hundred and fifty to a hundred and eighty thalers would make me perfectly happy. I pledge myself in return not to ask you for another penny till the end of the year. If you will grant my request, you will relieve me from a host of perplexities and distresses: . . . so do not be angry. This shall certainly be the last urgent request of the kind.

I remain cordially, and with deep respect, yours truly,

R. SCH.

This letter was unanswered. Meanwhile, Schumann and his schoolmate Röller made a journey to Strasburg, led thither by his lively interest in the July revolution. On his return, he addressed still another, the last, letter to his guardian : —

MOST HONORED MR. RUDEL, — Heaven grant that no misfortune in your or my home be the cause of your long silence! Or can it be that you did not receive my last *important* letter?

Once more I eagerly beg you to answer me at once, sending some money (if, in any way possible, a very large sum), and ease my troubled mind. You cannot conceive the anxiety and fearful suspense I suffer. I am the *only* student here, and wander about, deserted and poor as any beggar, head over ears in debt, through the woods and lanes. Be lenient with me, most worthy Mr. Rudel! Send me money this once, only

money, and do not force me to seek other means of paying for my journey hence, which would be very injurious to me, and could not be
agreeable to you.

I commend myself to your kindness and indulgence, and remain,

Yours very truly, but very poorly,

R. SCH.

His guardian gave ear to this pressing petition; but raised
objections to the proposed artistic career. No reply was made
to these; since, while matters stood as they did in Schumann's
mind, any intercourse between them would have been superfluous.

Schumann now prepared to visit Leipsic. He was ready to
consecrate himself exclusively and with firm purpose to the
pursuit of art. His path led him across the Rhine to Detmold;
whither he went, that he might once more see and enjoy his
friend Rosen, who returned home the last of June, that same
year, a doctor of laws.

II.

ROBERT SCHUMANN'S ARTIST-CAREER.

LEIPSIC.

1830 — 1840.

WITH a full, glad, hopeful heart, Schumann again greeted Leipsic, which he had once so gladly left. His dearest wish was now fulfilled. He could follow his soul's calling openly and without a fear : and the favorable opinion of a man on whom he relied must also have afforded him great satisfaction ; nor could he have found a city better suited to his plans than Leipsic.

The general idea that Leipsic's musical importance began with Mendelssohn's influential activity there, is (I say it with no desire to depreciate that illustrious master's merit) entirely erroneous. His incontestably great service to that city consists of his artist-life there, but more particularly does it owe to him its institute, which was under his sole direction, and to which he gave an animating, refreshing impulse, and a spirit until then unknown. But music flourished long before his appearance in Leipsic ; and all the musical institutions now existing, with the exception of the music school which was founded by Mendelssohn,* were standing in 1835. Even the Gewandhaus concerts, whose origin may be traced back to March 11, 1743,†

---

* See Neue Zeitschr f. Musik, vol. xix., page 201, in regard to the foundation of the Leipsic Music School.

† The Continuatio Annalium Lips. Vogelii, tom ii. page 541, anno. 1743. contains the following : " On the 11th of March, the great concert was

and which only suffered a temporary interruption during that period, so memorable to Leipsic (from 1813–1814), really began Nov. 25, 1781. * At that time Adam Hiller directed these concerts, — that is, the vocal compositions given at them; for these alone had a special director, while the orchestral works were led by the *concertmeister* from his seat at the head of the violins. Schicht succeeded him in 1785, and was himself succeeded by cantor Schultz in 1810, who held the office until 1827.

But, at the time that Schumann chose Leipsic as his permanent home, Pohlenz directed the concerts simultaneously with Matthäi, the leader of the orchestra, until 1835. At this time, Mendelssohn stepped forth as a regenerator,† and went so far as to use a bâton in directing the orchestral compositions. This innovation at first met with much opposition, although it had already been introduced in other places by Spohr and Weber. This was, however, changed to glad acknowledgment, as soon as the excellence of the method was recognized. But Mendelssohn's peculiar earnestness in business-matters, the admirable conscientiousness and artistic devotion with which he arranged and directed the Gewandhaus concerts, must in any case have brought it to a speedy and glorious consummation, to say nothing of the importance of its prime origin.

The number of the Gewandhaus concerts was originally limited to twenty-four. In 1827 it was reduced to twenty. This plan has been transmitted to the present time. Besides

founded by sixteen persons, both nobles and citizens, each person subscribing twenty thalers yearly and one Louis-d'or quarterly for its support. The musicians were also sixteen in number, all picked men. The first concert was given and held in Grimmisch Street, at the house of Counsellor Schwaben; the next (four weeks after) at the house of Mr. Gleditzschen, a bookkeeper, because there was not enough room at the first." And farther on, page 565, anno 1744, "March 9 was the day for the great concert, with a cantata, composed by Dr. Dohles, with trumpets and drums."

* The *true* beginning of the Gewandhaus concerts may be correctly given as 1781; since they were then first held at the Gewandhaus, whence they derive their name. See *Allg. Mus. Zeitung*, vol. xxxiii. page 801.

† The first subscription-concert led by Mendelssohn took place Oct. 4 1835.

the performance of vocal and instrumental works of every kind, the concerts were made more interesting by the appearance of famous foreign artists.

Some idea of the musical life in Leipsic during the last thirty years may be formed by a brief survey of the different musical institutions and clubs in existence there. Besides the Thomanerchor,* under cantor Weinlig, remarkable for its illustrious past, and which still assists at the Gewandhaus concerts, Leipsic possessed a royal theatre (municipal since August, 1832), an academy of singing, a musical union for popular and scientific vocal music (both societies under the direction of Pohlenz), the Pauliner Singing Society in its infancy, an orchestral club called " The Euterpe," founded in 1824, directed by C. G. Müller (afterwards conductor at Altenburg), and finally the Quartette concerts, under *concertmeister* Matthäi. It is evident that the music-saturated atmosphere of Leipsic was most fit to develop and form talent. How fully convinced of this Schumann himself was, is shown by a letter dated Oct. 28, 1846, in which he speaks as follows in regard to the culture of an artistic youth named Meinardus,† to whose father the letter is addressed : —

"I think the only way to confirm his future career is to send him to the conservatory in Leipsic. I am convinced that he will thus make the most certain and rapid progress. There illustrious men work together; there the best music is to be heard. Industry and emulation can nowhere else be so aroused as there, in intercourse with his contemporaries; in a word, there is no better school for a musician than Leipsic, in Germany, perhaps in the world."

On his arrival in Leipsic, Michaelmas, 1830, Schumann took possession of some vacant lodgings in Wieck's abode, Grimmisch Street, No. 36. This must have been the more desirable to him, that he could thus hope, by intimate intercourse with

---

* It is sufficient to name the cantor of all cantors, Johann Sebastian Bach.

† The composer, Ludwig Meinardus, still living in Dresden.

his teacher, to realize more speedily his plan of devoting himself to music; but the bright dream caused by this fortunate event was transformed, before he was aware, into a painful but finally expiatory reality.

Soon after he began to take lessons from Wieck, he was deluded by the idea, that the studies undertaken by his teacher's advice did not bring him on fast enough. To his misfortune, or, if you will to his good fortune, he now recalled the manipulations which he and his friend Töpken had devised in Heidelberg, and by dint of which he believed he could greatly shorten the tedious path to technical culture. However erroneous this idea was, as the result proved it to be, it was very natural that a mind anxious for technical ability would be very prone to hasten impatiently over the steps necessary to a normal technical development. Schumann did this with the best intentions, without mentioning it to his teacher; making the experiment with closed doors. During this time, he made no use of Fr. Wieck's instructions. He told his acquaintances, among them Julius Knorr, of whom we have spoken before, that he had found an infallible method of attaining a fine execution most quickly and surely: the secret, which he declared would be followed by most surprising results, could be discovered by no one. He fed all with hopes of the speedy arrival of the moment of demonstration; but, when it did arrive, he had lost the power of using his right hand in playing. The sinews of his third finger had lost their natural elasticity from excessive stretching; and the result was, that, instead of striking down, as desired, it moved upwards. Conceive the terror of the bold experimenter when he saw this. No one could agree which particular experiment caused this lamentable event. From occasional remarks dropped by Schumann, his friends concluded that he had fastened his third finger in a machine invented by himself, and had then practised unceasingly with the other four fingers, that they might attain the utmost independence. The great ardor with which he tried this experi-

ment is shown by the circumstance, that he composed a num
ber of studies expressly for this purpose.

Good advice was now precious: indeed, his only hope was
to repair his injury by rest and careful treatment.   With
incredible patience he tried every remedy suited to heal his
finger.   His faith in its final recovery is proved by the fact,
that he practised unremittingly with his left hand.   This
attained extraordinary dexterity, which was remarkable long
after he had given up playing.

The advantages which Schumann might have derived from
Wieck's instructions were now at an end.   His lessons were
never resumed.   On the contrary, he followed his original plan,
and began to study theory, under the direction of a certain
music-master, Kupsch by name; but this, too, was of short
duration.

In the course of the year 1830, the piano-concerto in F-
major, begun in Heidelberg, was continued, but apparently
never completed.

The year 1831 brought to light a work, which was afterwards published as op. 2, "The Papillons." *   It consists
of twelve more or less unimportant pieces, some of which were
composed in Heidelberg.   Schumann liked a certain mystic
symbolism, a veiled allusion to general poetic intentions, as
many of his ensuing compositions prove.   This mystic symbolism may be considered as the product of that romantic disposition which strives to express poetic combinations of ideas in
an ingeniously marked and profound manner, although it does
not thus attain that plastic purity and simple truth which
would directly impart those ideas to their enjoyers.   Thus the
title "Papillons" certainly has a deeper mystic meaning,
whose probable signification no one would suspect.

"The Papillons," dedicated to Schumann's three sisters-in-
law, Theresa, Emilie, and Rosalie, to whom he was bound by tender friendship, are aphoristical tone-movements, without special

---

* See Schumann's critique, with marginal notes, in the letters for 1833-
1852, No. 1.

artistic merit, and only interesting in so far as they reveal to us many contrasting forms, in which a mood of musical expression characteristic of the artist is plainly visible. The *finale* is rendered somewhat more full and attractive by the combination of the Grossvater dance * with the first piece, whose melodic figure appears in the treble, while the dance forms the bass. The formation of this work, as well as that of the Abegg variations, shows an evident awkwardness and stiffness, caused by ignorance of the art of composition. An almost fruitless struggle of ingenious musical ideas with form is everywhere apparent. Happy exceptions are evidently rather the result of musical instinct than of a conscious, clearly intelligent power of expression.†

A letter ‡ written in 1834 to his friend Henrietta Voigt, of whom we shall speak hereafter, proves that Schumann had some poetical idea as base for " The Papillons." It reads thus: " I could tell you much about this, if Jean Paul did not do it better. If you have a spare moment, I beg you will read the last chapter of the ' *Flegeljahre*,' where all stands in black and white up to the Riesenstiefel in F-sharp minor (at the end of the ' *Flegeljahre*,' I feel as if the play were surely done, but as if the curtain had not yet fallen). I must tell you that I put the words to the music, not the reverse; for else I should think it a ' silly proceeding.' Only the last, which the play of chance formed into an answer to the first, was evoked by Jean Paul."

There also date from 1831 the first movement of a sonata in G-minor (according to Schumann's list, published as Allegro, op. 7 §), and variations on an original theme in G-major.

---

* The " Grossvater dance, as well as the Marseillaise," plays a certain part in Schumann's life. They are often repeated in his works, especially the former, in a humorous manner.

† One number of The Papillons (No. 8) was first written in D-minor. He played it in this key to his friend Töpken at Heidelberg, pretending it was a Schubert waltz; and then, roguishly claiming to be the author, was greatly amused at the success of his trick.

‡ See letters for 1833-52, No. 2.

§ This must be an error in Schumann's list. The Toccata (E-major) is

The latter are entirely unknown. The sonata, if we are to consider the Allegro, Op. 8, as the same thing, as we cannot but believe, belongs in form and substance to Schumann's feeblest mental product. This composition is unrefreshing in its broad, irregular proportions, and affords no room for sympathy in its lack of all power and purity of expression. Schumann himself laconically says, in a letter to his friend Henrietta Voigt, Nov. 24, 1834, "That the composer is worthier than his work, but less so than she to whom it is dedicated." *

The pain in Schumann's injured finger was not yet entirely alleviated; in fact, in the autumn of 1831, his whole hand became lame. He could use it only so far as it was absolutely necessary in playing; but a real performance was out of the question. How characteristic is Schumann's manner of treating this event, and reviewing his Heidelberg life, in a letter to his friend Töpken, written in 1833 ! †

" We did indeed err, when we thought we could accomplish by capricious mechanism what the peace and leisure of later years would spontaneously bring; or, we grasped the handle so firmly that we lost the blade (the reverse is much worse). In this respect, and to make skill balance with the other powers, I have often been obliged to correct my ideas. Much which I once considered infallible has been discarded as useless and hindering. Often have I sought to unite the powers of opposing paths. For equal powers elevate and multiply each other here, as in the physical world; but the stronger kills the weaker, and, to apply it to art, a poetic whole can be formed only by the harmonious cultivation of skill and ability (culture and talent). I play but little on the piano now : don't be alarmed

known among musicians as Op. 7. An allegro for the piano-forte did, however, appear as Op. 8; still it is not in G-minor. The only imaginable explanation is the existence of two compositions both numbered 7. No one knows of such. We can only suppose it to be a slip of the pen in Schumann's note-book. A new edition of this allegro has recently appeared.

* The dedication was to Ernestine von Fricken. See letters for 1833-52, No. 5.

† See letters for 1833-52, No. 1.

(I am resigned, and consider it a decree of fate). I have a lame finger on my right hand; in consequence of the injury being slight in itself, it was neglected until the evil grew so great that I can hardly use the hand at all."

Thus almost unavoidably compelled by fate, Schumann at last trod the path whose soil nourished the seeds of creative talent dormant in his mind, and gradually converted them to a blossoming and fruitful tree, which, alas! soon withered: he devoted himself entirely to composition. As is evident, it was now necessary for him to retrieve without delay his long neglect of theory. He therefore applied, through an intimate friend named Von der Lühe, to Heinrich Dorn; who at that time held the office of leader of the orchestra at the royal theatre in Leipsic. On his introduction, spite of his lame hand, he played his variations on the name of Abegg to the celebrated musician. These were no very brilliant letter of recommendation: however, H. Dorn proved ready and willing to grant the wishes of the timid, quiet youth.

The instruction, of course, began with the A, B, C, of thorough bass; for the first task set him as a trial of his theoretic knowledge, which was simply to harmonize a choral melody, was performed in a manner contrary to all rules. But soon, by exemplary and constant industry, the scholar advanced from the elementary steps of theory to the study of simple and double counterpoint. Schumann was so anxious for a thorough knowledge of the latter, that he wrote to his teacher, requesting him to give him his lesson at home, since he could not tear himself away from his work. Dorn agreed to this; and, when he entered his pupil's room, he found him deep in the study of counterpoint and — champagne, with which they sociably moistened the dry task.

Schumann's letters to H. Dorn prove how grateful he was for this instruction, which disclosed the true nature of art to him.

If from one point of view the pursuit of this study rendered the latter part of 1831 of the highest consequence, it was equally important from another point. He aimed at nothing less than hoisting the banner of enthusiastic recognition of a newly-risen star in the musical world, who was as peculiar as interesting. Fr. Chopin, unknown and unnoticed, though often repulsed from the doors to publicity, with the products of a mind* baptized in the fires of French and Polish nationality, at last succeeded in publishing his Don Juan Fantasia (Op. 2). Surprised and attracted by the kindred spirit in this piano-composition, Schumann felt compelled to proclaim his enthusiasm to the world. This he did in a fantastic, highly eulo-gistic effusion, which resembled nothing less than an ordinary critique. It appeared in No. 49, vol. xxxiii., of "The Universal Journal of Music," † and even then displayed that almost su-perabundant wealth of Jean Paulistic fantasy by which Schumann's later literary labors are marked. The features of Florestan and Eusebius, afterwards so well known, were here introduced, although not at all as "Davidsbündler." They first appeared as such on the establishment of the "Neue Zeitschrift für Musik" (New Journal of Music.) Schumann's labors as a musical critic date from this time, although he did not continue this beginning for two years.

The claims of society, which Schumann purposely avoided during his residence in Heidelberg, were, and continued to be, limited in proportion to his peculiar timidity. With the ex-ception of the intimate but quiet intercourse with Wieck's family, he held but little converse with those of his own age. It is singular that there was always one among his few friends who was his constant companion in his silent walks, and will-ingly became a butt for all his jokes and caprices, although they were not always of the most pleasant kind. He generally

---

* Chopin's father was a Frenchman, his mother a Pole.

† The same number of that Journal of Music contains a critique of Chopin's works by an anonymous correspondent "from the good old times;" which is in every particular in strong contrast to Schumann's remarks on the new light. It is a well-established fact, that Chopin at first met with much and violent opposition from the critics.

went at evening to some restaurant with his chosen comrades, working diligently all day.

It was a habit of Schumann to collect Wieck's ch'ldren in his room at twilight, and to frighten them by the recital of the most horrible ghost stories of his own invention. Then he would sometimes shut the door, and appear suddenly by the light of a spirit-lamp as a spectre in a fur coat turned inside out, exciting universal terror. Another thing which afforded him great pleasure was to make one of Wieck's two sons stand on one foot for a long time, giving him some trifling reward, while he walked up and down the room with twinkling eyes, smiling merrily at his awkward attempts to maintain his equilibrium. The children were naturally very fond of him, the tricksy side of his nature * having a peculiar charm for them.

Substantially strengthened and improved by his lessons in theory, in 1832, Schumann wrote a few things, which, so far as they have been published, certainly prove the favorable result of more thorough knowledge : indeed, the study of the art of composition, although begun rather late in life (Schumann was then in his twenty-second year), and a sharply marked train of ideas, produced an artistically correct, round, and technically skilful manner. However, a perfect command of form, and a beautiful formation in the highest sense of the word, were still a stumbling-block which he could but seldom avoid. This was the natural result of his tardy studies : this was the Achilles' heel in many of his works.

Youth is certainly the most suitable time to acquire technical knowledge, — the handicraft of art. The more complete a mastery of technics is gained in early years, the more safe and easy it will be, productive powers excepted, to display the mental stores on the attainment of greater maturity. On the contrary, a man whose mind has been developed earlier than his ability to express himself with that freedom which is rooted in rules will be able to balance his power and ability but rarely

* Compare page 24.

and imperfectly, even by the most untiring industry. This
fact must be considered in viewing Schumann's career. His
compositions as clearly show the marks of his tardy study of
art. By the force of ideas, profundity, and fancy, he often
made his hearer forget his defects.

Of the above-mentioned compositions, the following are men
tioned in Schumann's list: Intermezzi for the piano, published
as Op. 4, in two parts, and the first movement of an orchestral
symphony in G-minor, which is wholly unknown; he also
transcribed six Paganini violin capriccios for the piano, which
appeared as Op. 3.*

In comparison with Op. 1 and 2, the Intermezzi possess
considerable musical interest; because in them independent
and extensive images belonging to the lied, or song form,
are given. They also plainly reveal an harmonic and thoroughly peculiar rhythmic style of expression, characteristic of
Schumann; but nevertheless, as a whole, they do not afford
complete satisfaction. The melodious figures are by far the
weaker part, proving that the composer always found great difficulty in the plastic shaping of his thought. One circumstance
probably in some degree aided this, namely, that, as he himself owns, he always composed on the piano, — a mode of labor
necessarily prejudicial to the creative process from within.
Moreover, the extent to which truth mingles with his work as
a fixed factor, is shown by No. 2 of the first part of Op. 4,
whose middle and end contain the words, "My peace is gone,"
as an indication of a certain state of soul, without which this

---

* Julius Knorr says, that an unpublished Fandango dates from this period.
Its existence is confirmed by the following notice, contained in No. 28, vol.
xxxiv., of the Allgem. Musikal-Zeitung: —

"Next in my list will appear, copyright retained: Robert Schumann, six
capriccios by Paganini, arranged as studies for pianists who wish to cultivate themselves in every way, second work.

"Intermezzi for piano, Opera 3.

"Fandango, rhapsody for piano, Œuvre 4.

FRIEDRICH HOFMEISTER."

LEIPSIC, July 1, 1832.

poetic hint would be but an empty show, such as Schumann never was guilty of.

The transcription of Paganini's violin capriccios, especially Nos. 5, 9, and 11 (only the introduction of this number is used), 13, 19, and 16 of the original edition, is a work which displays throughout a lofty spirit of conception. The loss sustained by these capriccios in being transferred to the piano is made good by an ingenious treatment and truly artistic handling. It is not surprising that this is far more fluent and finished than the other compositions of the same date; for, while in the Paganini capriccios he treated a given subject which prescribed its own harmonic, modulatory course, in his own ideal world he had first to clear and shape a leavening subject, to whose mastery he was in no way competent.

Schumann considered this work quite valuable as a study: it certainly was useful to him as such. A rather prolix preface, directly aimed at Mendelssohn, explains the occasion and motive of this work.

After a very busy winter (1832), he made a visit to his friends in Zwickau. Combined with this was a plan for having his newly-written symphony performed by the orchestra of his native town; for he wished to hear his composition with his own ears, which he lacked opportunity to do in Leipsic. It was publicly performed at a concert given by Clara Wieck, then thirteen years of age, in Zwickau, November of the same year. During the performance of his composition, he listened unnoticed in a corner. Two days after this concert, they went together (Nov. 20) to the neighboring mountain town of Schneeberg, where two of Schumann's brothers lived. Clara Wieck and her father then returned to Leipsic; while Schumann remained there, and spent most of the winter of 1832 and 1833 alternately in Zwickau and Schneeberg with his family. His chief occupation, as in the last part of his Leipsic life, was composition. He especially and eagerly practised counterpoint, urged thereto by the assiduous study of the great master Bach. He also wrote a few short pieces for the piano; namely, those published in "The Album Leaves," Op. 124, Impromptu, Scherzino, Burla, Larghetto, and Waltzes; also a second and third part to the symphony in G-minor. This kept him very busy, as is shown by the following letter to Wieck: —

ZWICKAU, Jan. 10, 1833.

MOST HONORED FRIEND, — In all haste an apology, if I can frame one. Great concert in Schneeberg — Thierfelder * wrote for the symphony — complete destruction of the first movement — re-writing of the notes and score — addition of other movements — up to my eyes in work. Can you frown, and question still? Seriously, it's an easy matter to write to you; but I did not feel competent to write one to Clara. Don't you believe me?

My hearty thanks for your kindness. I received the "Iris" review yesterday, and was much pleased: it gives me new strength and love for labor.† I think your idea very novel, but rather Frenchy. I'm as charmed with the Chopin works as a child. I'm sorry that he should print so many things at once, because it isn't prudent; for fame crawls on pygmy feet, and is not to be hurried: glory flies on storm-wings, as with Clara. Greet the dear, good girl for me: I hope soon to see and hear her mazurka. You are responsible for filling Zwickau with enthusiasm for the first time in its life. When you are mentioned, every eye grows bright and speaking.

I have really changed into a chrysalis here, and lie quite still in my cocoon; hence my silence. There's little food for the mind here, but plenty for the heart. I shall certainly come by the 1st of February, with my completed symphony under my arm. If you could in any way help me to have it performed,‡ it would be the best encouragement imaginable.

That Schumann at that time rode alone § seemed very funny to me, although my mother was beside herself. But I ask, Clara, who Schumann alone could have been? (It makes me shudder to write of myself, as of a third person). The symphonistic similes in Clara's letter are splendid, and have caused much laughter in Zw——, especially the naïve parenthesis, "here father helped me." It was just as if Clara whispered it in my ear.

* Formerly town musician in Zwickau.
† This refers to a review of Schumann's Op. 3, in Rellstab's Iris. vol. iv. page 3.
‡ The complete symphony was never performed.
§ Doubtless in reference to Wieck's departure from Schneeberg to Leipsic without Schumann.

Fink's review of the Euryanthe variations is too absurd.* He wants to be coaxed: I thought he deserved to be tickled and patted and pinched.

Hofmeister sends a thousand greetings. I've put him into a great state of distress. I wrote plainly enough that I hoped to win praise for the Intermezzi from the critics and artists rather than from the public. He, as was natural, replied, "Your confession alarms me. As a tradesman, public favor is all in all to me: the critic's opinion is immaterial to me." So you see I fared finely with my cosmopolitism.

My sister-in-law Theresa is in Gera. Your message shall be gladly and faithfully delivered to Rosalie, whom I shall see four days hence at Schneeberg. (The concert† is on the 17th.) My mother and brothers wish to be remembered to you and Clara. How often we speak of you!— almost every day.

I shall write more fully from Schneeberg to Clara. I think the piano-concerto must be in C-major or A-minor. Of your capriccios, I'm studying "Antonia Von Tilly." Burgomaster Ruppius,‡ who called me a sluggard, sends his regards.

Remember me most kindly to your wife and Clara. What do I not owe to you?

R. SCHUMANN.

Schumann did not return the 1st of February, as he intended, nor until the middle of March. He gave up his rooms in Wieck's house, though not his intimate relations with the family, and moved to a summer residence in Riedel's garden; where he spent the days in music, and the warm evenings with his friends. They were sometimes passed in a delightful, but sometimes, it must be owned, in rather a wild way; which, however, had always a touch of poetry about it. One evening, quite late, the Schumann circle, chief among which were the brothers G. and C. W., all fellow-students, left the restaurant that they always visited, and were about to seek

* Fink was at that time the critic of the *Allgemeine Musikalische Zeitung.* The review mentioned refers to Herz's piano composition of '62. This remark clearly reveals Schumann's dislike to the Leipsic critic; which he afterwards vented in the *Neue Zeitschrift für Musik.*

† It was postponed till Feb. 12, 1833; and at it the first movement of Schumann's G-minor symphony was repeated.

‡ Schumann's godfather. Compare page 15.

their nightly repose. They were deeply engaged in jovial talk, and soon decided to keep together, and, as a conclusion to the entertainment, to find some comfortable resting-place in Riedel's garden. Not even the bolted door and the impossibility of waking the porter could prevail against this enchanting plan. The first obstacle was overcome by the agility of expert gymnasts. Hardly were they seated in an arbor, when the amiable adventurers, in the mental excitement caused by their lively discourse, felt the need of some corresponding material restorative. They soon remembered that the well-filled cellars of a wine-dealer lay in this garden, and that he gave unlimited credit. 'Twas no sooner thought than done. The door was opened with the same skill and ease as had conquered the first obstacle. In spite of the darkness, they felt out the best kind of wine, and did it well. Of course the *extempore* drinking-bout, which doubtless was a very jolly one, was conscientiously paid for the next morning, — doubly on Schumann's part, since this night-revel resulted in an attack of ague.*

For the rest, Schumann's life in this idyllic home, as described by his quondam room-mate Günther, was not in strict accordance with the notions of propriety. By day he studied: at evening he visited a certain restaurant, where he spent several hours in a circle of friends. At such times he was usually silent, apparently passive: so that people who knew nothing more of him would have supposed that he was attracted thither rather by the beer, which he often drank in great quantities, than by social intercourse. When he went home at night, he half undressed, wrote down the events and occurrences of the day in his note-book, counted up his ready money, and closed the day's work with a record of the

* Dr. Brendel, who was one of this party, gives a rather anomalous account of it in No. 12, vol. xlviii., of the *Neue Zeitschrift.* Of course I cannot say which is the more correct, but must hold to my own story which came from reliable witnesses, whose truth and close observation are indubitable. Possibly there may have been two such parties.

musical ideas that had come to him during the evening. He often played this list over on the piano, and extemporized for some time, according to his humor. Since Schumann's mode of life was externally fixed and uniform, it doubtless continued steadily until his marriage.

His first composition in 1833 was the second part of the transcription of Paganini's violin capriccios for the piano, published as No. 10. It is the conclusion of the transcriptions undertaken the year before; from which, however, it is distinguished by a far more independent treatment. The capriccios 12, 6, 10, 4, 2, and 3 of the original edition are especially recommended to pianists.*

Then followed impromptus for the piano. This work first appeared under the title, "Impromptus sur une Romance de Clara Wieck, pour le Piano-forte, Œuvre 5. Dédiés à Monsieur Fr. Wieck, Publiée 1833, Août."

The base was, as the title indicates, a romanza, or rather a simple theme by Clara Wieck, shortly before published by her, with the accompanying variations, as Op. 3. The treatment of this theme was attractive to Schumann, on account of the lively, but as yet purely artistic, interest which he took in Clara Wieck. He wrote eleven different movements on this theme, which should have been called "Variations in a free Style," rather than "Impromptus;" since on the one hand they are too elaborate, and on the other too dependent upon the theme, for impromptus, which we expect to be improvisations.

The beginning is original enough : the bass, underlying the theme, flaunts forth as a solo, like a sentinel standing at an important post. After the theme has been introduced, the variations appear with interweaving and substructure of both theme and bass in differently-contrasting changes of time. Above all is revealed a luxuriant fancy, whose exuberant images are in

* Schumann himself gives further particulars of these transcriptions in his Jo·rnal, vol. iv., page 134.

perfect concord with the objective clearness. On the whole, there is an unmistakable progress in technique, as well as a more decided, powerful victory over the Schumann idiom, in comparison with his earlier compositions; although many crudities, and sharp, discordant modulations slip in, in which the need of formal mastery is clearly visible. Any one acquainted with Schumann's poetical style in variations No. 10 — an uncommonly fanciful piece — will see how large a part the moonlight and nightingale's songs in Riedel's garden played in this work.

The date affixed to the title had no other purpose than to determine the time of its publication, as in books. Schumann thought that this fashion was in many respects of positive value, and wished to introduce it: still he was satisfied with the mere attempt, which may have been principally on account of the publisher's dislike to the plan, for he unfortunately liked to have a composition preserve an appearance of novelty as long as possible.

The new edition of this work, prepared when Schumann was about forty years old, and edited by himself, varies greatly from the first one. Not only are the harmonies essentially altered, but two variations (one being the tenth, one of the most interesting) are entirely omitted, the third being replaced by a new composition. Finally, the *finale* to the whole has been judiciously changed. It is very interesting for a musician to note the special differences in the two editions; since he can thus see how and in what degree the composer altered his opinions in the course of the years.

Schumann afterwards undertook to remodel " The Toccata," composed in Heidelberg. He transposed it from D-major to C-major. He also outlined his piano sonatas in G-minor (Op. 22), and F-sharp minor (Op. 11). " The Toccata," published as Op. 7, was most probably suggested by a composition of the same name by Czerny; * to which in the beginning, though only there, it bears a faint resemblance. How could it retain the style of a study, with this apparently important com-

* Op. 92.

pass, without being of some merit from an inventive point of view? It seems chiefly intended for technical purposes, as is proved by a remark of Schumann's in his Journal, vol. iv., page 183. He there says, that it "is perhaps one of the most difficult of piano compositions." He also wrote during this year variations in two parts on Schubert's Sehnsucht waltzes, and on the allegretto in Beethoven's A-minor symphony. Both compositions are entirely unknown.

In September, 1833, Schumann left Riedel's garden, and took lodgings in Mr. Helfer's house, No. 21, Burg Street, up four flights. Here he was attacked by a fit of violent mental excitement, which greatly alarmed his friends. Rosalie, one of his three sisters-in-law, died; and the news of this event created emotions in him which, on one particular night, — he speaks of it in his note-book, — "the fearful night of October 17—," changed to morbid frenzy united with fearful anguish.* Dreading to be left alone, he begged Günther, who, as we said before, was once his room-mate, to return; which he did. No further signs of mental excitement appeared; but a "terrible melancholy" (so says the note-book), which time alone destroyed, took possession of him, and reduced him to a most apathetic state of mind. It is uncertain to what extent this state was induced by over-exertion, loss of sleep, and the use of spirituous liquors. However this may be, when we consider all his peculiar symptoms, we see how deep must have been his sufferings, — now waking, now slumbering for a long time, — but which gradually and unmistakably increased, and caused great anxiety by their frequent re-appearance. His later sufferings were decidedly similar to this attack. It is noteworthy, that after this catastrophe, and to the very end of his life, he had a pronounced aversion to living on an upper floor, and very soon after took rooms on a lower story of the same house.

His acquaintance with the painter Lyser,† formed at this

---

* From one source I learn that Schumann tried to throw himself out of the window on that night; but this story is contradicted by other parties.

† From Hamburg; although deaf, a great admirer of music. Also a co-laborer in the *Neue Zeitschrift*.

time, had a most salutary effect upon him, as did also his recent relations with the talented musician, Ludwig Schunke * of Stuttgart; who left Vienna, December, 1833, for a long stay in Leipsic. Schumann and Schunke, although of very different dispositions, inspired by the same enthusiasm for art, formed an intimate friendship soon after their first meeting.

The following year, according to Schumann's own words "the most remarkable of his life," was remarkably rich and important in events having great influence over him. These probably led to the establishment of the " *Neue Zeitschrift für Musik.*" Schumann speaks as follows of this in the preface to his collected works : † —

" At the close of the year '33, a number of musicians, mostly young, met in Leipsic every evening, apparently by ac- cident at first, for social purposes, but no less for an exchange of ideas on the art which was meat and drink to them, — music. It cannot be said that the musical state of Germany was then very pleasing. Rossini still ruled the stage. Herz and Hünten were sole lords of the piano. And yet but a few years had elapsed since Beethoven, C. M. von Weber, and Franz Schubert were with us. To be sure, Mendelssohn's star was in the ascendent; and wonderful things were reported of a Pole, Chopin by name : but they exercised no real influ- ence till later. One day the young hot - heads thought, ' Why do we look idly on ? Let's take hold, and make things better ; let's restore the poetry of art to her ancient honor.' So arose the first sheets of a new journal for music."

We thus see what was the first motive for establishing " The New Journal for Music." By its aid, not only was an intellec- tual struggle begun against the worthless, clumsy products of the day, founded on gross sensuality, and not only were the degraded tastes of the mass to be purified and elevated ; Schumann also wished to smooth the way for young and aspiring talents. In this connection, we must not omit to men-

* See Neue Zeitschr. f. Musik, for 1835, No. 36, p. 145; and vol. iv. p. 182.
† Published in 1854, by George Wigand, Leipsic.

tion, that disgust at the tame, slip-shod art criticism (particularly that of Fink in Leipsic *), which more and more had got
possession of the "younger musicians," was another motive for
the founding of an independent, impartial art-organ for candid
opinions. "It is almost inexplicable that this critical honey-
daubing should not have been put an end to long ago," writes
Schumann to Töpken.†

Besides Schumann, the following musicians were engaged in
this new undertaking: Ludwig Schunke, Julius Knorr, and
Friedrich Wieck ; although the co-operation of the latter three
was but transitory and occasional. ‡ But, soon after the publication of the " *Neue Zeitschrift für Musik*," several thousand
copies of whose first number left the press April 3, 1834, a man
was won who devoted himself to the interests of the Journal long
and zealously. This was Carl Banck, who had left Berlin for
Leipsic in the beginning of the summer of 1834, to publish some
of his lyric compositions, and was soon united by the most
friendly relations to Schumann ; being thus induced to take up
a permanent residence in Leipsic, that he might join in this new
artistic, literary effort. Finally Banck became not only a busy
assistant, — all the articles signed 6, 16, 26, B and C — k are his,
— but was also of service by his important share in writing reviews. Besides this, he provided the paper with such contributors as his friends in other cities, C. Koszmaly, Riefstahl, §
G. Nicolai, ‖ Schüler, ¶ and the artist Simon,** who wrote
under the name of Alexander.

* Compare page 75.
† See letters for 1833–52, No. 3.
‡ Knorr's contributions are marked with the figure 1. Schunke's are
signed 3. Fr. Wieck wrote under his own name. We can thus ascertain
which articles each wrote.
§ A violinist, who lately died at Frankfort, and then lived in Munich.
‖ A Prussian official in Berlin.
¶ Private singer to the king in Rudolstadt.
** He painted the Oberon pictures in the Wieland room at the Weimarauer
Castle : he also worked on the old building of the Wartburg, and in some
degree caused the recent attempt to restore it. In 1849, Simon went to Chili,
where he was unfortunately killed by savages.

The youthful, fresh, and fiery tone of the Journal formed a sharp contrast to the characterless, worn-out Leipsic criticism; and, soon after its rise, this organ of art won the warm sympathy of the musical public of Germany. Even in the August after its foundation, after the course of four months, Schumann wrote to Töpken,[*] " Prague alone takes fifty, Dresden thirty, Hamburg twenty copies." The list of its native and foreign contributors rapidly swelled; and soon a choice band of inspired intellects were working together to attain the purpose of the young artists of Leipsic. The " *Neue Zeitschrift für Musik*" for the present year gives a full account of them all.

Schumann repeatedly speaks of the tendencies of this new art-organ in the Journal as follows : " Our plan was formed beforehand. It was simply this, to recall the old times and its works with great emphasis, thus to draw attention to the fact, that fresh artistic beauties can be strengthened only at such pure sources, and then to attack as unartistic the works of the present generation, — since they proceed from the praises of superficial virtuosos,—and finally to assist in hastening the dawn of a new poetic age." And farther on, " The elevation of German taste by German art, whether by old and great exemplars or by a taste for younger talent, must still be considered as our goal. The red thread which spins out these ideas may be traced in the history of the Davidsbündler, an alliance whose members, however romantic may have been its plan, can be recognized less by outward signs than by an inward resemblance. They will also strive in the future to cast up a dyke against mediocrity in word and deed. If at first they are too violent, you must consider that ardent enthusiasm is always the distinguishing mark of the truly talented and artistic. We write, not to enrich tradesmen, but to honor artists."

The aims here explained were faithfully carried out during the first years of the Journal; which are by far the best.

No one will refuse to recognize the merits of Schumann's

---

* See letters for 1833–52, No. 3.

literary works. They do not indeed reveal the objective clearness, positive sharpness, and precision of criticism, suited to a reformer. On the contrary, they please by their luxuriant, flowery, imaginative current of thought, which occasionally reminds us of Jean Paul, and whose metaphorical form is also marked and striking. Schumann had a warm and deeply-rooted veneration for the masters of past ages, and a free, appreciative, animating, and encouraging feeling towards the promising young masters of the present day. He treated the great mass of mediocrity with a finely-seasoned, but always kindly, humor. He never, or but seldom, found severe fault with any one. Here he revealed all his natural amiability. The celebrated Lessing *Kunstkritikerskala* were not in complete concord with his nature.

He himself indirectly confesses, that his ardor sometimes carried him too far in his recognition of youthful talent, in the preface to his works, where he says that *most* of the opinions then pronounced (that is, in 1854, when the book appeared) are still the same; but not *all:* that would be too much to expect. Very few men can boast at an advanced age that they still hold to what they said or wrote in years of youthful enthusiasm. It is, however, certain, that the eventual errors to which he was led by his partial over-rating of individual artistic efforts — errors to which he always lent a charming face — were palliated by his love for the great and good. The columns of the *Neue Zeitschrift für Musik* proved that Schumann confirmed the growing fame of Franz Schubert, Mendelssohn Bartholdy, Ferdinand Hiller, and Wilhelm Taubert, and helped to found that of Norbert Burgmüller, Chopin, Robert Franz, Niels. W. Gade, Stephen Heller, and Adolph Henselt. Men like Bennett, Berlioz, and Verhulst were also introduced to the musical world by him. It may be said that these composers would have met with due recognition without Schumann's aid; but this possibility does not in the slightest degree derogate from Schumann's services. The *Neue Zeitschrift für Musik* unmistakably asserted itself as a valuable organ, essentially influencing and eagerly promoting the artistic interests of that period; nor can there be any doubt that its management considerably injured Schumann, from its pretensions to beat out a path for new artistic aims, of which plan he considered himself the chief support. This is clearly proved by many scattered expressions occurring in his letters: "I have a masterly gift at getting hold of unlucky ideas: it is the evil spirit which opposes my outward happiness, and derides it. I often carry this self-torture so far as to be a sin against my nature; for I am never satisfied. I should like to be in another body, or to pass over long eternities," . . . he writes to his friend Henrietta Voigt.* Schumann was never satisfied. His unquenched ambition thirsted to achieve some great and novel deed, like all conquerors of new intellectual spheres. He might have been such himself, if he had not lacked that quality by whose aid alone sure progress on unknown paths is possible, — objective clearness. Thence also arose the often paradoxical words and deeds, conformably to which he strove to call into existence new images, thinking that nothing more could be done in the established forms; thence also came his sudden return to and devoted emulation of classic examples.

Schumann's obscurity, often perceptible in this connection, could hardly have re-acted advantageously upon his creative powers; for although it never allowed him to realize his *dreamed-of* ideal, yet, in the ambitious struggles of his nature, he constantly hoped to attain it at last. It is thus evident that his works must often have been strained, morbidly excited, and fretted; while, in the very place where he wished to give as little as possible, he has provided really beautiful and significant matter. In the closest reciprocal action with this is Schumann's deeply-inrooted propensity to pursue a peculiar rather than a natural course as regarded his creative images, and to choose an original and ingenious expression, rather than a simple and beautiful one.

We must now discuss the idea of the Davidsbündlerschaft,

* See letters for 1833–52, No. 4.

which occurred at the time of the foundation of the Journal, and which emanated from Schumann. Of this he says in the already-quoted preface to his collected works: * " Here another alliance may be mentioned, which was more than a secret one; namely, the Davidsbündler, existing only in the brain of its creator. It seemed suited to bring out different opinions relative to art, and to invent opposing artistic characters, chief among them Florestan and Eusebius, between whom stood the mediating master Raro. This Davidsbündlerschaft ran like a scarlet thread through the Journal, combining 'truth and poetry' in a humorous manner."

The original idea of this alliance, which was derived from the story of the Philistines' war with David, can only be conceived as an immediate emanation of Schumann's inner nature. It afforded its creator the possibility of a suitable means of expression for those contrasting, romantic, humorous ideas, shifting from their very abundance, which floated confusedly through his mind. Meanwhile, he was not content with what, begotten by his fancy, was suggested by the spirit of Florestan or Eusebius,† or even by both united; but he also strove to draw into the circle of his ideal world, in some degree to complete it, those peculiarities which he discerned in his immediate acquaintance. With Florestan and Eusebius sprang up the figures of Raro and Serpentinus, by which names we are to understand Friedrich Wieck and Carl Banck.‡ A Jonathan also occasionally appears; perhaps this was Schunke. Thus

* See letters for 1833–52, No. 14.

† The choice of these two pseudonyms does not seem to have been gra-tuitous or accidental. In the name of Eusebius, at least, we can see a design. Schumann himself hints at this in the first of his Jean Paulistic " Fan-ciful letters to Chiara;" at the close of which he says, " Never forget to look out the 13th of August often in the calendar, where an aurora unites thy name and mine." In the Saxon calendar, the twelfth, thirteenth, and four-teenth days of August bear the names Clara, Aurora, Eusebius. In Flores-tan, Schumann sought to personify the powerful, passionate side of his nature, and in Eusebius the mild and dreamy side.

‡ Carl Banck sometimes wrote under the name of Serpentinus. See Neue Zeits. f. Musik, vol. iv. pp. 108, 130, 135, and 139.

it is perfectly intelligible when Schumann writes to Töpken, " We are now living such a romance * as perhaps no book contains : " † it was, in truth, a kind of intellectual game of bo-peep, which Schumann carried on behind the masks of the so-called Davidsbündler invented by him. In later years he fully recognized the shady side of such a proceeding ; which of course essentially limited the highest conception of an ideal world to a commonplace point of view, where it did not entirely forbid it. For not only did he write as early as 1836 to H. Dorn, " Florestan and Eusebius are my double nature, which I would gladly, like Raro, melt down into one man," but, as time passed on, he made less and less use of these fanciful images, until at last they vanished entirely from the theatre of his literary labors, with very rare exceptions, when the old fancies once more came over him. From an explanation issued by Schumann in the first volume of his Journal, p. 152, it appears that the origin of the truly protean Davidsbündlerschaft was often misconstrued, and gave rise to troublesome questions. It reads as follows : —

" There are many reports in regard to the undersigned alliance. Since we are unfortunately obliged to preserve our incognito, we beg Mr. Schumann (who is well known as a respectable editor) to allow us the use of his name in certain cases. THE DAVIDSBÜNDLER."

" I consent gladly. R. SCHUMANN."

The business management of the *Neue Zeitschrift für Musik*

* I have been assured by trustworthy people, that Schumann long intended to write a romance, " Die Davidsbündler;" but he never did it.

† See letters for 1833–52, No. 3. Schumann drew the confines of the Bündlerschaft still further, " The Davidsbünd is only intellectual and romantic, as you perceived long ago. Mozart was as great a Bündler as Berlioz is. You, too, are one, although you never received a diploma," he writes to Heinrich Dorn. See letters for 1833–52, No. 14.

is shown by the following letter, addressed by Schumann to Keferstein,* Dr. Phil. in Jena : —

DEAR SIR, — We are obliged to you for dropping your incognito, and doubly so for your resolve to aid us in the new plan, in which we are as deeply interested as in your true life.

Hartmann,† the publisher, is responsible for the undersigned editors. We are ignorant of how much you know of the Journal; otherwise, you should not be left in doubt as to its tendencies, which are, to acknowledge the remote past, to contest recent ages as unartistic, and to aid the coming of a new and poetic era. . . . We leave you to judge whether all this can be done in twenty numbers.

We would gladly leave the shape and size of your articles to your own judgment, gladly fulfil all your demands, were not some of them rather unnecessary, and opposed to the nature of a journal, and others to the various sacrifices made by a publisher when establishing any thing new.

We leave you to decide whether the length of one, or at most one and a-half (printed) pages, and the sum of . . . thalers per (printed) page is sufficient.

We should be glad to learn if you have any finished treatise (either æsthetic, fanciful, or in the form of a novel): you would also oblige us by annexing some pertinent motto.

We should like the manuscripts sent direct by post, by which your fee shall be sent at once.

Receive these lines in the friendly spirit which dictates them, and believe us, with the highest admiration for your literary talents,

The editors,

LUDWIG SCHUNKE, ROBERT SCHUMANN,
J. KNORR, FR. WIECK.

LEIPSIC, July 8, 1834.

A second important event occurred in 1834 ; namely, Schumann's intimate connection with a young lady, named Ernestine von Fricken, from the little town of Asch, which lies on the confines of Bohemia and Saxony. She came to Leipsic in April of that year, and lived in Friedrich Wieck's house, wish-

---

* He died minister of Wickerstedt, near Jena, and was an assistant of the *Cecilia* and the *Allgemein-Zeitung* under the name of K. Stein, before he joined Sch.

† Formerly a bookseller in Leipsic.

ing to perfect herself as a pianist under his tuition.   Soon after
her arrival, Schumann became acquainted with her, and speedily conceived a strong affection for her, which was fully
returned ; and for a long time he aspired to a matrimonial
engagement with her.[*]

According to authentic accounts, Ernestine was neither remarkably handsome nor intellectual.   It seems that Schumann
was led away by her youthful bloom and sensual charms, and
that only the poetry of love could perceive in her those qualities [†] which every man so gladly attributes to his love, even
when they do not exist.

Finally, we must mention here, as a third influential event,
his acquaintance with Henrietta Voigt, who lately went home,[‡]
the cultivated wife of Karl Voigt, a merchant of Leipsic.
He owed this to his friend, Ludwig Schunke.   It was formed
with great reluctance ; for, spite of all Schunke's persuasions,
it was long before he could resolve to subdue his aversion to
entering upon new relations, nor did he finally visit the hos-
pitable house without turning away many times.

For the better comprehension of his alternate relations with
his friends Henrietta Voigt and Ernestine, three letters are
here inserted, —

SCHUMANN TO HENRIETTA VOIGT.

LEIPSIC, Aug. 25, 1834.

Yesterday and the day before I was so wrapped up in myself that the
pinions hardly peeped out.   If a hand had touched me, at once I'd
have flown off and away, that no one might disturb my life, thought, and
love.   I flung down stones, and in return received diamonds ; or, rather, I
was as a Deucalion, breathing forth living shapes, which will educate
the future into something nobler and higher.

That which we would hide is always that awkward corner, which is

---

* The reason which Schumann gave, in conversation with me, for withdrawing from this engagement, cannot be mentioned now.

† See letters for 1833–52, No. 4.

‡ She died Oct. 15, 1839.   Schumann wrote a memoir of her in his Journal.
See Neue Zeitschr. f. Musik, vol. xi. p. 158.

seen by all; for I knew that you knew that it was Ernestine (although against her will) who held fast the veil between us.   But that you should gently lift it, and that I should press a warm, friendly hand behind it, was more than I dared to hope, since every other hand would have withdrawn from so silent and apparently repulsive a presence.   So, when I had read your letter, I closed it gently, and never read it again, even to this day, that I might preserve my first impression of it unadulterated for future years.   Ah! should a time come when I have nothing left but these lines, I will bring them forth, and clasp the shadow of that hand close and warm in mine.

NOON.

Some girl must have written the above — to some one else.   The treatise on Berger is progressing.   I have cast it in a daring mould, which will draw down your displeasure on me; * but I mustn't tell tales out of school.   Be prepared for the worst!   Didn't you tell me that the last study was taken from a situation in Dante's " Commedia " ?   What was the situation?   Do you know any thing else that I could use or build upon?   But to-morrow, or at latest the day after, I shall come myself. Don't think I'm obstinate if I'm silent again; † for the contents of your letter should have no other answer than an eye; but whose?

Ludwig ‡ is very, very sick.   The doctor only talks of one winter — these are very . . . . [illegible] prospects!   Heaven grant me strength to bear this loss!   What a comfort it would be if you would try to persuade Ernestine's father to let her return late in the winter for a month or more!   And you could do it, no one better.   Whatever may impend, my faith is firmer than ever that there are still glorious people in the world; and I will sum up this faith in your name, " Henrietta."

R. S.

To the Same.

LEIPSIC [undated, probably the last of August, 1834].

I really have nothing at all to tell you to-day.   This letter shall only be a shake of the hand, nothing more.   I was thinking over my wealth

---

* Henrietta Voigt was a pupil of Ludwig Berger.

† How patiently Schumann's silence and mysterious conduct in houses where he was intimate was borne, is proved by the following story· Schumann one evening walked into the room unannounced, nodded pleas antly, his lips puckered as if to whistle, took off his hat, opened the piano struck a few chords, closed it, and disappeared as he came, with a nod of adieu, but without a word.   All this was the work of a few moments.

‡ Ludwig means Schunke, who died of chest-disease.

this morning: three names compose it.* Then I thought that you might write the same of us, Henrietta. My pulse still throbs.

Forgive me for the ring! Precious stones call forth mental sparks, they say: it has witnessed many musical romances, which I will call "Scenes." They are really lilies of love, which hold together the Sehnsucht waltzes.† The dedication should be only to an A-major soul; consequently to one like yours, consequently to you alone, my dear friend.

ROBERT S.

TO THE SAME.

LEIPSIC [undated, probably Sept. 1, 1834].

I was completely exhausted yesterday, and your letter came. It soothed me like an angel's hand: that is for a day and night, and this morning . . . every nerve is a tear. I wept like a child over Ernestine's words to . . . [illegible]; but, when I read the other paper to you, my strength gave way. Is it a weakness to confess it? 'Tis my Ernestine whom I love beyond all measure; 'tis you, Henrietta, my beloved friend. You glorious creatures, what can I offer in return for your supreme favor! — 'Tis said that those who love each other shall meet again in some other star, where they shall live and rule alone. Let us hold this lovely saying to be true. When I wander out to-night, I will choose a very mild one, and show it to you if I have an opportunity . . . perhaps to a fourth also. Do not desert me! I am, as ever,

Your   R.

Schumann's musical productivity during the year 1834 can hardly have been great, since the Journal made special claims upon his time. Only two piano compositions occurred, which were published as "Etudes Symphoniques," Op. 13. They are based upon a theme which, according to the composer's account, was suggested by Ernestine's father. He here again reveals himself as a composer for special occasions, as in the "Abegg Variations," and "Impromptus." The "Etudes Symphoniques," twelve in number, form a companion-piece to the "Impromptus:" like them, although producing an entirely opposite impression, they belong to the category of variations.

---

* Namely, Ernestine von F., Henrietta Voigt, and Ludwig Schunke.

† He evidently refers to his variations on Schubert's Sehnsucht waltzes written in 1833. Compare page 79.

They again manifest his possession of a manifold rich power to work upon a given theme; but they are decidedly superior to the "Impromptus," are more clear and pregnant, — a fact which cannot surprise us, since between these works intervene the unpublished variations on the Sehnsucht waltzes, and the "Allegretto" from Beethoven's A-minor symphony, Schumann also having had much practice in the way of variations.

The last of the "Symphonic Studies" is, in spite of its partial relation to the theme, no mere variation, but an independent, finished piece of music, in the form of a rondo.

In 1852, Schumann published a new edition of this work; the first being out of print, Schubert of Hamburg having purchased the copyright from Haslinger of Vienna. It differed from the original not only in the title, "Etudes en Forme de Variations," but also in a judicious formal alteration of the last piece, fitly called "Finale," as well as in the omission of the third and ninth variations. The other alterations are unimportant.

The second tone creation begun in 1834, but not completed till the following year, was the "Carneval, Scênes mignonnes sur 4 notes pour Piano, Op. 9." No other work of Schumann's displays such direct relations to reality as this. The tone-poet himself says, "It originated in an earnest frame of mind and under peculiar circumstances." It is founded on fact; and his desire to express the emotions which had so recently and powerfully stirred his soul, through the medium of tone, in a cycle of unique, intellectual, closely connected compositions, was accomplished in a manner peculiar to himself. From their origin, they assumed the shape of a masquerade : hence the name "Carnival;" by which his experience was, as it were, personified or individualized, and brought out in a motley series. The characters are, "Florestan, Eusebius, Chopin, Chiarina (Clara), Estrella (Ernestine), and Paganini; among whom glide the typical masqueraders, Pierrot, Harlequin, Pantaloon, and Columbine." In "The Papillons," and the march of "David's Allies against the Philistines," we have before us equally significant reminiscences of the artist's life, while his other pieces, — we will confine ourselves to the titles, — such as "Préambule," "Aveu," "Coquette," "Replique," "Lettres dansantes," "Promenade," "Reconnaisance," &c., may be considered as supplements to the whole, conformed to it, and proceeding from the free play of fancy.

The following note, from Schumann to Henrietta Voigt, gives us some information as to the origin of this remarkable work : —

MY DEAR, EVER-WATCHFUL HENRIETTA, — Herewith an enclosure.* It vexed me to have to carry on the fond fraud against the father, under the mother's eyes. Yet I would like to have spoken to Ernestine herself. What do you think of my nice postscript? rather "pleasant that I'm coming at once, before the letter goes;" to which I add the wish, that she (Ernestine), (as well as others), may sometimes like to play the scale in E-flat (Es), C, H, and perhaps A: for I have just found out that Asch is a very musical name for a city,† that the same letters lie in my name and are the only musical ones in it, as the following figure shows, and which moreover greets you kindly.   ROBERT SCHUMANN.

At any rate, I'll come before eleven. How much trouble we give you! My postscript doesn't please me, for it is tasteless; but the chance ideas are peculiar and pleasant.

That sounds very melancholy. I'm in a perfect fever of composition: so pardon.   R. SCHUMANN.

LEIPSIC, 13–9, 34.

Although we are here permitted a pleasant peep into the laboratory of the creating artist, we learn more about the

---

* Probably a letter to Ernestine.   † Compare page 87

composition from a letter to Ignaz Moscheles, dated Sept. 22, 1837, saying, —

" This was almost all written for a special purpose; and all but three or four movements are built upon the notes A, S, C, H, which form the name of a little Bohemian town, where I have a musical friend, and which curiously enough happen to be the only musical letters in my name. I composed the titles afterwards. Is not music self-sufficient? does it not speak for itself? Estrelle is a name such as is put under portraits, to hold the picture fast.* Reconnaissance (recognition); Aveu (avowal of love); Promenade (the walk, such as is taken at German balls, arm in arm with your partner.) The whole has no artistic value: the different soul-states only are interesting to me."

We see by the above that Schumann criticised " The Carnival " very severely three years after its creation, denying it all artistic merit, which exceeded the truth. " The Carnival " is by no means destitute of artistic merit, especially when compared with his earlier productions. Even if the forms of the separate pieces are insignificant, but few numbers ever being played, they bear the marks of concise and organic culture. The musical construction of the separate parts is for the most part perfectly clear and transparent. To this is added an ingenious and characteristic expression and style, shown in the melodic, harmonic, and rhythmic figures; whose variety, in comparison with the insignificant motif at the beginning, proves a rich, elastic, and inventive faculty. In short, it is a true Schumann composition, full of his traits. Much of it is perfectly charming, sweet, graceful, and elegant; but the development of the *finale* is thoroughly humorous and comic to the last degree. The composer attained this effect by a skilful combination of the " Grossvatertanz " with the steady marked rhythm of "The Davidsbündler March," which strides

---

* Schumann, when I asked him at Bonn in 1853, told me that he meant by this name Ernestine, of whom he spoke at some length.

along solemnly, as if conscious of victory, in three-fourths tempo. The two motifs, when compared, afford a most delightful contrast. Their opposing direction is evidently meant to illustrate the spiritual contest between youthful aims and the Philistines of art; but we can easily guess which is victor. We might call this latter piece purposeless, meaning no reproach, since it is quite attractive as a composition. It is also useful as a proof that the meaning music which other and greater masters have occasionally essayed is perfectly possible.*

The close of 1834 brought a sad experience to Schumann: he lost, while visiting his family in Zwickau, his intimate friend Ludwig Schunke, whose death was caused, Dec. 7, by a wasting chest-disease. † This painful event, occurring at the time of Knorr's and Wieck's withdrawal from the Journal, had a powerful effect upon its future business management. Schumann, being the only one of the founders left, considered himself sole proprietor of it, and wished to have it published elsewhere, under the pretence of various irregularities, in consideration of which the publisher had run into debt. ‡ Hartmann, however, protested against this, saying that he had published the Journal at his own risk and at great pecuniary loss, and had carried it on for a long time without any special return for his outlay. The disputes on this subject were at length concluded (Carl Banck, at Hartmann's request, editing the paper for a few weeks) by the payment of a certain sum to the latter : so that, at the close of 1834, § all former relations were fairly dissolved. Henceforth Schumann was sole possessor of the paper, which

* It is proved that some of the pieces intended and prepared for "The Carnival" were omitted from the published edition, by Op. 124; which contains three pieces (Romanza, Waltzes, and Legends) on the letters A, S, C, H, dated 1835. The third piece in "The Album Leaves," taken into "The Parti-colored Pages," Op. 99, dated 1836, probably belongs to 1834 or early in 1835, since it is also composed on the four notes A, S, C, H.

† See Letters for 1833–52, No. 6.

† See Letters for 1833–52, Nos. 3 and 6.

§ See Hartmann's statement at the end of the first volume of the *Neue Zeitscher. f. Musik.*

he edited, aided by Carl Banck. The bookseller, Johann Ambrosius Barth of Leipsic, became the temporary publisher. Early in July, 1837, Schumann sold it to the bookseller, R. Friese.

The tone-creations of 1835 consist of the two sonatas, begun in 1833, in F-sharp minor, Op. 11, and G-minor, Op. 22. The first appeared under the singular title, "Piano-Forte Sonata, dedicated by Florestan and Eusebius to Clara." * It is a true "Davidsbündler composition," full of rich, though thoroughly opposite and contrasting forms; and it is therefore the more suitable to ascribe its authorship to the two ablest Bündler.

In no case does Schumann's own expression in regard to his early works, "dreary stuff," † assume such truth as in these sonatas. No one will deny that there are many significant passages, nor the bold, powerful course taken by Schumann; but neither can we overlook the fact, that the parts are not combined into a whole, that there is a total lack of organic development and unfolding of the idea, or that a turgid and even unlovely expression prevails. There is no doubt that this is in a great measure due to his ignorance of theory. In the first place, having but seldom essayed the sonata form, he had invincible difficulties in his path; and there must have been strong reasons for his taking up and finishing the sonatas begun in 1833. In the F-sharp minor sonata especially, a painful struggle with form ‡ is revealed; which, however, leads to no satisfactory result. Even if we cannot adjudge it any positive artistic merit, it is valuable as noting a stage of development. It forms a sort of mountain-border in Schumann's artistic development, whose narrow passes had to be evidently broken through, to prepare a

* Clara Wieck.

† This remark was made in the following connection: While in Dusseldorf, I once, while talking with Schumann, expressed a desire to hear his wife play some of his early compositions; to which he ironically answered, "Dreary stuff!" There is undeniably some truth in this reckless self-criticism.

‡ See *Neue Zeitschr. f. Musik*, vol. v., p. 135, for review of the F-sharp minor sonata, by Ignaz Moscheles, written at Schumann's special request.

smooth bed for the stream of ideas.* The G-minor sonata shows great progress; for it is decidedly superior to its sister, having great precision and purity of form, even if the idea is not always perfected; as, for example, in the middle part of the Andante. The most valuable piece — indeed, the last movement — was not composed until the end of 1838, during his temporary abode in Vienna; being also worked on three years later, to take the place of the original finale, as, on close comparison with the first three parts of the sonata, it showed a far more regular use of form. The organization and arrangement of the ideas and composition, the general formation, the precise intellectual expression, — all falls into a clear, round shape, just as the composer wills. The ground-note of this latter piece is united to the deeply melancholy expression of the foregoing movements, impregnated by the glow of concealed passion: so that the work, as a whole, gives a speaking picture of the agitated and excited states of feeling by which, as will be shown directly, Schumann was filled and swayed during 1836–1840.

The beginning of the year 1836 was important to him in a double sense. He first met with a bitter loss in the death of his mother, Feb. 4; † and almost simultaneously with this affecting event began a memorable period of his life.

His relations to Ernestine von Fricken, at first cherished with most devoted love, had gradually cooled. Not only was this coolness increased by the separation of the parties interested, when Ernestine left Leipsic, September, 1834, but reasons which cannot here be given rendered his withdrawal desirable. Therefore this connection was dissolved in January, 1836, by an amicable agreement.‡ He soon formed another passion, which lasted until his death. This was heartfelt love for Clara

---

* The new edition of this sonata, published several years since, only differs from the first in the correction of a few errors and in the title; which names Schumann as author instead of "Florestan and Eusebius."

† According to the register of deaths in St. Katherine's Church, Zwickau.

‡ This is proved by a letter from Schumann, which I have, but cannot quote.

Wieck, afterwards his wife, who had just attained to years of womanhood.

This turn of fate was also the beginning of a long struggle for the possession of his beloved, — a struggle calculated to stir the inmost depths of his nature, and to produce intense agony; but, as the storm-lashed, foaming, roaring sea tosses up from its depths wonderful treasures, so did the wild waves of contest bring to light rare pearls and jewels of art. In this import, he writes Sept. 5, 1839, to H. Dorn : * " Truly, from the contests Clara cost me, much music has been caused and conceived. The concerto, the sonatas, Davidsbündler dances, Kreisleriana, and novelettes owed their origin almost wholly to them."

A peculiar combination of circumstances soon removed him to a distance from the object of his love and ardor; for, from peculiar reasons, he did not visit Wieck's house for a long time : indeed, he could not believe that his passion was returned. And it is indubitable, that his relations with his future wife, at first constrained, were now for some time interrupted. "My stars are strangely unpropitious," he writes on the 2d of March to his sister-in-law Theresa; and again, April 1, 1836,† " We will talk of Wieck and Clara when we meet. I am in a critical situation, and lack the peace and clear sight requisite to recover from it; yet I am so situated, that either we must never speak again, or she must be all my own. " Added to this, Clara Wieck and her father made a concert-tour, which rendered their meeting even more difficult than before. But love, we know, is ingenious; so Schumann devised a plan for hearing from his chosen one through a third party, which gave him great comfort. It is explained in the following letter to Aug. Kahlert ; ‡ which leaves us at a loss to know how far its contents should be attributed to the play of imagination : —

* See letters for 1833–52, No. 31.
† See letters for 1833–52, Nos. 9 and 11.
‡ He was then an assistant of The New Journal of Music. See letters for 1833–52, No. 7.

LEIPSIC, March 1, 1838

MOST HONORED SIR, — I have nothing musical for you to decipher to-day, but lay before you (to come directly to the point) my heart's urgent prayer, that, if you will not spend a few moments of your life in carrying a message between two parted souls, you will at least not betray them. Your word on it in advance!

Clara Wieck loves and is loved. You might easily discover it by her gentle, almost heavenly look and mien. Pardon me if I omit, for the present, her lover's name. The happy pair met, saw, spoke, and became engaged without her father's knowledge. He has discovered it, would cut it down, forbids all intercourse on pain of death; * but they have braved him a thousand times. The worst of it is, that he has taken her on a journey. The last news came from Dresden. I do not know certainly, but think, and am almost sure, that they will spend a short time in Breslau. Wieck will of course visit you, and invite you to come and hear Clara play. Now comes my most heartfelt prayer, that you will let me know all you can learn, directly or indirectly, concerning Clara, — her feelings and her life, — and that you will guard what I confide to you as my most precious secret, as such, and not mention this letter to the old man, to Clara, nor indeed to any one.

If Wieck speaks of me, it may not be in the most flattering way; but don't let that disconcert you. You can tell him that I'm a man of honor, but a rattlepate. . . .

Now mark, it will be an easy thing for you to get into Clara's good graces and confidence, since she has heard of you before now from me (for I told my love every thing), and that I corresponded with you. She will be glad to see you on this account.

Your hand, my unknown friend, of whose generosity I have so high an opinion that it can never be altered. Write soon.

A heart, a life, depend upon it, — ay, my own; for 'tis for myself I have prayed.

ROBERT SCHUMANN.

Schumann's " critical situation," which he mentioned to his sister-in-law, lasted till 1837, as is indubitably proved by remarks in other letters. " Clara loves me as warmly as ever; but

---

* We must not forget that the poet in Schumann speaks here, as in all immediately preceding this passage, which relates to remote fancies. No acknowledged engagement existed at this time between Schumann and Clara. His desire for one is another affair. Peculiar considerations prevent more details.

I am completely resigned," he writes to Zwickau; and farther on : " In the mortal anguish which often seizes me, I have no one but you : you seem to hold and protect me in your arms." *

Meanwhile he relieved his oppressed heart by two composi-tions, rich in compass, and in many respects valuable. One of them was " The Concerto for piano *only*," mentioned before ; the other was " The Fantasie in C-major for the piano, Op. 17." According to Schumann's list, the latter work was specially caused by the summons issued from Bonn, Dec. 17, 1835, to the memorial festival in honor of Beethoven, a statue of whom was erected there in August, 1845. When he wrote this tone-piece, he meant to contribute the profits to the fund for the monument to the great master. Upon the titlepage was to be the word " Obolus ; " and the separate movements were to be called, " Ruins," " Triumphal Arch," and " The Starry Crown," whose symbolic meaning is clear to all. He afterwards gave up the idea of publishing this composition for the above purpose, as well as these titles. He placed as a motto upon the first page this strophe from Fr. Schlegel, —

> " Through every tone there soundeth,
> Drawn through earth's gay dreams,
> A gentle note that's heard alone
> Of him who listens from afar."

and dedicated it to Franz Liszt.

No more suitable name could be found for this composition than " Fantasie." All three movements, if we do not think of their effect, at the first glance, have some resemblance to the sonata ; but, on close examination, we find that the free mingling of diverse musical forms is but the characteristic force of fan-tasy. Thus the first section of the first movement unmis-takably bears the character of a sonata in the motif developed, which runs up to nineteen measures : then follows the middle movement in lyric form, which is interrupted but once by the passing vision of the leading idea, and the first section then goes on to the close, with some modification.

* See letters for 1833–52, Nos. 15 and 16.

The second movement, in general character a march, belongs in a great degree to the rondo: but this is also interrupted after the first section by a twofold lyric parenthesis, which then goes on, propping up and mingling with the staccato borrowed from the chief motif, and finally returns to the first theme.

The third and last piece belongs entirely to the lyric form. There are two leading themes in C and A flat, which finally mingle curiously and close.

The whole work, as far as the contents go, contributes nothing important to Schumann's works during the first productive period extending to 1840. The motifs are peculiar, uncommonly intense, and also of significant melodic charm; indeed, more like Beethoven than like Haydn or Mozart. There is something Titanic in them, which, rushing along on the wings of flaming fancy, would have exercised a fascinating power, if the conception of the whole, corresponding to the grand and deep design, had been more perfect and plastic. The obstacles opposed in this work to the flow of sympathy are chiefly produced by that peculiar, rhythmic, figurative style, which does not form a complete breach until later, and which here, as in earlier works, sometimes elevates the measure into a beautiful movement. The last part only forms an exception to this, more nearly approaching the requisitions of an adequate conception; although it is inferior to the two former movements in grandeur and power of primitive thought.

The second composition, first published as "Concert sans Orchestre" (Op. 14), was originally conceived as a sonata, and therefore was so called. The music publisher, Tob. Haslinger, however, insisted upon the thoroughly inappropriate name, "Concerto without orchestra;" and Schumann yielded to this whim, but felt obliged to omit an entire Scherzo, that the form might in some degree conform to the title.[*]

* Moscheles' opinion of this piece (which was dedicated to him), as expressed in a letter to Schumann, is most interesting.—See *Neue Zeits. f. Musik*, vol. vi. p. 65.

With the second edition, in 1853, the original shape and title were resumed. The other alterations which he made in the new edition (Schubert, Hamburg) are principally in the first part. Besides many changes in the harmony and rhythm, we notice the repetition of the measure 22–25, page 12 (an octave lower), which in the first edition (page 11) only occurs once. The third movement (Andante) is almost untouched: and the finale, with the exception of the time being $\frac{6}{10}$ instead of $\frac{2}{4}$, has undergone but few changes, and those are mainly at the close.

The whole composition is in that enlarged sonata shape derived from Beethoven. In mental expression, it is closely connected with the sonatas Op. 11 and 22, only this is much broader and nobler. It begins with an Allegro deeply emotional, passionate. Powerful soul-states are mirrored in it, and speak now in wild agitation, now in sadness. The second part, which approaches the minuet in style, is calmer, and more moderate than the first, forming a genuine contrast to it. Next come variations on an Andantino by Clara Wieck, mild and dreamy in expression, which enhance the effect of the first movement; while the finale "Prestissimo possibile" again takes up and pursues the thoroughly emotional, heaven-storming character of the first movement, with this difference only, there was no room for a second and peaceful element in it: it hurries on in an incessant storm, as if desperate to meet the end. Thus it offers no resting-point: the enjoyer, without being able to recover his senses, is torn away; and at last the sensation involuntarily swells into a sea of tone, whose waves perpetually break and overwhelm him.

The technical form of this sonata affords various points of comparison with "The Fantasie in C, Op. 17," just mentioned: therefore a repetition of our criticism seems unnecessary.

Besides the two works just mentioned, he also conceived in 1836 a sonata in F-minor (according to the list the fourth), which was apparently never written down, and composed several little pieces for the piano; among them those in Op.

124, with the exception of Nos. 5 (fantasie dance), and 7 (country dance).

The course which Schumann, as a creating musician, had hitherto pursued was followed by comparatively slight outward results. This is easily explicable. Although his former compositions in no way lacked deep fervor, true artistic effort, and rich creative power, united with poetic purpose, they almost always want two requisites for speedy and universal recognition of works of art, — plastic consummation and sensual gratification. This is unquestionably the reason why these works have met with so much less appreciation in musical circles than many of his later efforts. It was hard to introduce even the latter to the public. " The publishers won't listen to me," he writes to Moscheles ; and to Dorn,* "Moreover, you can easily believe, that, if the publishers did not fear the editor, the world would know nothing of me : perhaps it would be better for the world." Besides this, the critics did not take that interest in his compositions which they deserved. The Leipsic *Allgemeine Musik alische Zeitung* ignored them entirely for seven years ; and he himself, with few exceptions, always avoided any reference to his labors in the *Neue Zeitsch. f. Musik.* " ' The Cecilia ' is the only paper which ever mentions me. My Journal is for others ; and Fink is very careful not to say stupid things of me, as he would if he spoke of me in public," he writes to Keferstein.† In but two instances did he have the pleasure of sympathizing reviews of his works from important sources, — once from Moscheles, and once from Franz Liszt. ‡ He placed great weight upon these criticisms, and in later years considered them " the best ever written about him."

We can easily conceive that he sometimes sighed under such depressing circumstances, and are not surprised at such a remark

* See letters for 1833 – 52, Nos. 10 and 14.

† See letters for 1833 – 52, No. 17.

‡ We have already referred to Moscheles' opinion. That of Liszt in the *Gazette Musicale* is given in Appendix B.

as this : * "I often feel anxious. To stand upon the heights of time and vision, to assist others, to struggle to remain independent — unless I thought of all my inner and secret relations, I should be faint and sick." Every man has intrinsic need for recognition of his efforts; and Schumann, too, although he had received from Providence no trifling dose of self-esteem and self-consciousness, could not dispense with it. "No encouragement, no art. On one of the popular desert islands in a silent sea, a Mozart or a Raphael would never have been more than tillers of the soil," he writes to Fischhof † and to H. Dorn. ‡ "I should be very much pleased if you would put me into your gallery; for the world knows literally nothing about me. You know why. Sometimes one fancies that it's useless; but, on the whole, I prefer to agree with Jean Paul, when he says, 'Air and admiration are the only things which men can and must incessantly swallow.'" Schumann did indeed rejoice heartily at every recognition of his artistic efforts; but, as we have said, he sought them from a circle of intimate and chosen fellow-artists rather than from the world in general. In this respect his personal intercourse with men like Felix Mendelssohn Bartholdy, Ferdinand David, Moscheles, Chopin, Sterndale Bennet, Lipinski, Ludwig Berger, later Franz Liszt, and others, § some of whom lived in Leipsic, others of whom travelled to and fro, must have been salutary to him. We can hardly determine how far Mendelssohn, whose aims were very different, sympathized with him. ‖ However, soon after his arrival in Leipsic, late in the summer of 1835, Schumann was on intimate terms with Mendelssohn, as his expressions

---

* See letters for 1833 – 52, No. 16.

† See letters for 1833 – 52, No. 6.

‡ See letters for 1833 – 52, No. 31.

§ See letters for 1833 – 52, Nos. 15 and 37.

‖ Unfortunately Mendelssohn's recently published letters give no account of his relations with Schumann and his works. It is hardly credible that he can never have mentioned the latter in a letter; and it would surely be both interesting and valuable in more than one respect, to learn the composer of "St. Paul's" opinion of the author of "Paradise and the Peri."

of admiration for that master prove.   He writes, "Mendelssohn is a man to whom I look up as to some lofty mountain.   He is a true divinity;" and " no day passes in which
he does not utter at least two ideas worthy to be graven
on gold." *

One more circumstance must be considered here, which perhaps in some degree contributed to divert the attention of
the musical public from Schumann's creative talents, — his
literary powers as displayed in his Journal.   These were
indeed sufficiently attractive to cast the composer into the
shade.   His editorial duties also rendered it impossible for
him to devote himself and his energies entirely to music;
for Carl Banck, who had formerly been a pillar of support
to him in his literary labors, was prevented from assisting
him further, by his removal from Leipsic in the summer of
1836.   Schumann's intimate friends did not fail him in this
disaster; and Keferstein advised him, in a letter, to give the
Journal up, and consecrate himself exclusively to music.   To
this he replied, "To give up the Journal would be to withdraw the support which every artist should have, which
should come to him easily and spontaneously.   I really cannot think of large compositions now; so may there be at least
some small ones."   He afterwards altered his opinion, as we
shall soon see.   For the present, however, he went on as before; and, during the next year, only trifling compositions for
the piano were written, as his list shows.   The Fantasies, Op.
12, in two parts, and the " Davidsbündler" dances, occurred
in 1837.

The Fantasies † are among the best known of Schumann's
works: with them he enters upon a new department of composition, which he himself discovered, as Mendelssohn did, in
" The Song without Words," and which was afterwards attempted by other composers with more or less success.   Thus

---

* See letters for 1833 - 52, No. 11.

† " The Song without an End " is also to be ranked with these, — at least
it was composed in the same year, as the date affixed to it proves.

these tone-images were not only of importance in his development, but also in that of most of the present school of piano-
forte music. It lies in the nature of things, that no one else treated the fantasie in so peculiar a style, exactly hitting the accent
of the fanciful, since a copy can never equal an original.

The Fantasies, belonging entirely to the lyric realm, proffer
us "strength and tenderness," in agreeable contrast. The
single numbers enchant by their specific musical qualities as
much as by their soul-stirring and suggestive images. Schumann tried to indicate the latter more closely by words. The
titles arose in the same way, as also in "The Carnival." They
met with much opposition ; but, when we consider that they
were added after the completion of the pieces, and only give
poetic hints for their comprehension, they can neither disturb
us, nor seem unjustifiable. It is quite another thing if the
composer labors for a certain object; and even this dangerous
kind of composition has been occasionally essayed with success
by some masters of the past. A *master* may dare any thing :
he is perfectly aware of what he is doing, and will not engage
in problems unprofitable to his imagination, or absolutely ob-
jectionable from an artistic point of view. Schumann himself
speaks of the allowableness of such titles as the Fantasies bear
as follows : —

"Many consider too carefully the difficult question of how
far instrumental music should enter into the representation of
thoughts and events. It is certainly an error to think that a
composer should take up pen and paper on purpose to express,
depict, or paint this thing or that ; yet we must not rate accidental impressions and external influences too lightly. An idea
often works unconsciously with the musical fancy, or the eye
with the ear ; and this ever-active organ, amid other sounds
and tones, holds fast to certain outlines, which may be con-
densed and perfected with the advancing music into distinct
figures. Now, the more elements there are congenial to music,
and containing images or ideas begotten by sound, the more
poetic and plastic the composition will be ; and, the more fanci-

ful or acute the musician's conceptions are, the more praised and performed his works will be. Why could not the thought of immortality occur to Beethoven in the midst of his fancies? Why might not the memory of some great departed hero inspire his labor? Why not the recollection of a blessed past some one else? Or shall we be ungrateful to Shakspeare, for exciting in a young tone-poet's breast his most valuable work? ungrateful to Nature, and deny that we have borrowed from its beauty and sublimity for our own creations? Italy, the Alps, the image of the sea, spring twilight, — has music told us nought of these?" Further on, "It is indeed poetic to designate the leading thought by something akin to it." And finally, "The main point still is, whether the music is any thing in itself without words and illustrations, and especially whether a spirit dwells within it."

The music was the most essential and important part to him, while the concrete ideas added to it were merely hints at the spirit which inspired him in working. The Fantasies, therefore, bear most commonplace titles, such as, "The Flight," "Evening," "Caprices" (which no one could take seriously), "At Night," "Tangled Dreams," and "The End of the Song." In the "Wherefore" and the "Fable" especially, the limits of the allowable were rudely grazed.

After perusing the foregoing lines, we shall not be surprised to find some singularities in the Fantasies, which are contrary to impartial musical taste; such, for example, as the fourth measure in the middle movement (B-flat major) of "The Flight," some harmonic series in the middle movement of "The Tangled Dreams," &c. They are to be considered as the natural result of too tardy study, and are comparable to some wild shoot grafted on the stem of a lusty fruit-tree, which grows and improves all the spring until the bark is thick and hard; nor can we deny, that there is great general progress in command of technique, in comparison with his earlier works. The Fantasies form a luminous point amid the compositions of the first ten years.

The same importance cannot be attached to "The Davids-
•ündler dances." They bear the same relation to the Fanta-
•ies as clever sketches do to finished *genre* pictures. Their
musical marrow is less; the leading idea is but seldom perfected, to say nothing of perfect motifs. As in the writings
of the Davidsbündler, every thing is attributed to Florestan,
Eusebius, or Raro, so the authorship of these eighteen pieces *
is adjudged either to Florestan or Eusebius or to both (at the
end of every movement we find either the letter E or F, and
sometimes both) ; it is a formal thinking-out and writing down
of his own heart-life. In fine, the Davidsbündler dances are a
feebler echo of the sonata in F-sharp minor (Op. 11). While
in that there was at least an attempt to raise the world of ideas
with which he was filled into a higher artistic form, here a
succession of isolated images are set down. The following
titles make a singular and very Davidsbündler-like impression : "Something Hippish," † "Very lively and self-sufficient," "Here Florestan ceased, and his lips quivered sore,"
"Eusebius said too much about this ; but his eyes were full of
joy." He seems to have conceived a dislike to these genial
trifles; for, in the new edition, published during his lifetime,
they are omitted. Ay, even the motto on the titlepage of the
first edition, —

> "In each and every age
> Are knit together weal and woe :
> Be thou 'mid pleasure ever sage,
> And always be prepared for woe," —

which indicates the mental condition in which the Davidsbündler dances were written, is suppressed. The new edition
likewise differs from the old one only in the alteration of some
single notes.

Meanwhile Schumann was brought, during 1837, much nearer
to the realization of his heart's desires. "I am quiet, industrious, happy," he says in a letter to his sister-in-law, dated

---

* The titlepage of the new edition erroneously states them to be sixteen.
† "Hippish" means something stout and strong.

Aug. 31, 1837. Nothing but the consent of Clara's father was now needed to seal the union of souls. In a letter written about the middle of September of the same year, he sued for the hand of his betrothed. Friedrich Wieck, however, did not see fit to consent; and the motives which caused his scruples seem to have been approved of by Schumann; for he writes to his sister-in-law Theresa, Dec. 15, 1837, "The old man won't let Clara leave him yet: he's too fond of her. And he is really in the right; for he thinks we ought to earn more money first, so that we may live comfortably." He therefore took up the plan, entertained in 1836,[*] of removing to Vienna, where he hoped to find more fruitful sources of profit. This idea was rendered difficult, and finally impossible, by the abandonment of the Journal which was then contemplated. Very gradually and cautiously, as beseemed his reserved nature, he imparted his purpose to Fischhof, whom he chose for his confidant on this occasion. "Thanks for your information in regard to the Vienna cliques: such meanness in so large a city was new to me. My money still holds out: it would be hard to puzzle me or put me out of countenance. But I should like to see that city once. Perhaps this summer. Shall you remain in Vierna?" he writes to him April 3, 1838. When Fischhof replied, inviting him to his house, he answered,[†] "Am I really so seriously invited to visit you for Vienna's sake? It can't be done so hastily, and will cost me much labor before and after; but perhaps the gods will grant it. I need to travel. For eight years I've been a fixture." And again, in a letter dated May 8,[‡] "Of much else which will perhaps interest you, and is very important at present, soon."

At last, after a long interval, he comes to the point, and writes, —

LEIPSIC, Aug. 5, 1838.

MY DEAR FRIEND, — I received your kind letter just as I was sitting down to write to you upon matters of the utmost importance to me, in

---

[*] See letters for 1833–52, No. 11.

[†] See letters for 1833–52, No. 25.

[‡] See letters for 1833–52, No. 26.

which I need the advice of such a friend as I have found you to be. Don't be frightened, if, in two months from now, somebody knocks at your door, — my ghost, my very self; still more, if he tells you that he shall probably settle in Vienna next year and *forever*. I tell you all this in the STRICTEST CONFIDENCE, and with the request that you will not breathe it *to any one* (FROM LEIPSIC ESPECIALLY). The motives which bring me to Vienna are of a friendly nature: certain circumstances render it necessary for me to fix my residence in a larger city than Leipsic. I'll *tell* you more, which I may not trust to paper. *It is certain that I must be in Vienna by the middle of October at latest.* And the Journal? You will say, "Of course you won't give that up." During the three months from October till January, Oswald Lorenz * will take charge of it; and from that time forth it will be published in Vienna: and there I need your helping hand. Of course permission to publish must be granted, which it is the office of Count Sedlnytzky to concede. I am almost sure that no objections will be raised; since it is a purely art-paper, which has been sold in the Austrian States ever since its appearance. Still I know the circumspection of your officials and their tedious pace in such matters, by hearsay: so that I am already at work; that is, I should like to present my petition for permission to publish my Journal in Vienna as soon as possible, so that the first number of the next volume may be sent thence by the middle of December. Being entirely ignorant of the rules and forms by which such a petition should be shaped, I beg you graciously to assist a poor musician, who never before had any thing to do with officials and censors. *I shall never forget any thing you may do for me now.*

Therefore I pray you to learn from some lawyer in what form and to what address such a petition should be composed and despatched. Perhaps you can have one drawn up for me from the outlines written on the other side, and then send it to me, that I may have it copied neatly, and perhaps have it forwarded to Count Sedlnytzky through our ambassador, Prince Schönburg.

Do you know whether the authorities will require an account of my early life, my circumstances (in the best of order), &c., and whether it should be forwarded with the petition?

Lastly, whom would you propose as *joint publisher* with Friese? † We have already applied to Haslinger and Diabelli, but have not received a favorable answer. I should much prefer a bookseller, that I might nave nothing to fear from the publisher's eventual encroachments.

---

* An assistant of the Journal, then living in Leipsic.
† Then publisher of the Journal in Leipsic.

Friese is still publisher (I am owner); the change is agreeable to him, inasmuch as he can only profit by it. Friese's name and that of some Viennese firm would be on the titlepage.

I should have to take a fresh sheet of paper, did I attempt to tell you what high hopes I have for the future, for the growth and increased influence of the Journal, and for intercourse between North and South You are the only friend I have in Vienna whom I have learned to consider to be as skilful as good and modest. Have you been disappointed in me? Will you remain favorably disposed towards me? Do you not hope for much from the future which shall not delude us?

Thus I close, more agitated than ever, and with a most grateful heart. Assist me: *the happiness of my life* depends upon it. I am no longer alone. *All this is for your eye only.*

To-day is the 5th: on the 11th my letter will be in your hands; by the 19th you may be ready; and on the 24th I may expect an answer. I shall await it anxiously.   Yours,

SCHUMANN.

Petition, to be drawn out with the requisite legal formalities.

The undersigned, a Saxon by birth, living in Leipsic, musician, editor and owner of the *Neue Zeitschrift für Musik*, desires to change his residence from Leipsic to Vienna, on account of his love for music as well as of his business relations. The Journal, which has never touched upon any save musical subjects, has been licensed and widely read by the highest officials in the monarchy ever since its establishment (1834). He now seeks permission to publish it in Vienna from the 1st of January, 1839, or from the tenth volume. He is ready to produce all the necessary testimony to his former circumstances. Business prevents him from visiting Vienna until the middle of October; he therefore presents his petition in writing, and begs it may be favorably considered.

All this with due respect.

"I can write music better than petitions, eh? Once more let me thank you for your kind letter. I should like the diary to be continued. I have received all your letters punctually. The accounts of Liszt grew musty; and, when I first received them, I had no room for them. What is the *police music le?* As for the songs, you must make allowance for us: we always have at least *ninety* on hand to be reviewed, no matter how many Lorenz finishes off. We shall soon meet. I smoke a great many cigars, and look quite rosy. *How much does a decent lodging cost per year*, if possible, up *one* flight? From a hundred to two hundred thalers? Please help a stranger! Adieu."

Soon after receiving an answer to this letter, he wrote a second in regard to his removal to Vienna.

LEIPSIC, Aug. 25, 1838.

Many thanks for your pleasant letter, which helped me ever so much: to be sure, there are mountains still between you and Vienna and myself; but I must cross them.

> " With motives pure, and mind that's gay
> Man travels quickly on his way,"

says Goethe. Only remain faithful and friendly to me.

My departure from here depends only upon my letters of recommendation from Prince Schönburg to Metternich and Sedlnytzky, without which it would be foolish to undertake the journey. If I obtain them, I shall leave here the 22d of September; but I'm afraid that, *in spite of the recommendation*, the Journal won't appear in Vienna by the 1st of January. I should be very sorry; partly on account of losing time, which I must be sparing of; partly on account of the journey back, for I should have to pass several months more in Leipsic, since it would be impossible for the Journal to dispense with my presence until June, 1839. There is some hope that I may be ready by January; but if, now that you have reconsidered the matter, you have *strong doubts* as to whether I can carry my point by the end of this year, write to me at once, and I will remain here till March. Remember, too, that the Journal printed in Vienna the 1st of December must be sent off by the *middle* of that month. There also remain the October and November numbers to be attended to. Will it be possible to arrange with the censor in eight weeks ?

I followed your friendly advice in regard to recommendations from the authorities here at once. I obtained the usual police testimonials, and a special recommendation from the magistrate. The Austrian consul, who will soon hear from Vienna that I propose to come there, is an intimate (musical) friend of Mendelssohn, who promises to introduce me to him in a few days. I should prefer to bring ready money rather than letters of credit. Wouldn't a thousand thalers be enough? If not, I can bring securities from the magistrate for a larger sum. *Pray write me about it.*

I accept your invitation to visit you with hearty thanks, provided I come *alone.* It is possible that my publisher, Friese (a very pleasant, modest man), may come with me, to set things to rights at once. I couldn't very well leave him, nor could I expect you to harbor both.

But if you think it would be useless for Friese to come (if the Journal cannot be published by January, 1839), write me your honest opinion. Of course, I should like to have Friese do every thing himself, aided by an assistant there, since I know nothing about it. I thought of . . . the other day; perhaps he might be made sole publisher in time. Has he means? Do you know him, or Artaria?

Lewy is coming here soon. He is said to be a clever fellow. Write and tell me about him. He talks of establishing a musical paper in Vienna himself, and declares he will invite me there for that purpose. Partnerships generally fail. Nevertheless, I shall listen to his advice gratefully. You will be pleased with my paper in Vienna. I shall treat more *en gros* of local matters (in letters, &c.). But more of this when we meet.

Now, my dear friend, write to me again before the 8th of September if you can; and you shall then know all particulars, — my decision, the plan for my departure, and what progress I've made. What you now do for me is not for my temporary gratification, but for my life-long happiness. You write of mysterious hints; but, when we meet, all shall be made clear. Trust in my affection.

When does Thalberg leave Vienna? I agree entirely with your advice in regard to the *incognito*, if it is in any way possible.

Becker writes me, with regards to you, to say that he has just sent a copy of the Bach music to Mr. Fuchs, who will deliver it to you. The organ-records have long been attended to by . . . [illegible] and others. I will bring the missing numbers of the Journal with me. Send the enclosed letter to Besque * at once. Bennett will probably come in December: he is to take the room which I leave at Michaelmas. You would be charmed with him.

One thing more. How high up do you live? I always suffer from dizziness and nausea in high places, and can never remain long in the top story of a house.†

Besque knows my plan. Perhaps he could take occasion to speak to Count Sedlnytzky of me and my purpose. Say a word to him on the subject; ask him to do so.

After all your kindness to me, my dear friend, I may well believe that you will keep all this a profound secret, especially the mysterious hints.

Gratefully and lovingly yours,

S.

---

* Besque von Püttlingen, an official of high rank in Vienna, known as a song-writer, under the name of J. Hoven.

† Compare page 79.

Fear. — Will Sedlnytzky be in Vienna in October?

Postcript. — I have no time to write to Besque to-day, so I'll let this go as it is.

Do you really think that Haslinger will give up publishing the Journal?

Towards the end of September, Schumann started for Vienna, spending a couple of days on the way in Prague. The two following letters to his relatives in Zwickau give valuable accounts of his life there for several months, as well as of his hopes, plans, and wishes : * —

VIENNA, Oct. 10, 1838.

MY DEAR ONES, — I am not now calm enough to tell you all that has happened to me since our parting. Two days after my arrival here, I was horrified by such dreadful news from Leipsic that I could think of nothing else.† . . . So my plans have as yet progressed but little. The city is so large that one needs double time for every thing. I have been everywhere received with great kindness, even by the minister of police, who gave me an audience day before yesterday. He said that there was no objection to my living here, and that I might set to work as soon as an Austrian publisher could be found. If I could not find one, I might meet with great difficulties, being a foreigner, &c. I must try the first course at once, and then visit him again. I shall apply to Haslinger, — shall go to him to-day or to-morrow. You would hardly believe how many petty factions and coteries there are here: to get a firm foothold, one must have a great deal of the snake about him, which I don't think I have.

Be of good cheer! One chief hope is in Fr. von Cibbini: *all depends on her!* Clara has written her a splendid letter, confiding every thing to her; but she does not return till the 24th.

I have made all my most important visits. Thalberg is in the country. Seyfried was very cordial and kind. If all goes well, I shall live with Mr. von Besque and the Cavalcabo,‡ both of whom you know from the Journal. I dined with Besque day before yesterday. I never imagined such delicious cooking. At the Cavalcabo's I met Archbishop Pyrkner,

---

* See *Neue Zeitschr. f. Musik*, vol. xii. p. 84, for his life in Vienna.

† This news was in regard to his love affairs.

‡ Julia von Webenau, née Baroni Cavalcabo, a lady who lived in Vienna and had won some fame by different piano and vocal compositions. She was a pupil of Mozart's son.

the celebrated poet: he has a bright, expressive countenance, and in-
spires respect. My most intimate companions are Fischhof and young
Mozart. How much I should like to write you of other friends, and
of all I've seen and done! But to tell you a secret, I shouldn't like to
live here long and *alone:* serious men and Saxons are seldom wanted or
understood here. But the fine surroundings make amends for that. Yesterday I went to the churchyard where Beethoven and Schubert lie
buried. Think what I found on Beethoven's tombstone, — *a pen*, and a
steel one too. It was a good omen: I shall preserve it as sacred.

The Kurrers were very kind to me, as were all the inhabitants of
Prague. You would be astonished, Theresa, if you could see the old city
of Prague; it is far more remarkable externally than Vienna; but Vienna
is *ten times* livelier. I found a room in the city with very little trouble,
mark me well, No. 679 Schön Laternengasse, on the first floor; and it
only costs twenty-two gulden per month. Every thing is frightfully
dear for a stranger who doesn't know the ways, — at least, *three times* as
dear as in Leipsic; but, when I get accustomed to living here, I can do
very nicely with the same sum as in Leipsic. The cooking is superb.
Haslinger sent me some cigars of the nicest description, which are a
great comfort to me.

I am pining for news of you and Clara. Of course I've had no time to
find a confidant yet, so I keep every thing to myself. I should be
ill, had I not so much to think of. The splendid opera here affords me
the greatest pleasure, especially the orchestra and chorus. We in Leipsic could have *no idea* of it. The ballet, too, would amuse you. I have
not yet been to the German Theatre, acknowledged to be the best in
Europe, nor to the little Vaudeville Theatre. Perhaps you don't know
that I paid a visit to Serre in Maxen.* *I cannot describe* the life there.
All is overflowing with mirth and money: every one does just as he likes.
I could not bear to leave. There is always a certain danger in such
pleasant, merely sensual life. A Mrs. Von Berge, whom Clara calls her
mamma, — a strong, handsome, healthy woman of thirty, — pleased me
much, as did also Mrs. Major † herself, who is bubbling over with good
humor.

Clara is idolized here: wherever I go they tell me so, and speak in the
most affectionate terms of her. But it would be hard to find a more
encouraging audience: they are rather too enthusiastic. In the theatres
you hear more applause than music. That is very delightful; but sometimes I'm quite annoyed by it.

* A manor near Dresden, where Schumann afterwards spent some time,
when living in Dresden.
† Mrs. Major Serre, the owner of Maxen.

Our affairs will be settled by next week. If I cannot remain here, my firm purpose is to go to Paris or London.* I will not return to Leipsic; but I will be discreet : don't fear that I will act too hastily. As soon as matters are decided, I will write. Answer soon.

With love and longing I embrace you.   Yours,

R.

Schumann to his Sister-in-law Theresa.

VIENNA, Dec. 18, 1838, Wednesday.

MY THERESA, — I should like to write you whole pages and books, but can't find time. To-day you will only get a Christmas greeting. You will celebrate it as I shall, — your head buried in your hands, thinking of the past. I shall be at your house with my Clara in thought; shall see you deck a tree. Ah! the happy time will yet come when we three shall give each other Christmas gifts; perhaps 'twill be sooner than we think. It seems like a dream to me, that you should be in Leipsic; I can imagine just how you feel sometimes. Clara has been in Dresden: she is grieved to be unable to give you longer answers. Forgive her. You know she is all love, attachment, and gratitude. She makes me very happy in this matter-of-fact Vienna life. Believe me, Theresa, if it depended upon me only, I would return to Leipsic to-morrow. Leipsic is not so small a place as I thought. They prate and gossip here as much as in Zwickau. I must be particularly careful, being a well-known public character. I am also doubtful whether the famous Viennese good nature is any thing more than an empty, smiling face. For myself, I've had no bad experiences; but I often hear wonders from and of other people. In vain do I look for musicians; that is, musicians who not only can play passably well upon one or two instruments, but who are cultivated men, and understand Shakspeare and Jean Paul. Well, the step is taken; and it had to be taken. The Journal will plainly lose ground if I have to publish it here. I'm very sorry. But, if I can only get my wife, I shall forget all the trouble and sleepless nights she has cost me. I could tell you much about my fine acquaintance, — of the empress, whom I've seen and fallen in love with (she is a true Spaniard); of the Burg Theatre, which is really remarkable; of Thalberg, with whom I'm on very good terms; of my Journal, which is not yet licensed: so it must be published in Leipsic for six months more; and that I often feel very well, but much oftener melancholy enough to shoot myself; and that the Novello † bride

---

* This hastily formed plan for visiting Paris was never again mentioned; but it shows that he was inclined to do his utmost to attain his end.

† The famous English songstress, Clara Novello.

is with one of my dearest friends, which is exceedingly pleasant for me. I might relate all this at full length. But I don't know how the days fly here: I've been here three months to-day; and the post-time, four o'clock, is always just at hand. Now for the most important thing. Clara goes the 1st of January to Paris, and probably to London later. We shall then be far apart. Sometimes I feel as if I could not bear it. But you know the reason: she wants to make money, of which we are indeed in need. May the good God guard her, the good, *faithful* girl! Perhaps I shall spend a month in Salzburg this spring: perhaps I shall come to Leipsic, too, if it is necessary (on account of the Journal), which I must talk over with Gerold and Friese. We shall at any rate pass the first year in Vienna, if no obstacles are opposed. I shall end by turning into an Austrian citizen. It isn't hard to make money here: they need clever men. We shall come out all right. Have no anxiety, my dear Theresa. Didn't Laurentius bring you a copy of "The Humorist," which contained a notice of me, written by Lyfer? I gave it to him for you. What is Edward doing? Tell him he must write to me. I should be very much obliged if he could send me a cheque for twenty-five or thirty-five thalers. Although I wish to be economical, I must make a respectable appearance; and at first, when I didn't know the cheapest places, it cost me a *great deal* of money. Then I promised to pay for the new grand piano that I bought by the middle of January, and don't know where to get it all, since I should be *very* sorry to part with my government securities, which I intended for Clara. So if Edward can spare it, let him do so for my sake. Has Carl sold his . . . [illegible] yet? I read about it in the newspaper. Write and tell me about that and about every thing as soon as possible. It is high time to close, if you are to receive this letter on Christmas Eve: so receive a hearty kiss.

Think as kindly of me as I do of you. With my whole heart I'm

Yours,   ROBERT.

The two last letters show that his illusory notions of Vienna vanished when he learned to know it for himself. Although the musical atmosphere there was not what he had hoped, he determined to take up his abode in the imperial city for a time, in order to render possible his long-desired union with Clara Wieck. He remained in Vienna until the 1st of April, 1839, when he returned to Leipsic without having attained his object. His plans must have been impossible; for, after leaving Vienna, he said no more of settling there. In later years, however, the wish returned, — at least, he often spoke of it with visible delight.

Little as he accomplished by his stay in Vienna, he made it of profit to the musical world. He visited Franz Schubert's brother, and found in his possession the rich remains of the master who died so young, and whom he so loved. With his peculiarly praiseworthy enthusiasm for all in sympathy with him, he at once busied himself in publishing some of Schubert's manuscripts. He sent "The C-major Symphony" to Mendelssohn at Leipsic, who brought it out at a subscription-concert in the Gewandhaus, Dec. 12, 1839. This was probably the first public performance of this great work.

He now made every exertion to establish in Leipsic the domestic hearth which he had vainly sought in Vienna. He had many difficulties to contend with, since Clara's father thought it his duty to refuse his consent to the marriage. Schumann, therefore, appealed to the law; * and his marriage was rendered possible in 1840, when The Royal Court of Appeals at Leipsic requested the father to yield.†

We may here mention those works written in 1838, before his journey to Vienna. They consist of Novelettes in four parts (Op. 21), ‡ "The Scenes of Childhood" (Op. 15), and "Kreisleriana" (Op. 16). These three works are equally interesting from a musical and psychological point of view.

The Novelettes clearly owe their origin to special events: this is proved not only by their title, but by a statement already quoted from a letter to H. Dorn, according to which the Novellettes belong to the list of compositions "which Clara inspired." The contents of this work indicate the soul-state of a man who, being in love, now hopes, now doubts, now

* Peculiar considerations render a closer inspection of this step and its consequences undesirable at present.

† After this action, The Royal Court of Appeals published their decision for the benefit of the parties interested Aug. 1, 1840.

‡ He also wrote at this period No. 9, in Op. 99; and in 1838, Nos. 9, 10, 14 and 18 of Op. 124 were composed, as the dates affixed to them show.

exults, now sinks in despair. The scale runs up from melancholy to happiness, light, and strength.

The Novelettes, belonging in form to the lyric and rondo, from their aspect might be classed with the Fantasies (Op. 12); but they do less justice to the requirements of rule, and are not on the whole so concise and plastic in form. From this it is clear that he was not always able to govern musical material in the most graceful manner; for of course he tried hard to do every thing in the best style.

"The Kreisleriana"* may be considered as an improved continuation of the Novelettes, whose single numbers are also somewhat lyric and figurative in style. This work is in every respect more important, not only than Op. 21, but than all its predecessors. It reveals an almost superabundant force of passion, such as is to be found in but few of his works. Added to this are wealth of imagination, depth of feeling, and excellent command of material.

The title "Kreisleriana" is evidently derived from Hoffmann's writings. As in those, the sufferings of Kupellmeister Kreisler are painted in words: so Schumann traced back to musical expression the manifold emotions of love's pangs, which then shivered through his soul. He might just as well have called his work "Wertheriana" or even "Schumanniana;" but he thought Kreisler a more fitting figure; because we always think of him at his piano. What could Schumann have meant to express, if not the feelings of enthusiasm which filled him, and the sad longing for communion with his love, now chastely veiled, now passionately breaking forth? And he did it with the power of genius. In no other of his numerous piano-compositions does the composer offer us so rich and fanciful a world of sound, so poetically rich, soul-absorbing, and refined a vision. Never was he more a tone-poet in the deepest sense of the word than in this instance.

---

* A new edition of this work was published when the original Haslinger edition was out of print, several years ago, by Whistling of Leipsic, who purchased the copyright.

The "*Kinderscenen*" (Op. 15), which, as Schumann's list shows, were composed between the two works just mentioned, are poetic and retrospective views of childhood by a grown-up person, but by no means pieces for children. Events and oc-currences in the world of children, musically expressed in a pure and perfectly child-like way, form a series of tone-pictures; and, in most cases, it requires but a slight degree of imagination to follow the poet, who rather whispers than speaks a few shy words, begging indulgence for his darlings. The "*Kinder-scenen*" testify to a rare delicacy and sensibility of percep-tion of the naïve and tender; in them a note is struck with the most poetic strains, which will resound long after the quicksands of time have swallowed up all the imitations of this composition which have since arisen. The rare worth of this work was at first partially ignored by the critics, as is shown by the following quotation from a letter to H. Dorn : * —

"I never saw any thing more shallow and inapplicable than Rellstab's. criticism of my '*Kinderscenen*.' He thinks, for-sooth, that I set up a weeping child before me, and sought for music in its sobs. It is just the reverse. I won't deny that a few childish heads hovered before me while composing ; but the titles were of course given afterwards, and are merely sly hints for the execution and conception. Rellstab, how-ever, really sees nothing beyond A, B, C, and insists on accords."

These " Childhood's Scenes," which are thoroughly lyric in form, are widely known, and may be reckoned among those of his works which first established his fame as a composer in general musical circles. They are masterpieces, in which form and sense are in perfect unity.

During his residence in Vienna, during the months of Octo-ber, November, and December, 1838, he composed " Scherzo, Jig, and Romance " (Op. 32), — the fughettas found in this work were not written till the following year, — the last move-ment of " The G-minor Sonata " (Op. 22), and several short

* See letters for 1833–52, No. 31.

pieces; viz., Nos. 2, 4, and 5, of "The Album Leaves," published as Op. 99. He also wrote in Vienna during the months
of January, February, and March, 1839, "Arabesque" (Op.
18), "Flower Pieces" (Op. 19), "Humoresque" (Op. 20), the
first movements of "The Carnival Strains from Vienna" (op.
26), "Night Pieces" (Op. 23), and a few minor pieces; among
which those compositions contained in Op. 99, "Three Fragments," and "A Prelude," as well as No. 19 of Op. 124, are pre-
eminent. He also planned a Concerto-movement for piano and
orchestra, which was apparently never completed.

After leaving Vienna in 1839, he only wrote, "Fughettas in
G-minor" (contained in Op. 32), the last movement of "The
Carnival Strains" (Op. 26), and three Romanzas for the piano
(Op. 23).

"The Carnival Strains from Vienna" is the only one of
these compositions which invites remark. It was, as the title
proves, written on the Viennese Carnival; and the greater
part of it was written during that festival. No. 1 offers us a
picture of the merry, bustling, carnival life, in quickly changing and contrasting lyric melodies. If Schumann, as we cannot doubt, wished to represent this, he succeeded admirably.
With such an idea in view, we can scarcely speak of or seek
for regularity. Still the single, mosaic-like, closely-connected
movements are peculiarly characteristic and attractive. Amid
the tumult of the masquerade (p. 7), "The Marseillaise" peeps
humorously forth. He took pleasure again, afterwards, in slyly
introducing this allusion; since "The Marseillaise," as he says,
was then prohibited in Vienna. A dreamy but short and incomplete "Romanza" follows as No. 2, to which is annexed a
petulant, somewhat extravagant "Scherzino" as No. 3. After a
very fervent and fanciful "Intermezzo," No. 4, perhaps the most
valuable thing in the composition, there follows a "Finale," No.
5, in the usual sonata shape. In the last four movements, with
the exception of "The Scherzino," hardly any reference to carnival pranks is apparent. The author may have involuntarily
added them, to compensate for the want of form in the first
part

Before proceeding further, a general review of Schumann's career seems the more desirable that he henceforth, as will be shown, devoted himself to other provinces of art, piano-composition having hitherto exclusively occupied his thoughts. This one-sided perseverance in one and the same direction was one of his most characteristic traits : it indicates an effort to accustom himself to a certain sphere of art, and to become master of it. Unfortunately we cannot conceal the fact, that he was ignorant of the right way to acquire that medium by whose aid alone the command of any kind of art can be obtained.

As we have seen, he derived his first impulse to become a creative musician from the piano-forte : this is explicable in two ways. It was the only instrument upon which he had learned to express his emotions from childhood up, and consequently the only one with which he was familiar; then his early resolve to follow the *virtuoso* career * must have prompted him to write for that instrument. His study of composition, gradually causing him to recognize the defects of his early works, urged him the more strongly to piano-composition. His really artistic efforts probably aroused an ardent desire to produce something of musical importance in *one* department before attempting any thing new. If we consider that his deep and earnest relations with Clara Wieck afforded him a direct motive for composing for the piano, we shall understand the stability which marks the works of the first nine years.

The path he trod during this period is most peculiar, probably being unique in the history of music. It was in part based upon that kind of development which, when compared with normal education, must be in some degree opposed to it. While all productive and artistic men with whose lives we are familiar reveal a logical, organic progress, and a decided effort at creation, from boyish studies up to harmonious and polished masterpieces, Schumann labored like some musical and creative spirit from an ideal world, whose mental treas-

* Compare page 56.

ures, though unarranged and unruled, are richly developed, travelling on by gradual inner purification to transparency This was the necessary result of his insufficient and incomplete musical education. A normal mind, early skilled in schools and rules, slowly rising from small to great, from simple to complicated, merely needs to shake off the academic dust, to move on freely and easily in the path which leads to victory. But when Schumann, at an advanced age, determined to devote himself to music, and especially to composition, he lacked the technical skill and knowledge without which a composer is left to his own discretion or to chance. Without being at all to blame himself, he was deprived of a proper early musical education; and a singular prejudice for some time prevented him from repairing this neglect. Thence it is that we miss, during his first years as a musician, the clear, gold ground, the firm, secure basis, upon which alone a constant and healthy development is possible; for it was impossible that the studies which he took up to repair his ignorance should bear immediate fruits; impossible that they should, from a musical point of view, at once atone for the lack of early culture. He had to seek with unspeakable pains, and appropriate late in life, those things which are generally learned by children at play. This is plainly proved by most of the compositions hitherto mentioned. They resemble the rough ore drawn from the bosom of the earth; which, after undergoing various purifying processes, produces but a comparatively small portion of precious metal. *Strictly speaking*, of all the compositions occurring between 1830–39, only the "Fantasies" (Op. 12), the "Scenes of Childhood" (Op. 15), and the "Kreisleriana" (Op. 16) can be considered as such a portion, spite of all the beauties and merits of his other works. In those, form and contents are essentially one; and in originality of ideas and peculiar finish even of detail, we find so happy a union of the melody, harmony, and rhythm characteristic of him, that our enjoyment is never or but seldom disturbed. Whereas, all the other works which we have examined are more or less out of proportion either in melody, harmony, or rhythm. As we have already said, the melodious element is very seldom to be found; and in those rare cases it was a mere embryo. It gradually developed, and formed firmer images of characteristic pattern. Harmonic and rhythmic elements are more or less conspicuous, but often lack that power in whose train are purity and beauty. His harmonic combinations often lack organic development and the close and indissoluble web of logical modulation: so dull, discordant, and dead combinations of chords abound. The rhythmic proportions are not always clear and plastic in shape. We must confess that the latter, in their strange, Beethoven-like arrangement and limit, form a highly characteristic epoch in his music; and that through them an original, floating, flickering, and graceful motion is produced, which is in perfect unison with his nature. On the other hand, we cannot deny that their application sometimes results in too exclusive, monotonous, and partial a view; and, where this is the case, his music is often materially inconsistent. Afterwards, however, in the three works named above, which may be regarded as a happy result of the creative period just closed, the rhythmic element, at first predominant, was repressed, and united with the clarified melody and harmony.

Two more peculiarities of Schumann's music remain to be considered. The one specially concerns piano-composition, the other chiefly concerns the quality of his musical labor; that is, the general formation and completion of a composition. On examining the former, it is evident that he formed a style of execution peculiarly his own. It is revealed not only in the figurative images employed, but also in the use of widely separated accords, and the crossing and meeting of the hands. It is an indubitable fact, that Chopin's influence was first manifested thus: he afterwards pursued his own course, withdrawing more and more from kindred influences; and we may surely speak of a specific Schumann style of execution as correctly as of that of any other master. The best and truest insight into it is obtained by a thorough study and comparison of his piano-compositions with those of other masters who have influenced the technical development of this instrument.

In the second point, he also diverges from custom. But it is seldom that we find in any of his compositions — we speak of those already considered — what is called " elaborated work ; " that is, such a treatment of the subject as brings an organic formation to a fine point, constantly enlarging upon the chief motif, as in the works of Haydn, Mozart, &c. He generally does just the opposite. He picks to pieces his motives, —·which are often nothing but melodious figures, — builds them up again, creates new images from them, increases them; until at last the various combinations requisite to form a whole are obtained. He usually permits the leading thought to recur in its original shape, as if revolving in differently modulated positions, as if guiding it through various districts. It is as if we saw one and the same picture through different-colored glasses, the object remaining the same, the varying tints alone lending a new charm. Of course in smaller works, where the moods of feeling may be predominant, great effects may be thus attained, as was frequently the case; but in the larger forms of art, into which he also carried this manner, — we will merely remind the reader of certain parts of his string-quartettes, — it could hardly be used to good advantage. Such things require more than a fine, free action and a pleasing or expressive melodic figure, whose modulated recurrences finally become monotonous. A musician especially would feel dissatisfied. Thus, too, compositions in which the theme is hardly worked out at all strike us rather as spirited improvisations, than as perfected and completed compositions; and we may be sure that his habit, up to Op. 50, of composing every thing at his piano,[*] was injurious to the form of his creations

* Compare page 72.

III.

ROBERT SCHUMANN'S MUSICAL CAREER.

LEIPSIC. — DRESDEN. — DUSSELDORF.

1840 — 1854.

THE year 1840, as has before been said, marks an important epoch in Schumann's musical career. Before more closely considering this crisis, we must relate an event which occurred in the early part of this period; viz., his promotion to the degree of Doctor of Philosophy.

As is shown by his letters, he resolved in 1838 to win this honor,[*] but never attained it until now. He was aided by his friend Keferstein,[†] by whose advice he addressed a request for the title of doctor to the faculty of philosophy at the University of Jena. The following extract may be of interest: "My faith is often strengthened by the conviction, that I have been true to my aims and myself for several years; for error could not be so constant. I am also specially conscious of a sincere veneration for the past and future; but, nevertheless, I have sought to assist the talents of the present time, when they rely on the past like Mendelssohn, or devise something new and peculiar like Chopin. As a composer, I may have pursued an original course; but it is hard to speak of the soul's secrets.

---

[*] See letters for 1833–52, No. 23.
[†] See letters for 1833–52, Nos. 33, 34, 36.

Will you not consider my petition kindly, and trust in the future and that riper age which shall show what was reality and what mere hope ? "

The account of his life, given in this petition, reads as follows : —

"I was born at Zwickau in Saxony, June 8, 1810.   My father was a bookseller, a very active and intelligent man, noted for his pocket-edition of foreign classics ; for ' The Leaves of Memory,' much read in their day ; for many important business works ; and for a translation of several of Byron's poems, published shortly before his death. My mother was a Miss Schnabel of Zeitz. I was educated lovingly and carefully. From my earliest years I showed great taste for music. I recollect writing, unaided, choral and orchestral works when but eleven years of age.* My father wished me to study music ; but the plans which he formed with C. M. von Weber of Dresden were never carried out. I received the usual grammar-school education, pursuing my musical studies with perfect devotion, and composing according to my ability. In 1828, I entered the Leipsic University, chiefly for the purpose of hearing Prof. Krug's philosophical lectures. In 1829, I went to Heidelberg, attracted thither by Thibaut's fame as an excellent musical connoisseur and a bold thinker. Here I began to busy myself exclusively with music, and made considerable progress in piano-playing. For greater culture I returned to Leipsic in 1830, completed my study of composition under Heinrich Dorn, then director of music there, and published my first compositions. The critics treated me gently. Insured by a small fortune against the shadows of a musical career, I was free to devote myself to the study of greater compositions. At this time Europe being greatly agitated, and, in consequence,

* This statement differs from that to be found in his note-book; for this says in regard to the composition of the 150th Psalm, which must be the one referred to, since it is the only one of the kind, " 1822 or '23, the 150th Psalm, with orchestral accompaniment."

artist-life in Leipsic disturbed, I, in common with other musicians, chief among them my friend Ludwig Schunke, who died young, conceived the idea of publishing a 'New Journal of Music.' This plan was executed in April, 1834. The Journal gained applause, and was at once put upon a secure footing by the increasing interest of the public. In 1835, I became sole editor. Although I was thus obliged to divide my forces, productive power always had the upper hand, and often led me from other and perilous paths. I still occupy this post: it has brought me into intimate relations with most of the musicians now living, whose number increases yearly. I have been specially employed in aiding the efforts of the most talented young aspirants. Chopin, Clara Wieck, Henselt, and many others, were first brought into notice through the Journal.

"No other important events in my life can be related here. I was recently made a corresponding honorary member of the Rotterdam Association for The Promotion of Music, the German National Club in Stuttgart, and The Euterpe, a musical society in Leipsic.

"I have published twenty-two compositions, some of which have been played in public by Liszt,* Clara Wieck, Henselt, and others. I have also written under the names of Eusebius and Florestan. Most of the reviews of instrumental music in the Journal are by me, and are signed either by my name, that of Florestan or Eusebius, or the numbers two and twelve.

"ROBERT SCHUMANN.

"LEIPSIC, Feb. 17, 1840."

He had not long to wait for his doctorate. As soon as Counsellor Reinhold, dean of the philosophic faculty, laid the petition before his colleagues, which he did on the 22d of February of the same year, the diploma was made out and sent. It reads as follows: —

* See Appendix G for Franz Liszt's articles, written to introduce Schumann's music to the public.

Viro prænobilissimo atque doctissimo
Roberto Schumann
Zwickaviensi
complurium societatum musicarum sodali
qui rerum musis sacrarum et artifex ingeniosus
et judex elegans modis
musicis tum scite componendistum docte judicandis
atque præceptis
de sensu pulchritudinis venustatisque optimis edendis
magnam nominis
famam adeptus est
Doctoris Philosophiæ honores
dignitatem jura et privilegia
ingenii, doctrinæ et virtutis spectatæ insignia
atque ornamenta
detulit est.

Schumann's compositions in 1840 were entirely opposite in character to his earlier efforts. They were exclusively lyric. A rich stream of song gushed from his poetic soul, and this year is justly called "the year of song." On the 19th of February, 1840, he wrote to his friend Keferstein, "I write nothing but songs now, long and short, also male quartettes, which I should like to dedicate to that honored friend who now reads these lines, if he would kindly promise to deter me from composition no longer. May I? I can hardly tell you how delightful it is to write for the voice, in comparison with instrumental composition, and how agitated and excited I am when I sit down to work. Entirely original ideas occur to me; and I am seriously thinking of an opera, which would be easy, if I could only get rid of my editorial duties."

This sudden transition into a branch of composition with which he had but seldom meddled, and then before adopting music as his profession, was caused by a special influence. As he himself says in a letter to Dorn,* that Clara Wieck was "almost the sole inspiration" of many of the piano-compositions written during the latter half of his thirtieth year

* See letters for 1833–52, No. 31.

it is also clear that she was the cause of his labors in the lyric realm. It is evident that his delight at the speedy realization of his heart's desires drove him to express his feelings in words more fully than ever before. Thus arose the inspired glow of love and ardor with which he, loudly exulting and rejoicing, labored in the kingdom of song. But we still perceive that melancholy tone, apparently the reflection of love's doubts and fears. It is as intangible as the spirit of love. Yet we can see plainly in those love-songs — which, according to his list, were the first composed in 1840 — the human heart exalted and enkindled to the loftiest emotions by the power of a noble passion.

According to the list, one hundred and thirty-eight different songs, large and small, were written in 1840, — some for a single voice, some for several. We give them below in the order assigned by his list.

" Song-Wreath " from Heine, Op. 24 ; "Myrtles," 4 parts, Op. 25 ; 3 poems by Geibel for several voices, Op. 29 ; 3 poems by Geibel, Op. 30 ; " The Lion's Bride," " Red-haired Jane," and " The Fortune-teller," from Béranger, by Chamisso, Op. 31 ; 6 songs for a chorus of male voices, Op. 33 ; 4 duets by R. Burns, A. Grün, &c., for soprano and tenor, with piano accompaniment, Op. 34 ; 12 poems by J. Kerner, a series of songs, Op. 35 ; 6 poems by Reinick, Op. 36 ; 12 poems from Rückert's " Love's Spring," 2 parts, Op. 37 ; * 12 poems by Eichendorff, Op.

---

* This work contains three songs by Schumann's wife (the titlepage therefore gives both names), Nos. 2, 4, and 11. When Fr. Rückert heard of these songs composed on his poems, he published the following lines in a Berlin almanac for 1843 : —

TO ROBERT AND CLARA SCHUMANN.

It is long, oh, long,
Since of Love's spring was my song
From my heart's core
As it did pour,
In solitude it rang around.
Twenty years
Passed by ; and my fond ears

39 ; * 4 poems by Anderson, and one from modern Greek, translated by Chamisso, Op. 40 ; 8 songs from Chamisso's "Woman's
Love and Life," Op. 42 ; 3 ballads and romanzas for one voice,
with piano accompaniment, 1 number, Op. 45 ; "Poet Love,"
16 songs by Heinrich Heine. Op. 48 ; ballads and romanzas,
2 parts, Op. 49 ; the same, 3 parts, Op. 53 ; "Belshazzar," a
ballad by Heine, Op. 57 ; 3 duets for two female voices, Op. 43.

The above vocal compositions, whose number affords a
shining proof of the master's rich, varied, and quickly-formed
productive power, are in every respect the true children of his
mind. They reveal the whole inner man, with all his lights
and shades. We here find in singular accord depth and
warmth of nature, enthusiastic feeling, fancifully deep conception, ingenious and poetic wealth of expression, and a very
happy characterization, even in the smallest details, and
especially embodied in the piano accompaniment. But quaint,
even disagreeable notes slip in; and it is difficult to understand how Schumann, as an æsthetic and cultivated man,

> From the warbling throng
> Heard one song,
> Which repeated the sound.
> And now appear
> In the twenty-first year
> Two birdlings dear,
> Who tell me clear
> No note has fallen to the ground.
> My songs
> You repeat,
> My thoughts
> You sing sweet,
> My feelings outpour,
> My spring restore,
> Renew my youth
> With utmost truth:
> Accept my thanks, though others choose
> As unto me, all praises to refuse.

* In the new edition of this work (Whistling: Leipsic) the song, "The
Merry Traveller," found in the first, was omitted; and another, "Abroad,"
was inserted in its place.

could set to music such prosaic poems as the following by Heine : —

> " In Lapland they're a dirty set, —
>   Flat-headed, wide-mouthed, and small:
> They squat by the fire, and cook
>   Their fish, and chatter and squall."

or Burns: —

> " A happier wife than I
>   Ne'er lived on vale or hillie high:
> Then twenty cows had I.
>   Alas, alas, alas!
> They gave me milk and butter good,
>   And fed on clover grass.
> And twenty sheep were mine,
>   O woe! O woe! O woe !
> They kept me warm with whitest fleece,
>   'Mid frost and wintry snow."

or even poems like " The Fortune-teller," " The Treasure-digger," " Red-haired Jane," and No. 11 of Op. 48, unless we consider that his peculiar organization not only favored but induced extremes, both in life and in art.

Nevertheless he may well claim a place of honor among the great masters of song. For, aside from the lofty mental importance of his lyric compositions, he carried to a still higher pitch the German song handed down to us by Beethoven and Franz Schubert. He depends somewhat upon those masters ; but, in his struggles for complete unity, he aims at and attains a deep and forcible hold on the incidents of the poem, thus actively promoting this style of art. Fully appreciating his labors in this direction, he writes to Kahlert,* " I should like you to examine my vocal compositions more closely. They foretell my future. I dare not promise to do more (that is, in song) than I have already done, and am content therewith."

We said that Clara Wieck inspired his attempts at vocal

---

* See letters for 1833–52, No. 42

music, and that to her influence may be ascribed all the love
songs written in 1840. We must refer his further efforts in
the province of song to an analogous fact in his first creative
period. As there in the realm of piano-music a decided par-
tiality for a peculiar current of thought is evident, so here on
lyric soil the same thing is manifest. As already remarked,
this is obviously connected with his struggle to confine himself
to a certain sphere of art, and to be entirely subject to it.
This persistent toil in the kingdom of song was, however, allied
with the rare quality of melodious form, which cannot be too
highly rated, and which afterwards stood him in good stead:
for, while busily employed in vocal composition, he attained to
a great knowledge of melody. We learn that he at last realized his progress, by a letter to C. Reinecke, in which he says,
"The best way to cultivate a taste for melody is to write a
great deal for the voice and for independent chorus." To be
sure, he might have won more glorious results, especially in
vocal composition, had he gone one step farther, and fulfilled
the imperative demands of song as well as studied the pregnant and plastic perfection of melody. In this respect his
songs, with but few exceptions, only accidentally such, are
unsatisfactory. He lacked the requisite knowledge; and the
sentence in his writings, "Much may be learned from bards,
but don't believe all they say," proves that he considered the
more obscure claims made upon the composer by the nature of
song unjustifiable poetical caprices. This opinion must have
been in a great measure caused by his innate disposition to
ignore certain claims, which, however correct, were not obvious
to him. He thought that in vocal composition nothing was
necessary but melodious shape * and a regard for the vocal
compass: for the rest, the singer must accommodate himself to
the composer's designs, which, being purely spiritual, rank
higher. However true this may be, none but those who are
thoroughly familiar with the nature of vocal music should rely

---

* It is supposed to be self-evident, that melody and song are not identi
cal.

upon it. But Schumann never considered it, as his vocal compositions prove; on the contrary, his treatment of the voice but too clearly reveals his absolute independence. Songs like No. 1, in Op. 25 (" Consecration "), No. 1 in Op. 36 (" Sunday on the Rhine "), No. 9 in Op. 37, No. 4 in Op. 39 (*"Waldesgespräch "*), No. 4 in Op. 40 (" The Musician "), No. 15 in Op. 48, and No. 2 in Op. 53,* illustrate our remarks. In them we often see a sudden change, wearying and irritating to the voice, from far above to far below the middle range. This sometimes occasions great difficulty in springing from one note to the other.

Schumann shows great ignorance both in style and manner, when writing for certain voices, as, for example, in No. 2 of Op. 35, and No. 6 of Op. 36. They are written expressly for a " Tenor," but are far too low for such a voice, and are therefore useless. The same is partially true of the tenor parts in " Paradise and the Peri," and the soprano in duet No. 12 in Op. 37. When we read in reference to the second voice in this duet, " For tenor or baritone," we see clearly Schumann's naïve standpoint in vocal matters.

Otto Jahn says in his life of Mozart, " We can hardly consider it a favorable circumstance that song at the present day requires no musico-artistic culture." In this sentence we find the key to the inadequacy of Schumann's songs in regard to pure vocalism. This inadequacy is caused by the circumstances under which he essayed to write for the voice.

As we have seen, he grew up at the piano; and, during many years, composed almost exclusively *for*, ay, and without exception *at*, this instrument. He based his vocal compositions on this instead of on the voice; and thus it was natural that the latter, whose nature he had not studied, should receive a treatment suited to the piano.

The numerous lyric compositions which he afterwards wrote — some for a single voice, some for a chorus — are essentially of the same description; with few exceptions, they do not attain to the same spirit and depth of feeling as his earlier works.

* Only the most remarkable instances are selected.

Early in September, 1840, an important moment arrived completely changing his course of life: he was married. His betrothed was at this time visiting a friend, C. L., at the Thuringian mineral-springs in Liebenstein. While she was passing through Weimar, on her way to Leipsic, where she was to give a concert, the lovers met at the house of director Montag. Schumann entered unannounced, and excited not only delight in those most deeply interested, but gave a most charming surprise to all his friends in Weimar.

A few days later, on the 12th of September, the long anticipated marriage took place in the church at Schönfeld,* a village near Leipsic. He henceforth led a more quiet and contemplative life. In the course of time he became the father of eight children; † and his retirement was only occasionally interrupted by short pleasure-trips.

In 1841, he entered a new phase of development as a composer: he returned to instrumental music, but in another spirit. While his former works had generally resembled the Sonata in form, he now grasped the Symphonic elements, and showed himself devoted and industrious in this form of instrumental music. This re-action is easily explicable: so great a mind could no longer be content with the results hitherto attained in instrumental composition. As early as 1839, ‡ he wrote to H. Dorn, " . . . and then there is nothing of mine to be published or heard but Symphonies. I often feel tempted to crush my piano: it's too narrow for my thoughts. I really have very little practice in orchestral music now; still I hope to master it."

---

* The marriage-register of the parish of Schönfeld says, "Dr. R. Schumann, composer of music, and resident in Leipsic, only remaining lawful son of August Schumann, bookseller, of Zwickau, was joined in marriage with Miss Clara Josephine Wieck, lawful eldest daughter of the first wife of Friedrich Wieck, music-dealer, of Leipsic, on Sept. 12, Saturday before Dom. XIII. p. Trin. at ten o'clock, A.M.

† One of these eight children has already followed his father into eternity.

‡ See letters for 1833–52, No. 29

But this sudden conversion to other forms may be explained in another way. He had learned that, to compose with ease, he must master theory. In reference to this he writes to Mein-ardus: "If a man wants to compose in free forms, he must first master those binding and current in all ages." Here we see Mendelssohn's influence, perhaps for the only time; for the oc-casional appearance of kindred elements was caused by their living at the same time, — this being more or less true of all the composers then living. On the whole, both these masters were and remained true to themselves.

We can easily believe that so artistic a nature as Mendels-sohn's should impress Schumann, and spur him on to emula-tion ; for he found Mendelssohn's chief attribute to be the very thing he lacked, and had labored for years to attain, — *perfec-tion of form.* So it was very natural that he should seek to become master of form in the same way that Mendelssohn and all other masters of music had done; viz., by studying the masterpieces of the past. His surprising success is shown by the first work composed under these circumstances, "The B-flat major Symphony," Op. 38.* It heads a list of instru-mental compositions, which, in their masterly proportions, are incontestably the most valuable and enjoyable of his works. "The B-flat major Symphony" was followed in 1841 by a similar work, "Overture, Scherzo, and Finale," in E-major, Op. 52,† and by "The Symphony in D-minor," completed in 1851, and published as Op. 120. Here we again see exces-sive persistence in one direction, and finally by the sketch of a Symphony in C-minor, which was never completed.‡ He also composed what afterwards became the first movement of a Piano Concerto (Op. 54), an "Allegro" for piano and or-

* It was first performed with Op. 52, by Clara Wieck, at a concert at the Leipsic Gewandhaus, Dec. 6, 1841.

† The Finale of this work was remodelled in 1845.

‡ Schumann afterwards tried to complete it, but, according to his own statement, could find nothing more in the sketch.

chestra, and a vocal composition from Heine's "Tragedy," with orchestral accompaniment.*

Schumann conceived and treated the symphonic form in a peculiar spirit, based on the study of masterpieces, especially those of Beethoven. The ideas are thoroughly Schumannic : higher artistic value is bestowed on them by the fact, that these ideas are expressed in the old established form. They seldom reveal the arbitrary and formal abnormities which so often occur in his earlier works. We must, therefore, give more implicit recognition to the surprising power with which he handles an orchestra, with whose nature he could hardly have been conversant. There are exceptions, especially in the wind-instruments, which show a want of technical knowledge ; but these inequalities are easily overlooked, and we have no very difficult or daring technical problems to complain of. The tone-tint of Schumann's instrumentation is not always fine ; it has not that primary sense of harmonious tone-elements which is a special attribute of the greatest masters of the past, and which in Mozart compels deep admiration ; but it is always characteristic. We feel that the desired result is always attained.

In his Symphonic works, he solved the problem to which he had deemed himself incompetent;† namely, how to compose something *individual and remarkable* in a province which had been developed to the utmost degree. This is also true of the chamber-music composed the next year. This chiefly consists of three clever quartettes for two violins, viola, and violoncello, Op. 41, the well-known, always enthusiastically-received piano-

* Probably the term "Orchestral accompaniment" was a slip of the pen. I only know of one composition entitled "Tragedy," in three songs by Heine : it was published as Op. 64. Schumann must have undertaken *still another* composition, if this term is correct; but his list does not mention such. To the short works composed in 1841, not noted in his list, belong Nos. 1, 12, and 13 of Op. 99 (Album Leaves), and No. 16 of Op. 124.

† We see how irresolute Schumann was in his views, by a remark afterwards made, that there was nothing left to be done in the way of sonatas and overtures. Still he wrote two long sonatas and several overtures in the last years of his life.

quintette, Op. 44, and the piano-quartette, Op. 47. The "Fantasies," Op. 88, for piano, violin, and violoncello, which were also written in 1842, differ from the works just named: they are in no respect equal to them. They were originally intended to go together as a piano trio; but Schumann afterwards altered this title, which was hardly suitable. Even if the "Fantasies" do not form a comprehensive whole, they interest by their intrinsic moods.

The piano-quintette, Op. 44, not only ranks very high among his mental products, but is superior to any similar contemporaneous work, up to the border-line between more recent music and the "classic" period closing with Beethoven. It is unquestionably the greatest piece of chamber-music since Beethoven's gigantic efforts. For the terseness, finish, and polish, which form a beautiful, becoming, and noble image-veiling vesture, conceal such a strong and bold, though never extravagant, flight of fancy, such a happy polarization of all the forces and factors requisite to a true work of art, as has never been known in a similar composition of modern times. But we must consider it a merit peculiar to this tone-piece, that the flight taken is sustained evenly throughout the four movements, — ay, even at the close of the finale, when we might think the composer's powers exhausted, the whole soars aloft by the clever combination of the leading motives of the first and last movements. This work forms a picture of a wanderer, who climbs ever higher and higher, attracted by the blooming, fertile landscape stretching up the slope of the hill, longing to feast his eyes on the path he has left behind him, as he stands on the summit. The highest conditions of art are complied with in this composition. Ecstatic inspiration, lofty expression, fine mastery of passion, noble feeling, wealth of imagination, fresh and healthy images, and a happy issue, are here united in a rare degree.

The piano quartette, Op. 47, is, in many respects, equal to the quintette, and if not so nervous and powerful, not so complete, the treatment is finer and more accurate.

We have often spoken of Schumann's quiet, reserved na ture. This characteristic was greatly increased by his mar· riage. This was not only because he so seldom came into con· tact with the world, but also because his wife, with admirable womanly devotion, strove to keep far from him aught tha might hinder or disturb his professional labors. She thu, became the mediator between her husband and every-da· life, unless peculiar events forced him to come out of his shell. Under these circumstances, his nature, already reserved and silent, naturally became less inclined and fitted than ever for any great public work. This is proved by a glance at the fine sphere of action offered him in the Leipsic Music-School, which was opened April 22, 1843, under the direction of Felix Men- delssohn Bartholdy, assisted by the principal musicians then living in Leipsic, and the best instructors extant. According to a circular issued by the directors, Schumann taught piano playing, the art of composition, and playing from score. The object evidently was rather to learn from a *remarkable musi- cian* than from a *teacher*. As a teacher, he lacked that indis- pensable quality, a ready power of communication,* and ability to explain his meaning at all times with clearness and pre- cision.† It would be unjust to reproach him for this, as it would be unreasonable to require a man to exercise a faculty which he does not possess.

His connection with the Music-School lasted, with the ex- ception of a short absence from Leipsic in 1841, until his removal to Dresden soon after. It had no influence whatever

* Being myself a pupil of the Leipsic Music School at the time, I had ample opportunity to prove this from personal observation, especially as I entered one of Schumann's piano-classes, to play the violin part in a B-flat major trio by Franz Schubert, Op. 99, which one of the scholars was to play. The lesson was given with hardly a word from Schumann; although, as I well remember, there was abundant occasion.

† How well he himself knew this is shown by a letter beginning, —

" DEAR SIR, — The undersigned desires, if possible, to speak to-day on a subject of deep importance to him. As I might not be able to explain my meaning orally, I take the liberty to write you the following account, which is strictly true."

upon him, and he remained what he always was, — a musician, laboring zealously and silently. To this circumstance he owed the lovely, ay, charming variations for two pianos, Op. 46, and one of his most extensive works, written in 1843,* " Paradise and the Peri," † published as Op. 50. He was impelled to this by Emil Flechsig, the friend of his youth. He, amid his theological studies, had remained true to the love of poetry nourished in his boyhood with Schumann, and had translated the poem " Paradise and the Peri," contained in Thomas Moore's " Lalla Rookh." He gave it to his friend, hoping that he would set it to music. This occurred in 1841. Although Schumann enthusiastically admired this poem, which was not only of intrinsic worth, but peculiar in coloring, suited to a tone-poet's fancy, he did not set it to music until two years later.

Flechsig's close translation required many changes before it could be used for a great composition. Schumann undertook to alter it himself; ‡ and here he again shows that obscurity which always prevented him from mastering his subject : for, spite of many judicious alterations, the words, as set to music, decidedly lack perfect and regular unity. This is partially true of the poem itself; but a critical, clear, and correct hand could doubtless have given it a firmer and more consistent form. Its present shape renders it almost impossible to class this composition in any existing form of art. It comes nearest to the Cantata, but differs essentially from it in the introduction of a narrator, who, without any personal interest in the matter, only serves to bind together the special *epochs* of the action. This

---

* Nos. 11 of Op. 99, and 6 of Op. 124, were also written in 1843.

† First performed at the Leipsic Gewandhaus, under the composer's direction, Dec. 4, 1843, and repeated the next week to the great delight of all. These performances were greatly enhanced by the aid of Mrs. Livia Frege; who, although she had then retired from the stage, performed the part of the " Peri" (which was written and designed for her) with great spirit and grace.

‡ A contributor to the *Neue Zeitschr. f. Musik*, vol. lii., p. 211, thinks that Schumann used Theodore Ollker's translation (Leipsic Tauchnitz Jour.), since a third at least of this work agrees with Schumann's words to the Peri.

narrator is evidently copied from the Evangelist in Bach's "Passion Music," but by no means with a like necessity. Unquestionably the latter shared the conviction of his day, that not only the substance, but the words, of the biblical dogma were sacred. Schumann's case was not at all similar. He had before him, in the poem to be set to music, a work of art, which, although once remodelled, would still permit every formal change required by æsthetic considerations. How easy, for example, it would have been to abolish the narrator, as destructive of unity. At any rate, if the lame, monotonous, and prolix third part had been omitted,* since it contains no action, a suitable motive might have been inserted.

The variations in the text of "Paradise and the Peri" from the original poem were, as we have said, by Schumann. They consist, with the exception of occasional judicious abbreviations, in the addition of a chorus for "The Spirits of the Nile," the chorus of "Houris," the solo "Banished" for the Peri, the quartette "Peri, 'tis true," the solo "Sunken was the golden orb," and the concluding chorus. In the latter, the gifted tone-poet did not attain to a really poetic and effective close.

Spite of the defects in the text, at which we have but hinted, the work is uncommonly attractive in a musical sense, from the fervor and truth of expression, as well as the dazzling, shifting color (we might say, the Oriental, luminous warmth), which pervades and penetrates the whole. Schumann struck the key-note of the poem with a master-hand, and, aided by his wealth of imagination, reproduced it in music. The beautiful flow of melody, seldom marred by his early imperfections, and the simple arrangement of the musical ideas, are particularly praiseworthy. In the last respect, there is unmistakable progress, caused by his more rigorous labors for two years past. On the other hand, as in the lyric compositions of 1840, he

---

* The tedious action of the third part was somewhat lessened by the omission of all from "Slow sank the evening's golden light," to "She floated down in joyous hope." The bass-song in F-sharp minor may easily be omitted in performance.

did not fully comply with the requirements of song. The difficulties presented to the performer by the generally inadequate treatment of the voice are increased by an instrumentation, which, though rich and florid in itself, is too voluminous. In some passages, the fine balance which should be preserved between the vocal and instrumental parts is entirely wanting. So, too, discords between words and music, such as on p. 46, measures 10–11; p. 63, measures 12–13, and 23–26 ; p. 64, measures 24–25 ; p. 69, measures 3–5; p. 85, measures 19 ; p. 102, measures 21–22 ; p. 114, measures 3–5 ; p. 117, measures 6; and p. 118, measures 6–10 of the piano-score, work unfavorably, since they tear the poetical thoughts to tatters.

"Paradise and the Peri," together with the "Fantasies" (Op. 12), "The Kinderscenen" (Op. 15), a number of songs composed in 1840, and the piano-quintette (Op. 44) were the chief causes of public recognition of Schumann's creative gifts. This beautiful work soon became widely known, and survived many performances, even two in New York in 1848,* which gave Schumann great delight.†

The uniform retirement in which he lived and worked was interrupted, at his wife's request, in 1844 (the following year), by a long concert-tour. ‡ This journey had long been contemplated, as is shown by a letter to Keferstein, § in which he says, " I had to promise the journey to St. Petersburg to Clara in the most solemn manner, else she said she would go alone.   I believe she would have been capable of it, in her anxiety for our external welfare.   Pardon me if I forbear to tell how un-*willing* I am to leave my quiet home.   I never think of it without the utmost sorrow, and dare not let Clara know my

* See *Signale für die Mus. Welt*, vol. vi. p. 235.

† See letters for 1833–52, No. 58.

‡ Clara Schumann had made one grand concert-tour since her marriage, to Copenhagen, but without her husband; since his professional duties *or* bade him to accompany her farther than Hamburg.

§ See letters for 1833–52, No. 38.

feelings." And now it really came to pass. The artist-pair started the last of January, 1844, by the way of Königsberg, Mittau, and Riga. In the first-named city Clara Schumann gave two concerts; and in Mittau and Riga conjointly, five. In St. Petersburg four concerts were given, at which Schumann's compositions caused as much enthusiasm as his wife's matchless execution. The following letter to Friedrich Wieck gives us a full account of their life for several weeks in the city of the Czar:—

ST. PETERSBURG, April 1, 1844.

DEAR FATHER, — We have delayed answering your letter until to-day, that we might tell you the result of our visit here. We have now been here four weeks. Clara has given four concerts, and played before the empress. We have made many distinguished acquaintances, and seen much that was interesting: every day brings something new. So the time has passed; and to-morrow we return to Moscow, and, on looking back, may well be satisfied with our achievements. I have a great deal to tell you, and am very glad of it. We made one great mistake: we came here too late. In such a large city as this, many preparations are needed. Every thing depends upon the court and *la haute volée:* the press and the papers have but little influence. The Italian Opera took every one by storm. Garcia created a perfect furore. So it happened that our first two concerts were not fully attended; but the third was crowded; and the fourth (in the Michaelis Theatre) was the most brilliant of all. While other artists, even Liszt, have gradually fallen from public favor, Clara has always gained more and more, and could easily give four more concerts, if Passion Week did not intervene, and we were not obliged to leave for Moscow. Our best friends were of course the Henselts, who received us with exceeding kindness; then especially the two Wielhorskys,* remarkable men. Michael particularly has a true artist soul, and is the most highly gifted amateur that I ever met. Both have great influence at court, and see the emperor and empress almost daily. Clara, I believe, cherishes a silent passion for Michael, who, be it said, has grandchildren, — that is, — he's a man of over fifty, but fresh as a boy in soul and body. We also had a most friendly well-wisher in Prince von Oldenburg (the emperor's nephew), as also in his wife, who is the very incar

---

* These are the brothers Joseph and Michael, Counts Wielhorsky, well known as highly-cultured musicians, — one playing the piano, the other violoncello (at least in Russia). One of them recently died.

nation of goodness and kindness. They took us all over their palace yesterday. The Wielhorskys also have been very attentive: they gave a soirée for us *with an orchestra*, for which my Symphony * was practised, and I conducted. I shall tell you about Henselt when we meet: he is just the same as ever; but he's killing himself by giving lessons. He can't be induced to play in public: he is only to be heard at the house of Prince von Oldenburg, where he and Clara played my variations for two pianos.

The emperor and empress have been very kind to Clara: she played two whole hours to the imperial family a week ago. Mendelssohn's Spring Song † has become a public favorite. Clara always has to repeat it several times at every concert, — three times even to the empress. Clara will tell you when she sees you of the splendors of the Winter Palace. M. von Ribeaupierre (late ambassador to Constantinople) took us over it a few days ago: it's like a fairy story from " The Thousand and One Nights."

We are very happy; and we have the best news of the children.

Now imagine my joy: my old uncle still lives.‡ When we first arrived I was so fortunate as to meet the governor of Twer, who told me he knew him well. I wrote to him at once, and soon received a most affectionate answer from him and his son, who commands a regiment in Twer. He celebrates his seventieth birthday on Saturday; and I think that we shall go to Twer on that day.§ What joy for me and for the old man, who has never had a relative in his house!

We've heard shocking accounts of the road to Moscow; but, believe us, travelling in Russia is neither better nor worse than anywhere else, — *perhaps better;* and I can't help laughing at the frightful images my fancy drew in Leipsic. Every thing is *very dear* (especially here in St. Petersburg; for example, lodging one louis d'or per day, coffee one thaler, dinner a ducat, &c., &c.)

We intend to return to St. Petersburg in about a month, to travel by land to Reval, thence by steamer to Helsingfors, and by Abo to Stockholm, then probably by canal to Copenhagen, and so back to our dear Germany. ‖ By the 1st of June I certainly shall hope to see you again,

---

* The B-flat major Symphony, Op. 38.

† Vol. v. of the Songs without Words, No. 5.

‡ The eldest brother of Schumann's mother, Carl Gottlob Schnabel, who went to Russia, desiring to enter the army as a surgeon.

§ They did so.

‖ This plan was not executed: the artist pair returned to Germany by the usual route;

dear papa; and meanwhile you must write to us often, for the present at St. Petersburg, to Henselt's address. He forwards all our letters to us.

Alwin * has written to us several times. He don't seem to be getting on very well: we shall learn all the particulars in Reval. Molique left for Germany yesterday.

The musicians here have *all* been very friendly to us, especially Henry Romberg: they refused any compensation for their services at our last concert. Nothing was left for us to do but to send a carriage for them, which we were very glad to do. I have ever and ever so much to write you; but we are very busy to-day, preparing for our journey to Moscow: so accept this short letter with a great deal of love. Greet your wife and children most affectionately for us, and think kindly of me.

R. S.

P. S. To-day is a pleasant anniversary for me: you know it's the tenth birthday of our Journal. Send some of the enclosed slips to Leipsic; but please see that none of them go astray. One more request, write a few words to Wenzel: ask him if he finds any thing of general interest or special importance to me in the papers, to look at the dates, and write them down for me; for I seldom see a paper here. The poems † might also interest Dr. Frege.

After Clara Schumann had given three concerts in Moscow, the artist pair left Russia, and reached home by the 1st of June. Meanwhile, a purpose had ripened in Schumann's mind, which he executed soon after their arrival in Leipsic. This was nothing less than his withdrawal from the Journal. It almost seems as if his failure to publish it in Vienna rendered it indifferent to him; for he spoke very enthusiastically of the Journal and its future just before his journey to Vienna, and immediately after his return expressed himself with the utmost apathy concerning his plans for it, quite contrary to his former opinion. " On the whole, I'm very happy in my sphere of action ; but, if I could only get rid of the Journal, live only for music, not have to think of the many trifles to which an

---

* A son of Friedrich Wieck, once member of the imperial band at St. Petersburg.

† Schumann wrote a few poems while travelling in Russia, among others, one on the Kremlin in Moscow.

‡ Compare page 110.

editor must attend, I should indeed be at peace with myself and all the world. Perhaps this may yet come to pass," he wrote at this time to H. Dorn. And to Keferstein, Feb. 19, 1840, "I can only make the Journal a secondary consideration, fondly as I may cherish it. Every man is bound to cultivate his highest gifts. You yourself wrote the same thing to me, as I well remember, some years ago, and I've worked more bravely ever since. I write this, dear friend, because I thought you intended a slight reproach of my editorial duties in your last letter which I really didn't deserve, both because I do so much other work and because that is the highest purpose I have to fulfil in this life." And truly towards the end of the third year the *Neue Zeitschrift für Musik* showed that Schumann's original interest wore off. The letters, which at first were seldom inserted, encroached more and more upon the general reviews; and this of course caused its gradual decay as an organ of art. Still he might have retained the post of editor (which was given to Oswald Lorenz towards the end of June, 1844) * had not an alarming state of both mind and body rendered his retirement doubly desirable. His impaired health also compelled him to desist from literary labor, and to change his whole course of life; so that he left Leipsic forever, in the latter part of 1844, and took up his abode in Dresden. Before accompanying him thither, we must consider the tone-creations of 1844. Their number was small in comparison with preceding years, and they consist merely of the music to the epilogue of Goethe's "Faust" for solos, chorus, and orchestra, and a chorus and aria for an opera, "The Corsair," from Byron.†

* See Neue Zeitschrift f. Musik, vol. xx. p. 204. From Oswald Lorenz's hands, the Journal passed, early in 1845, into those of Fr. Brendel, who still edits it.

† In Schumann's book of plans for December, 1840, we see that he contemplated composing an opera to be called "The Corsair," from Byron's poem, — at least, this title is written by his hand under the heading "Subjects for Operas." Perhaps he had a libretto from which the above fragments, whi ;h are but little known, were taken.

In the autumn of 1844, Schumann went to Dresden; but his family did not settle there until December of the same year, — after he and his wife had taken public leave of Leipsic in a *matinée musicale* given on the 8th of December.

Misfortunes awaited them in Dresden. During the first year Schumann suffered much pain, led a more quiet life than ever, and thought of nothing but the restoration of his failing health. His symptoms were many and morbid, and are more closely described in the following account by Dr. Helbig of Dresden: —

"Robert Schumann came to Dresden in October, 1844, and labored so unceasingly on the music for the epilogue to Goethe's 'Faust' that, on completing it, he fell into a very morbid condition, manifested by the following symptoms: As soon as he began to use his brain, shivering, faintness, and cold feet set in, together with great pain and a peculiar fear of death, which took the form of a dread of high hills or houses,* all metallic substances (even keys), medicine, and infection. He suffered much from loss of sleep, and felt worse at dawn than at any other time. As he studied every prescription until he found some reason for not taking it, I ordered him cold plunge-baths, which so far improved his health that he was able to return to his usual (only) occupation, composition. As I had made a study of similar cases, especially among men who worked immoderately at one thing (for instance, accounts, &c.), I was led to advise that he should employ himself and distract his mind with something else than music. He first chose natural history, then natural philosophy, &c., but abandoned them after a few days, and gave himself up, wherever he might be, to his musical thoughts.

"The auricular delusions connected with his peculiar disposition and his highly developed sense of melody and hearing were highly instructive to the observer. The ear is the organ which is busiest in night and darkness, is the last to fall asleep, and

* Compare page 79.

the first to awake; through it we can influence men by a whisper even in sleep: it is most closely allied to the sense of touch,
and very near to the organs of foresight, revenge, offence,
and talent for music.* He who considers the attributes of
night and darkness, which we have not space to reckon, and
compares them with Schumann's disposition, will understand
his state. When we reflect that the eye could receive no light,
the brain conceive no thoughts, if the former could not create
light, and the latter thoughts, in itself, we shall have some idea
of his auricular delusions."

His morbid state was now so far relieved, that the master was
able to devote himself anew to labor; but his tendency to disease
rapidly increased, and could not be allayed. His former symptoms returned to a greater or less degree; and all the letters
written at the time contain complaints of his illness. He could
not bear the sight of Sonnenstein (an insane asylum at Pira,
near Dresden), as we shall see from a letter to F. Hiller; and,
after Mendelssohn's decease, he was in constant fear of a similar fate,† which made him very low-spirited. ‡ Even his friends
were astonished and alarmed by his abnormal condition; and
Dr. Keferstein says, " When I looked Schumann up in Dresden,
at the age of forty, I found him very ill, his nerves being so
shattered by labor that I was much concerned for his life. I
remember that he offered me some superior Stein wine, which

---

* Although pathological anatomy has never answered the question of
what use it has ever been in healing the sick, still the natural philosopher,
phrenologist, and psychologist will be glad to know the decision of anatomy
in regard to Schumann's brain-structure. A plaster-cast of his remarkable
head and a detailed account of the shape of his skull (according to Morson)
are highly desirable, not only for comparison with Beethoven, Mozart,
Haydn, &c., but for psychological purposes, and are the more to be expected
from the examining surgeons that the present realistic standpoint of this
science confines all theory concerning it to the purely objective. (Remarks
of Dr. Helbig.)

† Felix Mendelssohn-Bartholdy died of nervous apoplexy on the 4th of
November, 1847.

‡ Remarks by Dr. Helbig.

had been sent him at great expense from Brockenwirth, since he thought it was nowhere as good. He shunned all social intercourse,* and took lonely walks with his Clara." Prof. Kahlert of Breslau writes, Jan. 6, 1857,† "We (Kahlert and Schumann) met for the last time in the autumn of 1847 in Dresden. He had just returned from the sea-baths. 'Genevieve' lay upon the piano almost ended. I dispelled his doubts as to the construction of the text, as they came too late. He told me of his distressing mental condition before going to the sea-shore. 'I lost every melody,' he said, 'as soon as I conceived it: my mental ear was overstrained.'"

When we consider all the known facts, it seems highly probable that the mental obscurity into which he at last most pitiably sank was the result of some organic disease, which increased rapidly while he was in Dresden. We may consider as a forerunner thereof that excited state from which the master suffered at the time of his sister-in-law's death. There can be no doubt that his renewed and increased illness influenced his works; yet it would be a great mistake to suppose that the mental products of the following year bear *unmistakable* marks of the tragic doom hanging over him. Spite of their gloomy background, all but a few of those last composed are full of power. Occasional defects may be regarded as mere mannerisms. The natural results of his illness were: occasional intervals of rest from toil, and an astonishing and unnatural productivity, beginning in 1847, and reaching its height in 1849, during which year he composed thirty works of greater or less extent.

It is uncertain when he again resumed his musical labors

---

* He afterwards gradually returned to social life, especially with Berthold Auerbach, Edward Bendemann, Ferdinand Hiller, Julius Hübner, and Robert Reinick. He also took a lively interest in the subscription-concerts given at Dresden in the autumn of 1845, led by F. Hiller, but which gradually died out when he was appointed town-director in Düsseldorf in 1847. Schumann was one of the directors of these concerts. See letters for 1833-52, No. 48.

† To the author of these pages.

in Dresden. His list of compositions only contains the following notes : —

"1845 (Dresden). Many works in counterpoint,* — four fugues for the piano (Op. 72) ; studies for the pedal piano, first part (Op. 56) ; six fugues on the name of Bach, for the organ (Op. 60) ; sketches for the pedal piano (Op. 58) ; interlude and rondo ; finale, as a conclusion for my piano-fantasies, published as a concerto (Op. 54) ; sketch of orchestral symphony in C-major."

Here we again see persistence in one direction ; but, as most of the works mentioned are severe in style, it is evident that he was trying to handle form more freely than was then in his power. It was, as it were, the preparation for greater creative efforts soon to be begun.

The Studies (Op. 56) and Sketches (Op. 58) for the pedal piano † are attractive in combination and design. The former are more important than the latter. They contain resemblances to Bach's music, as he may have intended they should. Of the two sets of fugues (Ops. 72 and 60), the latter, consisting of six fugues on the name of Bach, is of extraordinary merit. The first five fugues especially display so firm and masterly a treatment of the most difficult forms of art, that Schumann might from these alone lay claim to the title of a profound contrapuntist. They show variety of plastic power with four notes only. The tone of feeling varies in all six pieces, and is always poetic, which, in connection with a command of form, is the main point in composition. These are serious character-pieces. The sixth fugue offers a difficult problem as to execution, since the mingling of even and uneven movement renders it very difficult to perform it properly upon an organ.

---

* The canon published as No. 20 in Op. 124 belongs to these.

† The idea of writing for the pedal piano is rather impractical, since that instrument is but seldom used. Schumann was incited to it by the introduction of a pedal piano in the Leipsic Music School for the practice of organ scholars. These compositions for a pedal piano can easily be performed upon a common piano, if a second person takes the pedal part an octave lower.

The piano-concerto (Op. 54), whose first movement (called "Fantasie") was written in 1841, is a master-piece in every respect: it is more than a piano-composition, it is symphonic; it was acknowledged as such on its first public performance.*

The C-major symphony (Op. 61), the third in order (1846), may be considered as an improved prosecution of the symphonic works begun in 1841. It is more mature, masculine, and power-ful, more profound than those, and far better suited to an orches-tra, both as a whole and in its single parts. The introduction to the first movement, "Sostenuto assai," was originally in-tended for something else, and was already composed when he conceived the idea of writing the symphony.† According to his own account, his conception of this symphony occurred when he was first taken ill. He says, "I sketched it out while suffering severe physical pain; indeed, I may well call it the struggle of my mind, which influenced this, and by which I sought to beat off my disease. The first movement is full of this struggle, and very peevish and perverse in character."

The year 1846 was very poor in a productive sense; his list, besides the completion of the work just considered, mentioning only the chorus songs (Op. 55 and 59).‡ Doubtless the state of his health was a great obstacle to composition, as was also a trip in November or December to Vienna, where his wife gave several concerts. The artist pair spent some weeks there, and, before their return to Dresden, gave a farewell party, Jan. 12, 1847, to which came a choice crowd of musical notabilities, such as Bauernfeld, Deinhartstein, Dessauer, Eichendorf, Grill-parzer, Besque von Püttlingen (Hoven), Jansa, Jenny Lind Adalbert Stifter, &c. § On their way home they gave two splendid concerts in Prague, when Schumann received a per-

* Mrs. Clara Schumann first performed it in Dresden, Dec. 4, 1845.

† The first public performance of this work took place at a Gewandhaus concert, Nov. 5, 1846.

‡ Schumann's list says there are five songs in Op. 59; but the published edition contains only four.

§ See Signals for the Musical World for 1847, p. 45.

fect ovation on the performance of his piano-quintette and some of his songs.* To this excursion to the South was soon added one to the North. He went to Berlin to direct, under very difficult circumstances, at a performance of his "Paradise and the Peri," given by the Academy of Singing.† After two concerts by his wife and a musical matinée at their lodgings, the artist pair returned to Dresden by the last of March. We must also mention a third journey, which he and his wife took after an interval of three months, — in July, 1847. They went to his native town of Zwickau. A small musical festival was to take place, at which some of his works were to be performed. The programme contains his second symphony in C-major (Op. 61), the piano-concerto (Op. 54), played by Clara Schumann, and the chorus "For Farewell" (Op 84). The tone-poet himself directed his compositions; the rest of the programme was conducted by Dr. Emanuel Klitzsch. Every thing was done to show due honor to the guests. A torchlight procession and a serenade were arranged, Dr. Klitzsch composing a dithyramb for the latter. The changes and distractions of this trip must have affected Schumann favorably; for a large number of works are marked in his list as written in 1847, whose titles are as follows : Two romanzas by E. Mörike, for solo voice and piano (Op. 64) ; ‡ orchestral overture to " Genevieve ; " the closing chorus to the scenes from " Faust " (" The ever-feminine attracts.") This and ensuing compositions from " Faust" were collected after the master's death, and published in three parts as " Scenes from Goethe's Faust," without number. Second trio for piano, violin, and violoncello, in D-minor (Op. 63); " Farewell song," for a chorus and wind instruments (Op. 84) ; third trio for piano, violin, and violoncello, in F-major (Op. 80) ; § ritornellos by Rückert, arranged as

---

* See Signals for the Musical World for 1847, p. 62.

† See Signals for the Musical World for 1847, pp. 84, 85.

‡ To this work, as published, also belong Tragedies, by Heine. Compare page 136.

§ The piano-trios, Ops. 63 and 80, are spoken of here as second and third,

catches for male chorus, eight numbers (Op. 65); * "Beginning," by Rückert, for four male voices; three songs, by Eichendorff, Rückert, and Klopstock for male chorus (Op. 62); Solfeggi for male chorus (not yet published); Solfeggi for a mixed chorus (not yet published); sketch for first act of " Genevieve; " song by F. Hebbel for two sopranos and two tenors.

The piano-trios (Ops. 63 and 80) are equal to any of the chamber-music composed in 1842 except Op. 88. The first is a serious, characteristic, and very important, as well as perfectly lucid work; the other, on the contrary, is a bright, cheerful tone-picture, with only one slight streak of melancholy in the two middle movements, like the deep red of sunset.

The greatest and most important work begun in 1847, but not fully completed till the 1st of August, 1848, the opera of " Genevieve," needs considerable examination. As we have seen, he contemplated as early as 1840 that most difficult of all musical tasks, the opera.† However little his musical nature corresponded to the requisitions of the stage, it is none the less plain that so richly endowed a mind must have longed to labor in that realm; and, although the master did not attain the same success which crowned his other works, this attempt to work in the most complicated known form of music seems perfectly clear and correct. This is not altered by the fact, that his only opera cannot be considered otherwise than as an attempt, and, if we measure it by its *pure* dramatic value, not always a happy attempt.

He was long undecided as to a subject. In his book of hints he marked the following, one after another: "Faust, Till Eulenspiegel, El Galan (Calderon), Hanko (Beck), Nibelungenlied, The Wartburg War, The Bridge of Mantible (Calde-

because Schumann originally called The Fantasies, Op. 88, the first trio. Compare p. 137. When this was altered, the other trios of course became first and second.

* As published, it contains but seven pieces.

† Compare page 128.

ron), Abelard and Héloise, The False Prophet (from " Lalla
Rookh "), The Last Stuart, Kunz von der Rosen, Atala (Cha-
teaubriand), The Noble Bride (König), The Pariah, The Corsair (Byron), Maria Stuart, Sacontala (Gerhard's translation),
War of the German Peasants (Kolhas), Sardanapalus (Byron), The Robbers of the Bell (Mörike), The Stone Guide-
post (Immermann), The Smith of Gretna Green, and The
Dead Guest (L. Robert)." We cannot here discuss the suita-
bleness of these subjects for dramatico-musical purposes : it
suffices to say that he used none of them. His plan of composing an opera was realized in quite another way. He first
conceived the idea from Hebbel's drama of " Genevieve,"
which he first saw in 1847. This work so pleased and delighted him, that he determined to found a musical drama
upon this and Tieck's " Genevieve." * He applied forthwith
to the well-known painter-poet Robert Reinick (who died in
Dresden, Feb. 7, 1852), asking him to outline a libretto from
that story. Reinick readily consented to his friend's request,
but thought it would be much more interesting to keep to the
legend of St. Genevieve. He very correctly considered that
a Genevieve without child or hind would be worse than none
at all; and he strongly opposed Schumann's desire to omit
these attributes. Perhaps he deemed it impossible to produce
a third vital work from two such opposite productions as
Tieck's romantic, melting poem, and Hebbel's monstrous,
bristling drama.

Reinick made two sketches : in one, Genevie e's exile was
treated in a prolix manner, with the intention of adding more
action. But Schumann did not like this ; and accordingly, at
his request, the exile and deliverance of Genevieve immediately succeeded each other in the fourth act.

Although Reinick sought to gratify Schumann's wishes, he
was by no means satisfied with the poetical treatment of the

* I owe these facts partly to Reinick's wife, partly to Pohl's account of
Schumann's transactions with Hebbel. — See *Neue Zeitschr. f. Musik*, l. p.
254.

subject. After finishing the first act, he wrote to Hebbel, asking his aid and advice.* The expected visit of the poet to
Dresden, which occurred in July, 1847, gave Schumann the desired opportunity for a personal interview with him; but it was
of no avail: he was reduced to trying his own skill at the text
just finished by Reinick. He availed himself of the author's
temporary absence to make such changes as he thought fit;
and the libretto of " Genevieve " thus received its present form.
This was so different from Reinick's version, that the latter felt
compelled, on seeing the alterations, to renounce all claim to
its authorship. Therefore the titlepage of the printed libretto
simply announces that it is " taken from Tieck and Hebbel."

Schumann was now satisfied with the material basis of his
opera, and not at all aware of its dramatic effect. " ' Genevieve ' ! but don't imagine it's the old sentimental one. I think
it's just a bit of biography, as every dramatic poem should be ;
for the text is principally founded on Hebbel's tragedy," he
writes to H. Dorn.†

This illusory remark is in direct opposition to the case in
hand.

The dramatic part of Schumann's " Genevieve " is, on the
whole, ill adapted for performance, and betrays a feeble hand
in the design and introduction of the great crisis.‡ The most
beautiful part of the legend is reduced to a minimum. The
sad, tearful life of the innocent but banished wife in the desert; the miracle by which she and her child were preserved,
indeed the child itself, — all this, which is so highly moral, so
productive of the deepest sympathy, so clearly and indissolubly
connected with the popular notion of " Genevieve," is omitted.
We can, of course, see that it would be very difficult, perhaps
impossible, to represent these portions of the legend dramati-

* See letters for 1833–52, Nos. 55, 56.

† See letters for 1833–52, No. 71.

‡ As I was an interested assistant at all the rehearsals of the three performances of this work in Leipsic, I consider myself justified in giving my
candid opinion.

cally: this is merely another proof that we should select no subject for the stage which cannot be easily represented.

So the "old sentimental" Genevieve was, for the most part, done away with; and perhaps with her was lost the sympathy felt by every sensitive nature for her simple, touching story. Hardly any thing is left but Golo's intrigue and its direct results. But how robbed of all illusion! Really, one need be no prude to be shocked at it, nor specially sharp-sighted to see into the flimsy plot. The man inspired to guilt by Golo is old and gray: it has a tragio-comic effect, that the count and his household should believe in the pretended intrigue with the countess; which is as much as to say that all believe in it. But it is repugnant to the spectator to see the poor old man killed, and by whom? By an insolent servant, who, just before, was ready to swear to the chastity and modesty of the countess, who is at the same time shut up in the tower. There is an uncomfortable mixture of truth and fiction, nature and affectation, in this part of the play.

Genevieve's exile takes place in the fourth and last act. It has hardly begun, when it ceases; and she returns to the count's castle as hastily as she left it. Further quotation would be superfluous. All is obvious; and we have already seen how much was sacrificed to the very contracted treatment of the subject.

So much for the text. The music is incomparably superior, revealing, as usual, a rare amount of creative power, combined with deep and noble feeling. Nevertheless, considered as dramatic music, it has many not surprising faults. These are innate in Schumann's disposition. He could not quite renounce his lyric nature, even to reach the heights of dramatic expression. His first vocal compositions, containing some fine dramatic touches, may have led him astray. His first and last dramatic work, however, shows that he was not born for the stage. The lyric portions are by far the best; while the dramatic portions are but partially satisfactory, being often lame and flagging The close of the second act is a laudable exception. The circuitousness of the recitative in " Genevieve" most plainly proves his lack of adequate dramatic talent. This work may be regarded as a struggle for greater unity of form; perhaps Schumann himself intended it for such. But the incapacity connected with his superabundant lyric feeling prevented him from recognizing recitative as one of the chief constituents of dramatico-musical art, and from subduing it in new forms. As we can lend an apparently honest but really deceptive color to all our weaknesses and defects, so Schumann * confessed, in regard to such parts of " Genevieve " as should have been recitatives, but were written as ariosos, that it was quite impossible for him to treat them as was customary " But there's not a measure," said he, "in the ' Genevieve, that's not thoroughly dramatic." He thus unconsciously verified Goethe's striking remark, " Characters often make a law of their weakness." There is no doubt that he erred as to the claims of the drama. Certainly no one ever dreamed of or demanded Mozartian or Gluckian recitative in his opera; but Schumannian they did. Recitative is the special support of the action in an opera; any circuitousness in it becomes stiff, monotonous, and prudish, as we see in the monologues and dialogues in " Genevieve " when sung. In fine, the whole thing is excessively tiresome, spite of its many musical beauties.

No more can be said of the treatment of the voice in this work than has already been said of his vocal compositions. The overture is a fine, characteristic composition, of high artistic merit, and to be ranked with his best instrumental works.

" Genevieve " was first performed upon the Leipsic stage † June 25, 1850, under the direction of the composer. Two more representations ensued, on the 28th and 30th of the same month. Since then this opera has been laid on the shelf, and has found its way to no other stages, with the exception of one

* On being asked by me.
† The overture was played at a concert given for the Leipsic orchestra fund, Feb. 25, 1850.

performance at the Weimar Court Theatre, and another by a musical society.

As already stated, this composition, published as Op. 81, was begun in 1847, but not completed until 1848, and, as his list says, on the 5th of August.

This list also names, as composed in 1848, "Three songs by T. Ullrich, F. Freiligrath, and J. Fürst, for male chorus, with an accompaniment of wind-instruments (*ab libitum* *). Chorus to Faust, 'The noble fellow's saved,' B-flat major."

From Aug. 30 to Sept. 14, "Christmas Album for Children who like to play the Piano" (forty-two pieces), (Op. 68).

In October, orchestral overture to Byron's "Manfred" (Op. 115). Up to Nov. 23, the rest of the music for Byron's "Manfred" (Op. 115).

From Nov. 25 to Dec. 20, "Thy king shall come in raiment poor," by Rückert. A cantata for chorus and orchestra (Op. 71).†

In December, three Pièces à Quatre Mains; three more Pièces à Quatre Mains (Op. 66); five piano-compositions à deux mains (Woodland Scenes).

"The Christmas Album," published under the title of "Forty ‡ Compositions for the Young" (Op. 68), is a gift as modest as lovely, unique in musical literature, spite of the many imitations which have arisen in the course of time. Schumann shows a rich and poetic conception of childhood and its mode of life. A remark made in a letter to Reinecke § proves that this charming work, of which it is often said, in a tone of malevolent reproach, that it was written for mercenary reasons, was peculiarly dear to its author ; also showing the purpose underlying it. "Many thanks for the time and trouble you've spent upon my elder children : my younger, too, — born

---

* Not yet published.

† First performed at a Gewandhaus concert for the poor of Leipsic, Dec 10, 1849.

‡ There are forty-three in the printed edition.

§ See letters for 1833–52, No. 63.

day before yesterday, — plead for sympathy. Really one always loves the youngest best; but these are specially dear to
my heart, and truly belong to family life. The first thing in
the Album I wrote for our eldest child's birthday; and in this
way one after another was called forth. It seemed as if I were
beginning my life as a composer anew ; and you'll see traces
of the old humor here and there. They are decidedly different from the ' Scenes of Childhood.' Those are retrospective
glances by a parent and *for the elders ;* while ' The Christmas
Album ' contains hopes, presentiments, and peeps into futurity
for the young."

The music to Byron's " Manfred " seems to have been singularly significant of Schumann's own nature: we can hardly
resist the thought that his own soul-life, and a foreboding of
his dreadful fate, are mirrored therein. For what is this Byronic " Manfred " but a restless, wandering, distracted man,
tormented by fearful thoughts; and the mad, soul-destroying
intercourse with spirits, — which must of course be taken sym-
bolically, — was also the culminating point of Schumann's last
illness. Doubtless he was strangely attracted to this subject
by a sense of affinity; for he once said in conversation, " I
never devoted myself to any composition with such lavish love
and power as to ' Manfred.' " Ay, and, when reading the poem
aloud before two people in Düsseldorf, his voice suddenly fal-
tered, he burst into tears, and was so overcome that he could
read no further. From this it appears that he unfortunately
penetrated too deeply into this dreadful subject: the ideas
themselves thus becoming rooted in his mind.

The music to " Manfred " consists of an overture and fifteen
numbers ; some melo-dramatic, some regularly musical in form.
The whole work, with the exception of " The Hymn of the
Spirits of Ahriman," — which is contrary to the laws of singing, — is deep in thought and masterly in conception. The
overture, indeed, might contend for superiority with all others :
it is a powerful soul-painting, full of tragico-pathetic flights, and
quite surpassing all his other instrumental works in intellectual

grandeur. We feel that it was composed with rare devotion and unusual outlay of mental power. Its nature is in concord with the poem, — of a gloomy, melancholy, but sometimes passionate and demoniac tint.

One theatre only has thus far attempted the scenic representation of "Manfred," — all three parts of the poem have been altered and abbreviated for the purpose; * and that theatre was in Weimar, where the performance was repeated in 1852. We could hardly expect this work to be extensively performed; since the poem, although it contains many ingenious features, is too unpleasant. There are no flesh-and-blood men in it, so we cannot sympathize as with men. The spirit-world, floating " 'twixt heaven and earth," which is introduced here, proves interesting for a time, but never truly and lastingly satisfactory. Add to this the morbid, self-tormenting character of the hero, who terrifies rather than touches, produces dislike rather than true sympathy, and excites us to repel rather than to assist him. Schumann's music is incomparably more delicate and harmonious (in the key-note of gloom and despair) than Byron's poem; and, in comparison with his other compositions, forms one of his most conspicuous and significant memorials as a true poet.

"The Advent Song" (Op. 71) is the first of his works at all "religious" in character. It is founded upon a poem by Rückert, which describes in a reflective manner Christ's entry into Jerusalem, and closes with an appeal to the Lord "of great mercy and truth." It is noteworthy that he chose *this* way of expressing his religious feelings and opinions, when the Bible was at his command. This cannot be considered accidental. The cause must be sought deep in his creed and nature; for the music written during the next year for Rückert's poem, "Despair not," for two male voices, which he himself calls a "religious song," is similar in sense and spirit to "The Advent Song."

* I do not know by whom these alterations are.

Schumann writes Jan. 13, 1851,* to a friend of his latter days, Strackerjan: † " A musician's highest aim is to apply his powers to religious music. But in youth we're all rooted to the earth with its joys and sorrows; in riper age the twigs struggle upwards. So I, too, hope that this struggle will not be too faint." In 1852, he wrote a mass and a requiem, both to the Latin words : but we can ascribe a pure and sacred signification to the mass only; for, on completing the requiem, he said, " *That* is written for the individual; " and he considered it less a contribution to religious music than his peculiar protest. This single case is of slight importance, since his religious opinions in 1852 were no longer free, but had assumed a morbid character, which, as his mind was obscured, degenerated into a sort of mysticism. In 1854, he revealed singularly weak powers of judgment, which Brendel says were peculiar to him in youth.‡ He met with the poems of Elizabeth Kulmann, and wrote § to Dresden in regard to them on the 11th of June of the same year : " I have also been studying a remarkable book, 'Poems by Elizabeth Kulmann,' which have kept me busy for a fortnight. Try to obtain it. I can say no more than that ' it is a miracle displayed to us.' If you see Bendemann, Hübner, Reinick, or Auerbach, remember me to them ; tell some of them, especially Auerbach, about the Kulmann. I think they'll feel grateful." He, however, found no one to share his enthusiasm. It was by no means contagious. In the autumn inspired sentences again flowed from his lips in regard to this young girl, whose talent is indubitable, but not so great as he believed. He went so far as to hang her portrait, with a laurel-wreath above it, over his writing-table, and honored it as if holy.

The matter mentioned just before lay much deeper, and is hardly explained by his letter to Strackerjan.

* See letters for 1833-52, No. 73.
† An officer in the service of Oldenburg.
‡ Compare Neue Zeitschr. f. Musik, vol. xlviii. p. 160.
§ To the author of these pages.

He was in thought and action thoroughly a "free-thinker.' His views of life and the world, based on true religious feel ings, were pervaded by a deep moral fervor. Throughout his life he was free from church dogmas; he was never subjected to any rigid influences of the sort in his parents' home. He regarded the religion of humanity as the only authorized stand- ard for conduct. "If a man knows the Bible, Shakspeare, and Goethe, and has taken them into himself, he needs no more," he once said. Under these circumstances, it is not strange that he *never* employed his creative powers in what is called *religious* music, which, according to the common notion, is to be used only in church, or that he chose to express his sense of religion by these two Rückert poems. Who would venture to remonstrate with him? This is the point in mor- tal life where book-lore ceases to be of avail, where there can be no compulsion, and where each must judge for himself, fol- lowing the wise remark of a great prince: "In my kingdom every man shall be happy in his own way."

Besides this, as his book of plans shows, he fully intended to write an oratorio "Maria;" which, however, he never did.

The "Advent Song" cannot be classed with any existing form of music. Schumann was himself undecided in regard to it. In his list he calls it a "Cantata," in his letters a "Motet." But, correctly speaking, it is neither. The printed edition, there- fore, has no general title. One remark may be made in regard to the musical treatment of the text: that is, it seems too broad and large, the contents of the song being unsuitable for such rich and expansive musical expression. The music itself is noble, though devoid of any inspired or inspiring ideas.

The Dresden Chorus Club,* founded in 1848, was of some importance in Schumann's career, as he became the director of it, after taking charge of the Liedertafel in 1847, Ferdinand Hiller having removed to Düsseldorf. To this dear friend he wrote, Jan. 1, 1848 :† "We often think of you. Especially in

* See letters for 1833-52, No. 58.

† The Dresden Chorus Club was established by Schumann Jan. 5, 1848,

the Liedertafel, which gives me great pleasure, and urges me
to action. . . . The chorus-club, too, is waking up. Jan. 5 is
the first meeting. Up to the present date we have a hundred
and seventeen members; that is, fifty-seven active ones, the
rest being passive."

The direction of the clubs in question was not only a welcome bit of practice for him, but also a salutary interruption
of his excessive mental labor. It forced him, as far as possible, to mingle with men and the external world. This probably had a favorable effect upon his morbid state. He wrote
to F. Hiller,* "My strength increases with my work. I see it
clearly; and, if I can't keep myself perfectly well, still it's not
so bad as a close inspection of trifles led me to suppose." And
again, a year later,† "The Leidertafel has done much to restore
my consciousness of directive ability, which, in my nervous
hypochondria, I thought was gone."

But he soon resigned the charge of the Liedertafel, confining
himself to the chorus-club. "My chorus-club gives me the
greatest delight (sixty to seventy members). I can have all my
favorite music performed there at will. I've given up the män-
nerchor. I found too little musical ambition, and felt I was
not suited to the post, they were all such fine folks," † he
writes farther on.

The chorus-club, which was evidently very dear to him, un-
doubtedly inspired many vocal compositions; the list for 1849
containing a large number. This was the most productive
year of his life in regard to quantity. He wrote April 10,
1849 (also referring to 1848), to Hiller, "I've been very busy
all the time. It has been my most fruitful year, — as if the external storms moved men to greater inner action: as for me, I
found it a counterweight to the fearful load from without."

and directed by him until his removal to Düsseldorf in the summer of 1850.
It did not then break up; but it had no regular meetings, and did not resume
action until 1855, upon the anniversary of its foundation, Jan. 5, under the
direction of Robert Pfretzchners.

* See letters for 1833–52, No. 58.

† See letters for 1833–52, No. 66.

And at the end of 1849, "As I told you before, I've been exceedingly busy all the year: we must work while the day-light lasts."

By the "fearful load from without," he meant the politica excitement of 1848, and particularly the May insurrection in Dresden in 1849. This drove him, as well as many other peace-lovers, from the city for several weeks. During that time he took up his abode in Kreischa, near Dresden, not from any strong convictions of the injustice of the thing, but because the wild, lawless state of affairs was unpleasant to him. These events form a curious contrast. He was a free-thinker in poli-tics as well as in religion. He always took a lively interest in all historical events. But his disposition was far too passive to permit of his expressing his opinion frankly and unreservedly, far less of his taking an active share in politics. He was therefore a liberal in spirit, but a conservative in appearance. We never think of him at a political meeting, but at his desk, in his hand the pen from which at this time flowed the "Marches" (Op. 76). The time of their origin is established by the date 1849 affixed to them.

The compositions written in 1849, according to the list, are as follows: —

"1849 (Dresden) four more * piano compositions for two hands, "Waldscenen" (Op. 82).

February, three Soirée pieces for clarionet and piano (Op. 73); Feb. 14, Romanza and Allegro for horn and piano (Op. 70); from the 18th to 20th, concert-piece for four key bu-gles and full orchestra (Op. 86).†

In March, fourteen ballads and romances by Goethe, Mö-rike, Uhland, Eichendorff, and J. Kerner, for a chorus (Part i. Op. 67, Part ii. Op. 75); ‡ twelve romanzas for female chorus

---

* This "more refers to the five pieces belonging to Waldscenen," written at the close of 1848.

† First performed at a concert for the orchestral school-band at the Ge-wandhaus, Feb. 25, 1850.

‡ Ops. 67 and 75 only contain ten poems instead of fourteen.

four, five, and six voices (Op. 69, Part i., Op. 91, Part ii.);
Spanish vaudeville for soprano, alto, tenor, and bass, twelve
numbers, with piano accompaniment (Op. 74).*

In April, five easy compositions on popular melodies for vio-
oncello and piano (Op. 103). April and May, thirty-five to
urty songs for my " Album of Youth " (Op. 79). " The Album
f Youth," as published, contains but twenty-nine songs. The
itle was also altered to " Song-Album for the Young." This
work forms a companion-piece to Op. 68. " You, of all men,
can best explain its meaning, — that I strove to select poems
adapted to the young from the best poets only, and that I tried
to pass from the simple and easy to the difficult ones: Mignon
closes, bending her bodeful gaze upon a wilder mental life," he
writes to E. Klitzsch in reference to it. The idea is excellent,
but the aim is not always fulfilled, the songs being, with few
exceptions, but ill adapted to childish voices. Almost all require an accomplished and artistic singer, and the musical
matter is not always sufficiently important for such a one.

At Kreischa, near Dresden, May, 18–21. Five hunting-songs
for male voices, with an accompaniment of four horns (Op. 137,
No. 2 of the posthumous works). 23d to 26th May, " Despair
Not," by Rückert (Op. 93), a religious song for a double male
chorus (organ ad lib.). 1st to 5th June, German Minnespiel
from F. Rückert's " Liebesfrühling," for soprano, alto, tenor, and
bass (eight numbers), with piano accompaniment (Op. 101).

In Dresden, 12th to 16th June, four grand marches for the
piano † (Op. 76). 18th to 22d June, four songs of Mignon from
Goethe's " Wilhelm Meister " (the first is also in the " Album
of Youth "). Also the ballad of the " Harper," and Philina's
song.

July 2 and 3, sketched the Requiem for Mignon ‡ (Op. 89[b]).
6th and 7th, the three songs of the " Harper " (all from " Wil-

* The Spanish vaudeville, Op. 74, contains but ten numbers.

† The " Quick March," published as No. 14 in Op. 94, dated 1849, was
evidently composed at this time.

‡ First performed at a Düsseldorf subscription-concert, Nov. 21, 1850.

helm Meister," Op. 98), to be published together. The songs
and ballads from Goethe's "Wilhelm Meister" appeared as
Op. 98ᵃ. There are nine in all.

July 13 and 14, cathedral-scene from Goethe's "Faust."
15th, garden-scene from the same. 18th, "Incline your Ear."
24th to 26th, scene between Ariel and the awakening Faust.

August, the scenes from "Faust" furnished with instrumenta-
tion; end of August, four songs for soprano and tenor: "Dance
Melody," "He and She," "I think of Thee," and "Cradle
Song" (Op. 78).

10th to 15th September, childish *pièces à quatre mains* for
the piano, in two parts (six numbers). 18th to 26th September, Introduction and Allegro for piano and orchestra (in G,
Op. 92). From Sept. 27 to Oct. 1, two more parts of the childish *pièces à quatre mains* for the piano, six numbers (Op. 85).

From 11th to 16th of October, three double-chorus songs for
large singing-societies, — "To the Stars," by Rückert; "Uncertain Light," "Trust," by Zedlitz. End of October, "To
God belongs the Orient," for a double chorus, No. 6 of the posthumous works, was published with these three songs as
Op. 141.

Nov. 4, sketched "Night Song," by Hebbel, for chorus and
orchestra. 8th to 11th, furnished it with instrumentation* (Op.
108). Up to the last of November, worked on the second Spanish vaudeville, with four-hand piano accompaniment (ten
numbers), published as "Spanish Love-Songs" (Op. 138), No. 3
of the posthumous works.

4th and 5th December, 1849, three of Lord Byron's Hebrew
Melodies with harp accompaniment (ad lib.) also piano (Op.
95). Middle of December, 1849, three romanzas for oboe and
piano (Op. 94). Dec. 22, "Fair Hedwig," by Hebbel, for declamation, with piano accompaniment (Op. 106). Dec. 27 to
Jan. 3, 1850, "New-Year's Song," by Rückert,† sketched for
chorus and orchestra (Op. 144).

* First performed at a Düsseldorf subscription-concert, May 13, 1851.
† First performed at a Düsseldorf subscription-concert, Jan. 11, 1851.

The intense creative activity of 1849 was immediately followed by a period of rest, which was prolonged by two trips from Dresden early in 1850.

His wife and he first went to Leipsic, Bremen, and Hamburg. Clara Schumann wrote of this journey to Ferdinand Hiller, May 7, 1850, "In February and March we made a very pleasant excursion. We first spent four weeks in Leipsic, then in Hamburg, being treated with great regard. Most of our time in Hamburg was spent with Jenny Lind, who sang at my last two concerts." The performance of his opera " Genevieve " in Leipsic caused his temporary absence from Dresden.*

It is thus doubly evident that comparatively few compositions occurred during the first eight months of 1850. The list names them as follows : —

1850, April, " Resignation," " Submission," " The Hermit," — three solo-songs with piano accompaniment (Op. 83); the same, " Not so Fast," by G. L'Egrü.†

From 25th to 28th April, scenes from " Faust," " The Four Gray Women," and a sketch for " Faust's Death," completed with instrumentation by May 10.

The complete cycle of scenes from Goethe's " Faust," set to music by Schumann, comprises, in the order given by the dramatic poem, " Garden Scene," " Prison Scene," " Ah ! bend thine Ear," &c., " Cathedral Scene," " Scene between Ariel and the awakening Faust," " Scene with the Four Gray Women," and " Faust's Death." The epilogue to the second part forms the finale. Schumann divided these fragments into three parts; the first including the scenes of the first part, the second those of the second, and the third closing with the epilogue. To the whole, which would occupy an evening, he afterwards added an instrumental introduction.

* See page 156.

† This song is printed as No. 5 in Op. 77; which also contains " The Merry Traveller," published in the first edition of Op. 39, as well as three other songs: " My Garden," " Spirits are Near," and "The Mute Reproach," the last of which is not to be found in Schumann's list. The songs contained in Ops. 27 and 51 are also missing from the list; also the music to Schiller's " Glove " (Op. 87), probably written in 1849-51.

May 10, "The Evening Sky," by Wilfred von der Neun. May 11, "Autumn Songs," by the same. The same up to May 18. Four more poems by Wilfred von der Neun (Op. 89).

July, "The Wanderer's Evening Song," "Snowdrops," "Spring Delights," "Her Voice," "Spirits are Near," "Spring Song," "Hussars' Retreat," "Song," "Heaven and Earth," "My Garden," "My Old Horse," * songs for one voice and piano.

August, six solo-songs by N. Lenau, with piano accompaniment (Op. 90); Requiem to an old Latin text, for one voice and piano (Op. 90).

The latter part of the summer of 1850 brought with it an event of the utmost importance to Schumann; namely, his acceptance of the post of director of music in Düsseldorf, which had been vacated by Ferdinand Hiller's departure for Cologne. The latter mediated between Schumann and the General Musical Association, as is shown by the three following letters:—

DEAR HILLER,—Many thanks for your letter. Your offer is very attractive; but there are some objections to it. In both respects, I think it would be well to compare notes before deciding to accept the situation. I particularly remember Mendelssohn's opinion of the musicians there; which was not favorable.† Rietz, too, discussed it with me when you went from here to Dresden, and said "that he could not imagine why you took the place." I didn't tell you at the time, for fear of discouraging you.

Dear Hiller, tell me the plain truth. Of course I can't expect much culture in an orchestra; and I am prepared to meet common musicians but not rude or malicious ones.

* Of these songs, "The Wanderer's Evening Song," "Snowdrops," "Her Voice," "Song," "Heaven and Earth," are taken into Op. 96; "Spirits are Near" and "My Garden" may be found in Op. 77; "Spring Delights," "Spring Song," "Hussars' Retreat," and "My Old Horse," are in Op. 127, which contains a "National Song" (composed in 1851), as the fifth song.

† As is well known, Mendelssohn was director in Düsseldorf before taking charge of the Gewandhaus concerts. Julius Rietz, now court conductor at Dresden, succeeded him, and was succeeded by Ferd. Hiller.

Please inform me on these points; or, better, let me ask you my own, questions: —

1. Is the office municipal? Who is my superior officer?

2. The salary is seven hundred and fifty *thalers* (not gulden)?

3. How strong is the chorus? How large is the orchestra?

4. Is living as dear there as here? What do you pay for your rooms?

5. Can furnished lodgings be found?

6. Would not a reasonable sum be allowed me for removal, and the expenses of my journey thither?

7. Could not the contract be so worded, that I could break it if any thing better offered?

8. Does the club practise all summer?

9. Should I have time in winter for short journeys of from a week to a fortnight?

10. Could my wife find any sphere for action? You know her: she can't be idle.

And now the main point. I could not come before Easter, 1850. My opera is to be performed in Leipsic in February, and probably soon after in Frankfort. Of course, I must be present. Please answer all my questions, and then we will discuss the matter further. It would be very hard for me to leave Saxony; and yet it's healthy to vary the old round of daily events. We are all very busy here. Clara and Schubert * are giving very popular *soirées:* I'm engaged in a representation of " The Peri," and am always occupied with a multitude of things. More in my next letter. Accept my hearty thanks for having thought of me. May a gracious Spirit aid me to decide! A thousand greetings from my wife to you and yours. R. Schumann.

Dresden, Nov. 19, 1849.

A second letter soon followed this, in answer to one from Hiller : —

Dresden, Dec. 3, 1849.

Dear Hiller, — I suffer incessantly from headache, which prevents me from working or thinking. Hence my delay in answering.

Your letter and all that you wrote increased my desire to go to Düsseldorf. Be so kind as to write me *how soon* you think the directors will require a *decided* answer from me. I should prefer not to decide until Easter. I will tell you later why. One thing more: I looked in an old geography recently for remarks on Düsseldorf, and found mentioned. among other buildings there, three nunneries and an insane

* Royal Concertmeister in Dresden.

asylum. The first are all well enough, but the last is most disagreeable. I will tell you my feeling in regard to it. Several years ago, as you may remember, we lived at Maxen.* I discovered that the chief thing to be seen from my window was Sonnenstein.† This prospect became horrible to me: indeed, it spoiled all my pleasure. So I thought the case might be the same in Düsseldorf. However, perhaps the book was wrong, and the establishment may be merely an ordinary hospital.

I have to guard against all such melancholy impressions. You know very well, that, if we musicians live on sunny heights, the misfortunes of life cut all the deeper when they rise before us in their bare outlines: at least, it's so with me, having so lively an imagination. I remember reading something similar in Goethe (*sans comparaison*).

I have read your poem to Chopin's memory,‡ and admired your versatile talents. I had a celebration here too. But the authorities refused me the use of the Frauenkirch. We were very much vexed about it.

It just occurs to me to ask you whether there'll be a Rhenish musical festival next year, and in what city. I should be very glad to assist at it; and I think it would be a good opportunity to introduce myself in the Rhine Provinces; write me what you think of it.

As I told you before, I've been very busy this year; we must work while the daylight lasts. And I see with joy that the world's interest in my efforts is increasing rapidly. This spurs me on. Is there no hope of your coming here before settling in Cologne? Every one expects you.   With cordial greetings, yours,

                                        R. SCHUMANN.

After the scruples mentioned in this letter had been allayed, he still hesitated to accept the position of director in Düsseldorf.

But he shall speak for himself: —

DEAR HILLER, — "The Peri" has been brought out twice during the last week. You know what that means, and will forgive me for not writing before.

---

* Schumann, as we said before, often visited Mrs. Major Serre of that place.

† Sonnenstein is an insane asylum near Pinna.

‡ Hiller wrote a poem for the celebration in honor of Chopin, arranged by him in Düsseldorf.

Friendly and acceptable as your propositions are, as a man of honor I can say nothing but what I have already told you. The committee must wait a while for a definite answer. In confidence, dear Hiller! Some influential people *here* are working for me; * and, although I'm not sure of it, I have been advised to postpone my decision until another offer is made me. I have explained to them that I could delay no longer than April.

You cannot tell how glad I should be to save the expense of removal to Düsseldorf, and in how many respects a residence here is preferable, if I could obtain the post of director here, or the certainty of it within a year.

Now you know what you may have guessed before. I beg you will mention the matter to no one not immediately interested.

The first performance of "The Peri" went off very well: the second (of the third part), owing to the Schwarzbach's † brilliant singing, succeeded wonderfully; which delighted me.

Everybody is wild about "The Prophet:" so that I have much to contend with. I think the *music* wretched: I have no words to express my disgust.

Farewell, dear Hiller! Remember me kindly to your wife, and think kindly of   Yours truly,

DRESDEN, Jan, 15, 1850.   R. SCH.

The feeble hope of finding a public sphere for action as a director in Dresden vanished; and Schumann went to Düsseldorf, where both he and his wife were received with open arms. Mindful of the fact, that in him they welcomed a master of extraordinary merit, the people arranged a reception for him; which took place on the arrival of the artist-pair in Düsseldorf, Sept. 2, 1850. It consisted of a banquet, preceded by a concert by the choral and musical societies. Among the compositions performed was the second part of "Paradise and the Peri." The most delicate attentions were paid to the new director and his wife; and all showed that the coming of such gifted artists was considered a most joyful event.

---

* For the place of second conductor at the Royal Court Theatre in Dresden.

† Francisca Schwarzbach, then court-singer in Saxony, now in Munich.

His first performance as municipal director was at the first subscription-concert for the season of 1850–51, Oct. 24. The programme was as follows: Grand overture (C-major, Op. 124), by Beethoven; Concerto (G-minor) for piano and orchestra, by F. Mendelssohn-Bartholdy, played by Mrs. Clara Schumann; " Advent Song," by Rückert, a motet for chorus and orchestra, composed by R. Schumann; Prelude and Fugue (A-minor), by J. S. Bach, played by Mrs. Clara Schumann; Comala, by N. W. Gade.

Schumann's official duties, besides the direction of these concerts, consisted of weekly rehearsals of " The Choral Club," and musical performances, recurring at regular intervals every year, in the high mass at the Catholic church.

We see by a letter to E. Klitzsch how comfortably situated he now was. He says, " I am very well contented with my situation here, and hardly know a more desirable one, since my physical strength is not too severely taxed (though directing costs severe exertion ").

He had as little talent for directing as for teaching.* He lacked the qualities most requisite for both, and the ability to put himself in close rapport with others, and to make his meaning clear to them: this was because he either was silent, or spoke so low that he could not be understood. He also lacked the physical energy and endurance requisite for a director: he was always easily exhausted, and was obliged to rest at intervals during a rehearsal. Nor did he exercise any sort of care or oversight. On the other hand, he had in his favor considerable fame, and an artistic, earnest, and impressive personal presence. The favorable results which for a time followed his labors in Düsseldorf may be ascribed not only to this, but also to the fact that he found the chorus and orchestra in a state of high training. Most of the performances under his direction were satisfactory if the measure of technical perfection was not applied.†

* Compare page 138.

† Being then a member of the orchestra, I can state that this was perfectly true.

The inadequacy of his directorial powers was, however, veiled from the uninitiated for the present. It was first made manifest when his increasing illness and a certain disposition to indolence prevented him from continuing to do what had once been easy to him : this of course created, and by degrees confirmed, a spirit of discontent and evident uneasiness in the circle of his labors. No one will therefore question or wonder that those malevolent men, who are to be found every· where, gained the handle they desired against him. Never· theless, his engagement was prolonged from year to year on the plea of reasonable love and reverence. But this did not prevent the dissolution of the connection, so far as Schumann's direction was concerned, in the autumn of 1853, after the first of the usual series of winter concerts, which took place Oct. 27.*
The cause of this almost unavoidable result was as follows : †
The " Acting Committee of the General Musical Association," in consideration of his rapidly-lessening directive powers, believed it would be for his as well as their interest should he cease for a time to direct (except in the case of his own compositions), that he might recover his health. Julius Tausch, who had been associate manager of the Choral Club with him, offered to fill his place temporarily. An arrangement of this kind was attempted through his wife, but he took the offer very ill. At the next rehearsal, they waited half an hour for him in vain. As he did not appear, they concluded that he did not wish to direct; and the committee requested J. Tausch to take his place, since the concert had been announced, and could not well be postponed. Thus ended Schumann's career as a director.

After thus rehearsing the chief points of his practical work in Düsseldorf, a few remarks concerning the compositions of that period, and other external events, remain to be made.

No sooner had he become accustomed to his new relations

* See letters for 1833–52, No. 89.

† I have confined myself to the simple statement of facts as learned from credible witnesses.

than he began to do justice to his passion for work. The list names the following as written in Düsseldorf in 1850 : —

End of September. — Instrumentation of Rückert's "New-Year's Song " * (Op. 144, No. 9, of the posthumous works).

From 10th to 16th October, sketched a concert-piece for violoncello, with orchestral accompaniment (Op. 129).

From Nov. 2 to Dec. 9, symphony in E-flat major (in five movements), sketched, and instrumentation completed (Op. 97).†

1850, Dec. 29–31, sketched overture to Schiller's "Bride of Messina " (Op. 100). ‡

The symphony in E-flat major, the fourth composed, may be truly called "The Rhenish;" for the idea was first conceived, so the composer said, on seeing the cathedral at Cologne. During its composition, the master was greatly influenced by the festivities consequent upon the elevation of Von Geissel, Archbishop of Cologne, to the rank of cardinal. To this fact the symphony probably owes its fifth movement, not usual in symphonies (the fourth in order), originally headed, "An Accompaniment to a Solemn Ceremony." When the work was published, Schumann omitted the heading. He said, "We must not show our heart to the world : a general impression of a work of art is better; at least, no preposterous comparisons can then be made." He adds, in speaking of the other movements, "I wished national elements to prevail, and think I have succeeded : " in two parts (the second and fifth) there plainly is a popular vein as far as was possible to Schumann.

The E-flat major symphony may, on the whole, be considered equal to any of his orchestral works. Many regard it as inferior to earlier symphonies ; but they are wrong. It reveals, as they do, rare invention, originality, and fancy ; and is dis

* This work was first performed from the manuscript at a Düsseldorf subscription-concert, Jan. 11, 1851.

† First performed at a Düsseldorf subscription-concert, Feb. 6, 1851.

‡ First performed at a Düsseldorf subscription-concert, May 13, 1851.

tinguished by many beauties of conception and fine execution. The defects of which it is accused are more or less visible in all his orchestral works.* The works of 1851 are, —

(January.) 1st to 12th January. — Overture to " The Bride of Messina," instrumentation completed (Op. 100). Five songs for a mezzo-soprano, by Ullrich, Mörike, and Kinkel, —" Heart-ache," " The Window-Pane," " The Gardener," " National Song," and " Evening Song " (Op. 107).†

Jan. 23 to Feb. 2, sketched and arranged for instrumental performance the overture to Shakspeare's " Julius Cæsar " (Op. 128). ‡

March. — " Legendary Pictures," four pieces for bass-viol and piano, Op. 113 ; four hussar-songs, by Lenau, for bari-tone and piano, Op. 117 ; " Spring Greeting," by Lenau ; another song by Lenau.

April to May 11. — " Pilgrimage of the Rose," for solo and chorus, with a piano accompaniment (twenty-four numbers). (Op. 112.) §

May 12 to June 1. — " The King's Son," a ballad, by Uhland, for chorus and orchestra (six numbers, the last is missing), Op. 116 ; ‖ Maiden Songs for two voices, by Eliza-beth Kulmann (1–4), Op. 103 ; seven poems, by E. Kulmann, for one voice (Op. 104) ; " Bridal Song," by Uhland ; " The Minstrel," by the same, for a chorus.

June, 1851, five more four-hand pieces for the " Children's Ball " (Op. 109) ; accompaniment and instrumentation for the ballad of " The King's Son." ¶

---

* I will not now mention them.

† Only the first three and the last of these songs are in Op. 107. The Na-tional Song is omitted, and inserted in Op. 125 ; two others being taken into Op. 107, — " In the Woods," composed 182–; and " The Spinner." The latter song cannot be found in the list.

‡ First performed at the male choral festival in Düsseldorf, Aug. 3, 1852.

§ First performed Feb. 5, 1852, at a Düsseldorf subscription-concert.

‖ First performed May 6, 1852, at a Düsseldorf subscription-concert.

¶ At this time, the end of July, a pleasure-trip to Switzerland occurred

August, 1851, song, by W. Müller; * three compositions for piano only (romanzas or fantasies, Op. 111).

September, 1851, sonata in A-minor for violin and piano (Op. 105).

" The Cottage " and " Warning," two songs from Pfarrius's " Woodland Lays " (Op. 119). †

Oct. 2 to 9, trio in G-minor for piano, violin, and violoncello (Op. 110).

Oct. 26 to Nov. 2, two sonatas (D-minor) for piano and violin (Op. 121).

Nov. 7 to 27, " The Pilgrimage of the Rose," arranged for orchestra.

Dec. 1 and 2, " The Scherzo of the Symphony," by N. Burgmüller, arranged for instrumental performance. ‡

Dec. 3 to 19, piano-score and new instrumentation of the old symphony in D-minor.

Dec. 19 to 23, finished the overture to Goethe's " Hermann and Dorothea." (" I wrote this overture with great pleasure in a few (five) hours.")

Let us now say a few words in regard to Op. 109. The little word " more " added to it in Schumann's list (see above) refers to four other four-hand piano compositions, which the master meant to mark as Op. 109 in his list, but probably forgot to do so. He originally intended to call the cycle of tone-pieces contained in Op. 109 " The Children's Ball." When he played them through with his wife on their completion, he jocosely interpreted at the " Préambule," " Here the servants pass among the guests with dishes." Farther on he said, " Gradually the grown people mingle in the crowd, and the affair becomes more serious." The composition may afterwards have seemed to him too grave for a " Chil-

---

* Contained, as already remarked, in Op. 125.

† Besides these two songs, Op. 119 contains a third by Pfarrius, " The Bridegroom and the Linden-Tree," not mentioned in the list.

‡ The manuscript of this composition, without the instrumentation, was extant in Düsseldorf, and so interested Schumann, that he completed it.

dren's Ball," and he chose the title of " Scenes at a Ball." His creative spirit is here displayed in its most agreeable light. But he did not abandon the idea of a " Children's Ball," and carried it out in 1853.

The music to the poem, " The Pilgrimage of the Rose," by Moritz Horn,* was intended for a composition of more moderate compass and modest form. Accordingly, it was at first written for the piano only. It was performed in private in this form soon after its completion. He wrote concerning it, Aug. 9, 1851, to E. Klitzsch, " We, too, had a small musical performance last month : it was a legend, ' The Pilgrimage of the Rose,' by a young poet of Chemnitz, Horn by name. I have set it to music for solo, chorus, and piano. It's somewhat akin to ' The Peri ' in form and expression, but, as a whole, more rustic and German."

After he had heard his work, he concluded to add an orchestral accompaniment, thus rendering it accessible to larger circles ; which he did in November of the same year. The fine spiritual instrumentation is only adapted to increase the charm of coloring, no idea of which can be given by a piano. " The Pilgrimage of the Rose " is almost identical, in regard to form, with " The Peri : " therefore the remarks respecting that work need not be here repeated. For the rest, " The Pilgrimage of the Rose " offers us many charming and agreeable tone-pictures. We might, perhaps, call it a " musical idyl ; " yet we must say, that, from its rather weak and sentimental nature, it belongs to that school which has been known of late in novels and poetry as " the lovely school."

In " The King's Son," Schumann sought, for the second time since his first creative period, to open a new field for musical productivity. He felt so perfectly at home in the forms handed down to us and " valid for all time," † that he thought he could rely the more implicitly upon his own strength.

* For the correspondence between Schumann and the poet, see letters for 1833–52, Nos. 74–76 and 78–80.

† Compare page 135.

Throughout " The King's Son" we see a struggle to call into being various new shapes and forms; but the result *by no means* corresponds with the struggle. His intentions were far from clear: indeed, his firm conviction of the excellence of his projects, for a time prevented him from hearing the reproaches of others. It was therefore impossible that the productions which he evidently intended for concert-music, headed by " The King's Son," should be otherwise than inadequate in form. In fact, they lacked unity and organic articulation of form, not only *of one given* form, but of all corresponding to the requirements of musical truth. This defect is based on the involuntary mixture of lyric and dramatic elements, which might have been avoided. In " The King's Son " he holds to the poem, even to a stanza, when all which elevates the unity of a musical work into something noble must have long left it. Only the last verse of the closing song is omitted; because Schumann did not consider it fit to conclude an important composition, and replaced it by another.* Here we may ask why this should have been altered when the rest of the poem was unchanged. And again: why should not the whole have been submitted to a proper change, especially when the poem's stability was thus impaired? And, finally, the question comes up, whether it is æsthetically correct to strain a species of poetry like the ballad into larger, broader, musical forms, and to employ the most artificial means; for this use of intense and artificial means seems out of all relation to the narrow and confined nature of the ballad. In some instances, too, this narrow, confined nature is copied in music: while in others a verse is strained to the utmost, and repeated again and again; as, for example, in No. 4, and particularly No. 5, of " The King's Son." These are contradictions which cannot be overlooked, even in the pleasure excited by many beauties and merits: what is worse, they cannot be explained. These remarks on " The King's Son " hold good for all the ballads afterwards

* I do not know the name of the author of this verse.

12

arranged by Schumann for chorus, solos, and orchestra. Time alone can decide whether they contain the germ of some new and poetic style : at present, his effort seems futile.

The D-minor symphony, the second written, composed in 1841,* then set aside and first arranged for instrumental performance, and published in 1851, has many of the qualities of the best works of the second creative period ; indeed, it seems specially marked by power, purity, and conciseness of conception. It consists of four movements, after the manner of most great works of the kind, but succeeding one another with no pause between. This may have been caused by his desire for short, incomplete romanzas (instead of tiresome movements), or by his struggle for greater finish of form. The instrumental changes made in the manuscript are chiefly confined to the wind-instruments ; the string quartette was retained as originally written. One instrument, which played a prominent part in the first sketch, was omitted ; i.e., the guitar. He feared it would not work in well with the other instruments.

The first composition for 1852 was a second attempt in that province of art opened by " The King's Son," — Uhland's ballad, " The Minstrel's Curse," for soli, chorus, and orchestra (Op. 139, No. 4, of the posthumous works). It was sketched between the 1st and 6th of January, and arranged for instrumental performance between the 10th and 19th of the same month.† It was followed, according to the list, by, —

Feb. 13 to 22, Latin Mass (in C) sketched (Op. 147, No. 10, of the posthumous works). From Feb. 24 till March 5, and from March 25 to 30, furnished the mass with orchestral and piano parts.

April. — From April 26 to May 8, sketched a Latin requiem (Op. 148, No. 11, of the posthumous works).

May. — From the 9th to the 15th, instrumentation of the

* Compare page 135.

† This ballad was first performed from the manuscript-score at the Lower Rhenish Musical Festival at Aix-la-Chapelle in 1857. The words are by R. Pohl.

double chorus motet, "Despair Not," for an orchestra (composed in 1849). From the 16th to 23d, instrumentation of the whole requiem.

June 18 to 22, sketched the four ballads "Of the Princess and the Page" (Op. 140, No. 5, of the posthumous works).*

"The Fugitives," by Schelling, for declamation, with piano accompaniment.†

July 28 to Sept. 12, instrumentation and piano-score of the ballads "Page and Princess." (The first ballad was arranged by Clara.)

October and November, piano-scores of "The Minstrel's Curse," Requiem, and the second part of the "Faust" scenes.

Dec. 9 to 16, five songs, "Queen Mary Stuart," for mezzo soprano and piano (Op. 135). Piano-score of D-minor symphony.

Strong as was his fever for production in the first part of this year, when he made a trip to Leipsic between March 6 and 23, the latter part was dull in comparison : he busied himself almost solely with arrangements. This was caused by his increasing illness, which may be regarded as the immediate precursor of the sad catastrophe of the early part of 1854.

Even in 1851, alarming symptoms of this terrible, slowly-developing, and anxiously-watched disease, appeared. He wrote of it, ‡ June 11, 1851, "We are all tolerably well, except that I am the victim of occasional nervous attacks, which sometimes alarm me; especially a few days ago, when I fainted after hearing Radecke § play the organ." These "nervous attacks" increased in 1852, and were accompanied by peculiar symptoms. Pre-eminent among them was that difficulty of enunciation from which he had always suffered, though never to such a degree. It was also noticeable, that, on hearing

---

* The poem is by E. Geibel. It was first performed from the manuscript score, Dec. 2, 1852, at a Düsseldorf concert.

† Contained in Op. 122.

‡ To me.

§ Robert Radecke, director in Berlin, who was then visiting Düsseldorf

music, he always thought the time too fast; longed to have it slower, and insisted upon it when he led. This was clearly because he was no longer able to follow a brisk movement His demeanor was sad; and his reception of intimate friends, spite of apparent cordiality, revealed great apathy. He took little interest in the male choral festival held at Düsseldorf on the first four days of August, 1852, although he had been chosen one of the directors; and it was evident that he was exhausted, both mentally and physically, by the slight exertion of leading a few pieces.

By medical advice, he sought by cold-baths to alleviate his illness; and was sent by his physician to a water-cure at Scheveningen, whence he returned at the end of September. His health did not, however, permit him to resume his official duties at once: wherefore, at his request, Julius Tausch assumed the direction of the first two winter concerts. At length he so far recovered, that he was able for the last time in his life to devote himself, with ever-lessening powers, to his profession. He directed, as usual, all the subscription-concerts, dating from the third, and composed a number of works in the year 1853. They are, according to the list, —

1853, January, harmonized the six sonatas for the violin, by J. S. Bach.

Feb. 27 to March 12, sketch and instrumentation of the ballad, "The Luck of Edenhall," for male chorus, soli, and orchestra (Op. 143, No. 8, of the posthumous works).*

March 15 to April 10, piano-score of "Edenhall," and harmonization of six sonatas for the violoncello, by J. S. Bach (not yet published).

April 15 to 19, festal overture, with an air from the "Rhine Wine Song," for an orchestra (Op. 123)† (planned in the summer of 1852). April 20 to 24, two-hand piano arrangement of the "Overture, Scherzo, and Finale" (Op. 52).

* First performed at a musical festival in Düsseldorf, May 17, 1853.
† The words are by Dr. Hasenclever.

May 28 to June 9, seven fughettos for piano (Op. 126).

June 11 to 24, " Scenes of Childhood" for the piano, in G-major; two easy sonatas for the young, for the piano (in D-major and C. major), Op. 118.

Aug. 4 to 11, two-hand arrangement of the string-quartettes, Nos. 1 and 2 (Op. 41).   Aug. 13 to 15, sketched overture to "Faust."   Aug. 16 and 17, arranged for instrumental performance.*   Aug. 20, "Birthday Song for Clara," for four voices (unpublished).   Aug. 24 to 30, Concert Allegro, with piano and orchestral introduction (Op. 134).

Sept. 2 to 5, sketch for Fantasia for violin and orchestra (Op. 131).   Sept. 6 and 7, instrumentation.†   Sept. 15, ballad of "The Shepherd Boy," by Hebbel, for declamation, with piano accompaniment.‡   Sept. 18 to 20, "Children's Ball;" six four-hand piano compositions (the minuet dates from 1850), Op. 130.§

Besides these compositions, he wrote in 1853 and 1854 "Legendary Tales;" four compositions for piano, clarionet, and bass-viol (Op. 132); a violin concerto, with orchestral accompaniment;‖ romanzas for violoncello and piano,¶ and "The Songs of Morn" (Op. 133).   A number of songs for three voices (Op. 114), written shortly before, are omitted from the list.

The morbid symptoms so often recurring in 1852 not only re-appeared in 1853, but new ones were added.   This was the time of "table-tipping," which put Schumann into perfect ecstasies, and, in every sense of the word, captivated him.

* He had worked on a " Faust " overture for several years without ever writing one. He considered it a difficult and almost unending task.

† First performed in public by Josef Joachim, at a Düsseldorf concert, Oct 27, 1853.

‡ Contained in Op. 122.

§ Schumann's abstract of his works reached thus far when he sent it to Bonn for my use in the autumn of 1853.

‖ As yet in manuscript.

¶ The existence of this work is proved by a letter to Strackerjan. It is not yet published.

" Table-tipping " troubled many prudent people at that time, when it went the rounds of the boudoirs and tea-parties of nervous ladies, and the studies of otherwise earnest men ; but their feelings were different from Schumann's nervous frenzy. While visiting Düsseldorf in May, 1853, I one day entered his room, and found him on the sofa, reading. To my inquiry as to the subject of his book, he replied in an excited tone, " Oh! don't you know any thing about ' table-tipping ' ? " I laughingly answered, " Well ! " Upon this, his eyes, generally half shut and in-turned, opened wide, the pupils dilated convulsively, and with a peculiar, ghost-like look, he said, slowly and mournfully, " The tables know all." When I saw that he was in serious earnest, rather than irritate him I fell into his humor, and he soon grew calm. He then called his second daughter, and began to experiment with her aid and a small table, which accented the beginning of Beethoven's C-minor symphony. The whole scene struck me with terror; and I well remember that I expressed my distress to acquaintances at the time. He wrote of his experiments to Ferd. Hiller, April 25, 1853,* " We *tipped the table* yesterday for the first time. Wonderful power ! Just think ! I asked for the first two measures of the C-minor symphony ! It delayed longer than usual with the answer : at last it began,

$$\gamma \quad \flat \quad \flat \quad \flat \mid \, \natural \mid$$

but rather slowly at first. When I said, ' But the time is faster, dear table,' it hastened to beat the true time. When I asked if it could give the number *which I was thinking of*, it gave it correctly as *three*. We were all filled with wonder." And to the same, April 29,† " We have repeated our experiments in magnetism : we seem surrounded with wonders."

There were also occasional auricular delusions, which caused him to hear an uninterrupted sound, and in his nervous excitement he really heard it, although there was nothing in the slight-

* See letters for 1833–52, No. 84.
† See letters for 1833–52, No. 85.

est degree approaching a sound. The violinist Ruppert Becker of Frankfort on the Main, who then lived in Düsseldorf, told me that he was at a beer-saloon with Schumann one evening, Suddenly Schumann threw down the paper, saying, "I can read no more : I hear an incessant A" —

Nevertheless, this symptom was ignored, since it often disappeared. It is plain that he was very ill, from a letter written in July, 1853, in which he says, " Nor do I feel perfectly well : I must avoid all over-work." He was only able to share in the musical festival held at Düsseldorf in 1853 by directing at the first concert (at which he won a decided triumph for his D-minor symphony), and leading two pieces on the third day, which fatigued him much. Two letters to F. Hiller* prove that this arrangement was made by himself. In them he begs Hiller to assume the direction of the other concerts.

While Schumann was visiting Bonn in July, 1853, something occurred, early one morning, which led him to suppose that he had had a paralytic stroke. He got into bed again; and the physician, Dr. Kalt, who was quickly summoned, had great difficulty in persuading him of the contrary, and inducing him to rise. This doctor, however, expressed decided apprehensions for the future.

The close of 1853 brought two joyful events to Schumann, — the latter especially delighting him. In October he met Johannes Brahms, whom he had himself introduced to the musical world as the "Messiah of art" by an enthusiastic recognition of his merits in the columns of his journal.† In November he and his wife took a trip through Holland, which was a triumphal procession. "We made a journey to the Netherlands, which was, from beginning to end, guided by good fairies. In every city we were welcomed with joy ; ay, with honor. To my great surprise, I find that my music is almost as well known in Holland as at home. Everywhere

---

* See letters for 1833–52, Nos. 84 and 85.
† See *Neue Zeitschr. f. Musik.*, vol. **xxxix**. p. 185.

there were fine performances of my symphonies, even the most difficult, — the second and third; and, in the Hague, my 'Rose' was given," he writes to Strackerjan.

The "Signals for the Musical World" says of this journey in No. 51, vol. xi., "Robert Schumann and his wife achieved great triumphs in Holland. In Utrecht, after the performance of some of his works, he was repeatedly called out, and loaded with garlands." And in No. 52, "Robert Schumann and his gifted wife were received here (in Amsterdam), as in all the principal cities of Holland, with enthusiasm. Never have I heard Clara Schumann play so beautifully as here in Holland. Schumann always found the concerts arranged, and had nothing to do but to take his place, and direct. In Rotterdam and Utrecht, his third symphony was performed; and in the Hague, the second, and also 'The Pilgrimage of the Rose.' The Dutch people, who have cultivated the best tastes, know and honor not only the old masters, but the new, and received the artist-pair with delight, overwhelming them with attention."

Dec. 22, he returned to Düsseldorf from his trip in Holland. The dreadful event was fast approaching which tore him forever from art and the world. With the exception of a short visit to Hanover, he lived quietly in the bosom of his family during the months of January and February, 1854. Besides the edition of his "Collected Writings" which he was preparing for the press, he was very busy with a literary labor, which he called "The Garden of Poets." The idea, which was to collect all said of music by the poets from most ancient times down to the present day, had occurred to him in his youth; and he had made extracts from the writings of Shakspeare and Jean Paul for the purpose. He was now searching the Bible and the Greek and Latin classics. This was quite difficult, since he had entirely neglected the dead languages while at school and in college. But he was not destined to complete his task; for, when it was but half done, the dangerous symptoms of the preceding year not only returned, but increased to such a degree, that the morbid mental darkness, from which he never recovered, soon gained the upper hand.

The auricular delusions again appeared. He imagined that he heard a tone, which pursued him incessantly, and from which harmonies, ay, whole compositions, were gradually developed. Spirit-voices were heard whispering in his ear, now gentle, now rude and reproachful. They robbed him of sleep for the last two weeks of his wretched existence. One night he rose suddenly, and called for a light, saying that Franz Schubert and Mendelssohn had sent a theme which he must write out at once, which he did, in spite of his wife's entreaties. During his illness, he composed five piano variations on this theme. This was his last work.

One of the ideas that occupied his mind was the belief that " he could never be cured at home," but must resign himself to the care of some physician. On one occasion he sent for a carriage, arranged his papers and compositions, and prepared to depart. He was perfectly aware of his condition, and, when violently excited, would beg his family to help him. His wife made every effort to dissipate the phantoms and delusions which haunted his fevered imagination. Hardly did she succeed when some new fancy would disturb his distracted brain. He declared again and again that he was a sinner, who did not deserve to be loved. Thus the unhappy master's agony increased, until at last, after a fortnight of terrible struggle against his disease, he gave way, and his sufferings drove him to a desperate step.

On Shrove Monday, Feb. 27, 1854, he received a noonday visit from his physician, Dr. Hasenclever * (a member of the board of health), and his musical friend, Albert Dietrich. They sat and chatted together sociably. During the conversation, Schumann, without a word, left the room. They supposed he would return; but when some time passed, and he did not come, his wife went in search of him. He was nowhere

* Now director of music at Coblentz.

to be found. His friends hastened out to look for him, — in vain. He had left the house in dressing-gown and bare head, gone to the bridge that spans the Rhine, and sought to end his misery by plunging into the stream. Some sailors jumped into a boat, rowed after him, and pulled him out. His life was saved, but to what purpose! Passers-by recognized the wretched master, and he was carried home. The news was broken to his wife, who was not permitted to see him in this lamentable state. A second physician was called in, for a fearful paroxysm at once ensued, which finally ceased. He now required constant watching.

The doctors agreed that the scene must be changed, and great care and attention devoted to the sick man. An arrangement was therefore made with his wife to remove him to Dr. Richarz's private hospital at Endenich, near Bonn. Dr. Hasenclever, with true friendship, undertook to execute the plan, and took the patient in a carriage, with two nurses, to his destination, on the morning of March 4, reaching it at night. Here he remained until the end of July, 1856.

It seems fitting to complete the sad picture of his illness by a more minute account. I will make but one more statement. Before leaving Bonn in the summer of 1855, I went with my friend, Otto von Königslöw, to Endenich, to inquire for the health of my honored master, as I had often done before. He was sitting at the piano which had been given him at my request, playing extempore melodies. We watched him long and unnoticed through the half-open door. It was heart-rending to see this great and noble man with all his mental and physical powers gone ; the master to whom music owes so much that is beautiful ; who devoted his quiet but fertile life so zealously to the highest aims. His playing was far from pleasant. It seemed as if the force whence it proceeded were injured, like a machine whose springs are broken, but which still tries to work, jerking convulsively.

During his sojourn at the Endenich asylum, he was visited, with the doctor's consent, by Bettina von Arnim, Joachim, and

Brahms; but as the visit was followed by great excitement, it was never repeated. He corresponded with his wife for some time. She never saw him again until he parted with earth, on the 29th of July, 1856, at four o'clock in the afternoon, when the angel of death called his weary spirit home.

The mortal frame of this immortal master was brought to Bonn, July 31, and borne through the city, amid a throng of people who felt that this was no common death, to the churchyard by the Sternenthor, and there buried with the priestly blessing.

Ferdinand Hiller, who came from Cologne to see his sleeping friend laid in his last resting-place, wrote a fine memorial of him in the Cologne paper.*

Robert Schumann was of middling stature, almost tall, and slightly corpulent. His bearing, while in health, was haughty, distinguished, dignified, and calm; his gait slow, soft, and a little slovenly. When at home, he generally wore felt-shoes. He often paced his room on tiptoe, apparently without cause.† His eyes were generally downcast, half-closed, and only brightened in intercourse with intimate friends, but then most pleasantly. His countenance produced an agreeable, kindly impression : it was without regular beauty, and not particularly intellectual. The fine-cut mouth, usually puckered as if to whistle, was, next to the eyes, the most attractive feature of his round, full, ruddy face. Above the heavy nose rose a high, bold, arched brow, which broadened visibly at the temples. His head, covered with long, thick, dark-brown hair, was firm, and intensely powerful, we might say square.

The expression of his face, although firm, was sweet and genial : the rich soul-life was hardly mirrored there. When he assumed a friendly, confidential manner, — as he but seldom did, — he could work upon his friends at will.

* See his collected essays, "From the Tone-Life of our Day" (Leipsic, published by Mendelssohn).

† Of course I can only speak of the last years of his life, when I knew him well.

When standing, — long standing was painful to him, — he either held both hands behind him, or but one, stroking his mouth or chin reflectively with the other. If he sat or lay idle, he would twist his fingers together.

The nature of his intercourse with others was simple. He spoke but little, and in disconnected sentences, which, however, always showed his mind to be occupied with the subject discussed. There was no premeditation. His style of talking resembled a soliloquy, the more so that his voice was weak and unsonorous. He never conversed on common, every-day subjects (for empty chatter was odious to him) ; and it was rarely and unwillingly that he expressed his opinion, even on important matters most interesting to himself. One had to watch for a favorable moment. If you hit upon the right time, he could be eloquent in his own way. He made significant and intellectually fine remarks, which threw a strong light, from one side at least, upon the question in hand. But it was only to his dear and trusty friends that he vouchsafed this favor, although he sometimes spent whole hours in their company without entering into conversation. But no one could argue from his silence that he liked or disliked a person. It was merely a characteristic habit formed in early life. The following anecdote from Heinrich Dorn forms an amusing illustration : "When I saw Schumann in 1843, after long separation, there was a musical party in the house (it was his wife's birthday). Among the guests was Mendelssohn. We had barely time to exchange a couple of words, for new guests were constantly arriving. When I went away, Schumann said in a regretful tone, " Oh, we haven't been able to talk together at all ! " I comforted him and myself with the hope of a speedy meeting, and said laughingly, " Then we'll be silent to our hearts' content ! " — " Oh ! " he answered blushing, " then you've not forgotten me ? " This incident shows how his peculiarity was to be taken. It is very evident that none but an intimate friend could interpret him aright, and that his chariness of words on chance meetings in society caused much offence and many unkind and unjust criticisms.

Strangers, or people whom he disliked, might easily take offence at his manner. He was as easily aggrieved by uncalled-or confidence and cordiality as by importunity. He was not wholly free from whims and peevishness, especially during his latter years, when sorely tried by ceaseless pain. Still his heart was always so good and noble, that the disagreeable side of his nature was easily overlooked. He always was and appeared the best in a small circle of friends over a glass of beer or wine. At certain times he preferred champagne, and would say decidedly, "This strikes out mental sparks." On such occasions, he was never without a cigar. He used very fine and strong cigars, which he jestingly called "little devils."

In the family-circle he was rarely accessible; but, if any one could enjoy this privilege, he received the most charming impression. He loved his children no less than his wife, although he did not possess the gift of showing his love by outward signs. If he happened to meet them in the street, he would stop, put up his eye-glass and look at them a moment, and say kindly with pouting lips, "Well, you dear little things?" Then he would resume his former manner, and go his way as if nothing had happened.

His habits during the last years of his life were exceedingly regular. In the morning he worked till about twelve o'clock: he then usually took a walk with his wife and one of his intimate friends. At one o'clock he dined; and, after a short rest, worked until five or six. He then generally visited some public place or private club of which he was a member, to read the papers, and drink a glass of wine or beer. At eight he usually returned to sup at home.

He but seldom went to tea or evening parties. He sometimes assembled a few of his musical friends and acquaintance at his own house, and could, if in the mood, make a very agreeable host. While in Düsseldorf, he was often uncommonly gay and good-natured. Once, after music and supper, he even proposed a general dance, in which he took a brisk share, to the great astonishment of all present.

He was severely conscientious in his profession, hardly ever allowing himself to speak hastily or angrily of it under most irritating circumstancès ; and, when he did happen to do so, he soon spoke again in a conciliated and conciliating tone. This was also the case when he had been pettish to a person of whom he was fond : he perceived his fault at once, and sought to atone for it.   When present at controversies, he was generally silent : this was always a sure sign of unexpressed opposition, in accordance with which he acted.   At a committee meeting of the General Musical Association of Düsseldorf, a resolution was once about to be passed of which he did not approve.   Without a word, he seized his hat, and left the room.   He was inexorably severe against malevolence and vulgarity ; and, where they had once been shown, he never forgot nor forgave them.

His manner towards artist-friends (especially musicians and critics), has already been illustrated : in this respect he is worthy of imitation.   He recognized with cordial warmth all that was great, wise, and talented, particularly when attracted by kindred spirits.   He also showed (which was surprising with his thoroughly *German* disposition and mind) enthusiastic interest in foreign art, although ever averse to the new dramatic music of Italy and France, and never valuing them correctly from an objective point of view.   During the last years of his life, he showed but little interest in some of the great masters of the past, particularly Haydn and Mozart.   Indeed, he sometimes let fall disparaging remarks concerning their famous works, so that he must have been misunderstood by many : for his illness caused these expressions ; and it is probable that the fancies of his own ideal world, increasing with years, had also much to do with it.

In his death, the modern world of music lost one of its most richly and highly gifted creative spirits, one of its most devoted priests.   His life is important and instructive for the history of music, — important for its moral and intellectual grandeur, its restless struggles for the noblest, loftiest objects, as well as its truly great results; instructive through the errors by which he, as all earth-born beings must, paid tribute to finite conditions. But a man who strives and errs *thus* may be considered fortunate.

LETTERS FOR 1833-1852

IN CHRONOLOGICAL ORDER.

LETTERS FOR 1833–1852,

IN CHRONOLOGICAL ORDER.

"Letters are among the most important memorials which any man can leave." — GOETHE.

1.

TO TÖPKEN, AT BREMEN.

LEIPSIC, Good Friday, April 5, 1833.

. . . I am very glad that you know the "Papillons," many of which originated in my happy Heidelberg life with you, since they must give you at least a hint of my feelings. Your review will be very acceptable. If I have room, I will add to it a Viennese one, which pleased me much. You will also find favorable notices of me in the Berlin "Iris."

I have written Intermezzi (two parts, longer Papillons) and an Allegro di Bravura, of whose publication I will notify you, for the Easter fair. During the past winter, my time has been occupied by a grand orchestral symphony, which is now finished. Without vanity, I expect the utmost from it in the future. I play the piano but little now: don't be frightened (I am resigned, and consider it a dispensation of Providence). I have a lame, broken finger on my right hand; from an injury insignificant in itself and neglect, the evil has grown so great, that I can hardly use the hand. Expect full accounts in my next letter of this, and of my present circumstances (which are very pleasant), my reception in the musical world (which could not be more encouraging), my plans for the future, and my quiet life, which, in contrast with . . . [illegible] prospects in Heidelberg, is temperate, busy, and orderly. Your letters will always reach me through Wieck. The old teacher is now my oldest friend. You probably have read about Clara: imagine the utmost, and I will subscribe to it. Moscheles has been most kind, both when we met and in regard to his music. Kalkbrenner will be here in three days. I am exchanging friendly letters with Hummel: if you like, you shall read his opinion of me, which quite coincides with yours.

If Easter, 1830, had been the same day as it is this year, to-morrow would be the day on which a one-horse carriage bore us to Frankfort and Paganini. I quote the following from my diary: "First coachmen — current of clouds in the sky — roads unexpectedly bad — Melibocus — Auerbach — Benecke (I met him here, seated in a stage-coach, on his way to Berlin) — the little waitress — Lichtenberg's auction (I've taken up half a sheet by mistake; beg indulgence; promise to amend) — bills and laughter — Forster — Malaga — then Schädler and Eckmayer — drinking-match — bed on the floor, &c. *Easter Sunday:* Töpken's oath — sorry faces — Darmstadt — picturesque weeping-willows in the hotel courtyard — April weather black and blue — watchtower before Frankfort — lame nag, and tedious journey — arrival at the Swan — evening, Paganini — Weber (I've never heard of him again: have you?) — enthusiasm (was it not?) — with Weber, Hille, and you at the Swan — distant music, and bliss in bed. *Easter Monday:* Pretty girl by the willow-bush — evening, "Tell," by Rossini (then the diary says, "Töpken's sound judgment") — headlong plunge into the willow-bush — the lovely girl — bombardment of eyeglasses — champagne. *Easter Tuesday:* Looked at pianos with Töpken — Al. Schmitt — Schubert waltzes — Braunfels — wax-work show — parting with Weber, perhaps forever (it was indeed) — departure from Frankfort — my artful evasion in Frankfort lanes — Darmstadt (now I transcribe literally) — charming condition after a pint of wine — splendid Melibocus in the evening glow — wine in the stomach — horrid horse — changed reins — final arrival in Auerbach — Lottie. *Easter Wednesday:* Bad weather — mountain-roads bright with blossoms — vicious Prussian foxes in Handschuchsheim — arrival in Heidelb. — end."

It is long since I have known any manuscript (except my compositions) to give me such pleasure as these lines. Your image is so vivid, that I would fain add a second and longer letter to this, which should tell you how I love and esteem you. With friendship and affection, I send you a . . . [illegible] greeting. May your hand soon remove the cloud which veils the last two years: perhaps it may fall in warm drops on the hand of your friend,　　　　R. SCHUMANN.

As I have room, I enclose the promised critique: —

"1.　Thème sur le nom, etc.

"2.　Papillons.

"It is always well to use one's own feet, and need neither crutches nor another's shoulder to lean upon. The tone-poet, whom we now meet for the first time, is probably still young. He belongs " (here I was excited, visibly alarmed) " to the rare phenomena of the day; he belongs to no school, creates from his own mind, makes no boast of odd ideas collected in the sweat of his brow; has made himself a new ideal world, wherein he roves at will, and with great originality: for this reason, and because phœnix-like peculiarities are innate in him, he deserves support. Many, indeed, to whom Jean Paul's profound pictures of life are all Greek, or who abhor Beethoven's grand lightning-flashes, will feel as if an emetic were offered them. Probably, I say, these gentlemen will take offence at A-flat and E-flat, sneer at the boldness of this obscure neophyte, and make an uproar about it. Perhaps they'll consume a few quires of paper and wear out half a hundred quills over " how it is " and " how it ought to be." No matter. A gift to the public is always subject to public criticism, which is scorned by self-conceit alone, but gratefully received by one who strives to rise, remaining true to his own genius, which will not be apt to lead him astray.

" A few words only on our subject, although too many could hardly be said. No. 1 is based on a motive of five notes,— A, B, E, G, G." (Don't be alarmed about Countess Pauline, whose father I alone am. I had reasons for this mystery, which will some day be declared to you.) " No. 2 consists of six introductory measures, and twelve rhapsodical movements of varying length and in different keys, measures, and tempo; mostly variegated, fickle, and coquettish: a true picture of butterfly nature." (The Papillons are something very different. In my next letter, you shall have the key to the mystery.) " They are not at all easy to play: the execution requires character: careful study and practice are requisite to a proper conception of the work. The publishers, new in name at least, begin their work most pleasingly." 76.

Copying this review has almost lulled me to sleep, as the writing plainly shows. Reward this great sacrifice by a speedy answer, if you can. We find it more convenient not to prepay letters. Write me of your musical studies: I always take a deep interest in them, as I need not assure you. I think I can conscientiously recommend the Paganini capriccios to you as excellent practice, and await your opinion. The concealing "76" above, stands, as I afterwards learned, for Grillparzer the Viennese poet.

My address is, Riedel's Garden (or through Wieck).

Adieu, dear, best friend!

2.

TO HENRIETTA VOIGT, AT LEIPSIC.

LEIPSIC, Summer of 1834.

MOST HONORED LADY, — The fashion (I don't know if the word suits —I mean the manner) in which I have often received and repelled the various proofs of your interest in poor me, forms so curious an enigma of polaric attraction and repulsion, that I should now like to place myself in a more favorable light in regard to certain circumstances. But the constellations move so confusedly, my present life refracts such tints that I must delay answering you until my relations grow clearer and calmer. I tell this to *you*, my honored friend, to no one else, — dared I hope that an avowal and assurance of sincerest sympathy in all that concerns you were of any value to you, 'twould comfort, if not excuse me, since it would contradict my past mode of showing interest. However, judge me gently, if you can, I beg! Your last letter is inexpressibly dear to me. I have read and re-read it, and silently rejoiced over the future advice which I shall give you. Would we could trust Eusebius! who, on reading your words, gave his promise (or, properly speaking, his pledge) to finish the essay on Berger, which should still contain your reflections.

When Florestan read the letter, Fate made a right clever anagram. You wrote, "Rochlitz, who has been for years a faithful friend to every aspiring artist," &c. But Florestan read it "every expiring"! I think that's a good description of R., a loving father, who has so often, with tears of sorrow, closed the eyes of so many noble men, and spoken at their graves. Florestan said it made him think of Lafayette, who stood boldly up at a nation's last gasp as defender of the corpse. "Whither do your thoughts conduct you, Florestan?" said I. That makes a bridge to the Papillons, for it's pleasant to think of the Psyche hovering above the faded body. You might learn much from me in this connection, did not Jean Paul teach it far better. If you have a spare moment, I pray you read the last chapter of the "Flegeljahre," where all stands in black and white up to the Riesenstiefel in F-sharp minor (at the end of the " Flegeljahre," I feel as if the play were indeed done, but the curtain not yet fallen). I must mention that I set the words to music, not the reverse; for that I should think a "silly proceeding." The last only, which the act of playing forms into an answer to the first, was occasioned by Jean Paul. One question: Are not the Papillons self-evident to you? It is important that I should know.

Receive these few lines, which are but a faint echo of all I had to say to you, with the favor I should be proud of did I deserve it better.

ROBERT SCHUMANN.

One request. I promised Ernestine theatre-tickets for to-night, but am obliged to make a long excursion into the country, which will prevent me from delivering them in person. Will you be so kind as to forward them?

Apropos, henceforth I shall call you, not Eleanor, but Aspasia. Eleanor shall still stand in the Davidsbündler. I would like to close my review of Berger with your letter. May I? Yes? R. S.

3.

TO TÖPKEN, AT BREMEN.

LEIPSIC, Aug. 18, 1834.

You have yet to learn, good Theodore Töpken, how a man feels when he has begged his host to have patience from one fortnight to another, and continues to ask for delay; for you always have money. On account of the lingering illness of our secretary, the business falls on my shoulders, so that I can pay but part of my debt to-day, and that little ill, for my head still buzzes from proof-sheets. Added to which, I've cut my pen three times to no avail. I now do it for the fourth and last time. If I don't succeed, you'll get no letter to-day. But I hope for the best. . . .

First, many thanks for your works, all of which please me much, for various reasons. The mystery of their publication on the day of departure from Bremen is funny, but plain enough; since we unfortunately were so long delayed by the publisher, that we are a fortnight behind-hand. But yesterday, at a solemn conference, such serious measures were taken, that all will be in fine trim in less than a month. It would also be unfair to the public, who support us so strongly as to delight us. Prague alone takes fifty copies, Dresden thirty, and Hamburg twenty.

All that there is in youth, consequently futurity, shall soon echo through the land. It is almost inexplicable that this critical honey-daubing has not been put a stop to long ago. So strike right at the People, although it is like a flock of sheep, who look up once when it lightens, and then quietly go on grazing. The flock shall look up for one moment, at least.

So your projected review of Hünten's piano-method will be just the thing for us, if it's not too much like the first. Perhaps you could write it in a simpler, sharper form. At any rate, you will deeply oblige us by sending any thing you have in hand, and as much as possible: any thing that comes from you can be sent to press without revision. The faulty proof-sheet is all right. I am the guilty one. I don't like pseudonymes ín so good an article. I've given little thought to externals. Adieu! The clock strikes ten. I'm going for a fine walk.

I've returned from the fine walk; and it was good. Now to your letter again.

"Three" does not stand for me, but for Schunke. Still I have a great îeal to do with his articles, since he handles his pen a thousand times worse than his piano. I seldom sign with numbers; but, when I do, I take the *twos*, — as 2, 12, 22, 32, &c. "Father Doles," who is to be rated far higher than "Beethoven" in the last number, originated with my friend the deaf painter, Lyser. He will give two similar portraits, — Haydn and Handel. The Davidsbündler contribute seldom, but moderately well: at present they're working on large sketches closely (historically) connected, Beethoven's last symphony (as the turning-point from the classic to the romantic period), Franz Schubert, Mendelssohn, Chopin. But I am prudent, almost timid, and shall hold back a fortnight longer.

Klein's story about the origin of the Hummel studies doesn't seem credible. Only examine them, and you can neither mistake the master's hand, nor the weaknesses of age.

Your rhapsodies will appear in 35 and 36. Go on! Also gratify us by shorter articles on "Music in the North," which are very scarce. If you desire pay, it shall not be withheld; but if you will be generous, and spare the publishers, who have many sacrifices to make, you will oblige us doubly.

The next number will contain something humorous by K. Stein, a long sketch of Schröder-Devrient's musical doings, and a magazine review which will be interesting.

We are very much pleased with your musical life in South America. Fink will swear!

The notes ordered will soon be sent. Have you read Gottfried Weber's review of me? * It was really refreshing. You will greet an old friend in my Toccata: only he speaks more politely than of yore; he's not so wild. If you have a mind to write a criticism of the Toccata and the Intermezzi (of course, a candid one), setting aside all personal feelings, *signed with your name*, we should like it much. I would also draw your attention to Schunke's new sonata (published by a miracle).

All the editors and the Davidsbündlerschaft salute you with high esteem. We now live such a romance as perhaps no book contains. For·get me not.   Your   Sch.

* In reference to a short general notice of Op, 12, 4, 5, — See Cecilia, vol. xvi. p. 94.

4.

TO HENRIETTA VOIGT, AT LEIPSIC.

ZWICKAU, Nov. 2, 1834.

I have just read your last letter.

This sheet was really meant for Ernestine. Dare I confess to my dear Henrietta that I hardly care to which I write? Ludwig* just said that you were now really represented by me as I by you; at least, in Zwickau. Oh, how I wished for some of my regard for friends, shown by deeds rather than words; some of my haste in writing to a lonely friend! Yes, I wished to own all my own qualities. I might easily turn this into an excuse, and say, " It's enough for me to write to Henrietta and Ernestine; I won't write to myself; " but think a simple recommendation, "Don't be angry," will answer the purpose. By the by, I don't remember to have written a letter for years without a tedious excuse for delay, which must have been a perfect bore to the recipient.

My dear friend, I love and esteem you so truly, that I believe you will consider my silence a mere pause, that is, a stupid interruption, but not an end. I turn poet when I think of you, as all my relations know; for you stand before me like a vision, now musing, now advising, seldom sulky, sometimes gloomy, oftener merry, ever loving and kind. Then Ernestine appears with her Madonna face, her child-like devotion, soft and bright as a heavenly eye, blue piercing the clouds; then Ludwig embraces you, gentle in aspect, anguish and noble scorn in his face, — the group is complete. I draw the veil.

(Four days later, Nov. 5.)

The Sunday after our Friday farewell, I came here. In truth, a traveller should never have to reply — for those who are left at home, at least retain the place which chains the images of the past more surely than can imagination. The traveller is distracted by new faces and new relations: he stands, as it were, at the junction of strangely fluctuating and confusing seasons. Besides, the whole misses a link from the chain, less than the individual does a failing in the whole.

Nov. 7.

Every moment swells my debt. How your images — yours and Ludwig's — torment me! Now I have seated myself, firmly determined not to rise until my letter is done.

Could I be with you but for an hour, you should know more than

* Ludwig Schunke.

this fragmentary epistle can tell you. How much I intended to do and to complete here! — to carry on a correspondence with certain people in Leipsic; to work for the Journal and the " Ladies' Conversation Book," * — none of which I have done. My studies consist of a letter to Ernestine, from whom I received a note the day after my arrival, directed by you. Since then my distractions have been endless. The thousand familiar faces of my native city all demand a word and a smile, from our old cook up to the colonel. What flattering absurdities one has to swallow and to answer! But the recovery of old friends, tested by long absence, richly compensates for all this; as does the lovely vale of my childhood, where all is so familiar. One learns it unconsciously, so deeply does habit mark our minds. All this delights and distracts me; but the state of my soul is, as ever, fearful. I have a masterly gift for getting hold of unlucky ideas: it's the evil spirit which opposes my happiness, and derides it. I often carry this self-torture so far as to be a sin against my nature: for I am never content; I would fain be in another body, or pass over long eternities. . . . Ernestine wrote to me most blissfully. She asked her father, through her mother; and he gives her to me. . . . Henrietta — he gives her to me. . . . Do you understand me? And yet this fearful state! — as if I dreaded to accept this jewel because I knew my hands to be unworthy. Would you bid me name my anguish? Alas! I cannot. *I think it is, just, anguish:* I cannot express it otherwise. Alas! perhaps it is love, and longing for Ernestine. I can bear it no longer; and have written, bidding her hope for a speedy meeting. But, if you would feel true delight, think of two souls who have bestowed upon your soul their holiest emotions, and whose future bliss is inseparable from yours.

How confusedly I write to-day! But the letter burns beneath my fingers, and must leave the house within the hour. It is now my turn to console. May your heart receive true peace! Write me all you know of Ludwig: I will shape my letter accordingly. How can I bear to give him up? If he dies, for Heaven's sake don't write to me, or let any one else do so. I did not need to ask you that.

I just looked up to heaven. The clock has struck five. White, fleecy clouds float above. There is no light in your room; but in the background I discern a slender form, her head on her hand. I gaze at her with melancholy eyes, as she wonders whether she shall still retain what are generally considered most sacred, — friendship and love. Glad-

---

* Schumann, for a short time, worked for the "Ladies' Conversation Book," published by Herlossohn, furnishing many short articles on music for it. — See *New Jour. of Music*, vol. xii. p. 132.

ly would I venture nearer, and humbly kiss her hand; but she turns away.

Well, be ever mine, my dear friend,

ROBERT SCHUMANN

5.

TO HENRIETTA VOIGT.

Like Cordelia, I am last to offer my good wishes. Shall I repeat what worthier men have already expressed in more glowing words?

Were you Lear, and did you ask, "What do you wish for me?" I should answer, "Nothing: by that I mean, there is indeed much which you do not possess."

If you angrily insisted on a wish, I should reply, "All; for, in truth, you deserve all."

If you were not satisfied, I'd say, "Well, then, I wish that you may always have something to wish for; for I consider it a happy thing to have one wish succeed another as fast as they are gratified."

So may it be, my friend! Be content with this trifle. On such a day I'd gladly gaze an instant longer into your eyes, and be silent; for loud talking is forbidden in church.

My mother begs leave to add Bulwer's works to her good wishes; and Ernestine and I send the Allegro, with the assurance that the author is better than his work, but worse than she to whom it is dedicated.

Of the rest, next time. A thousand friendly greetings to my esteemed Mr. Voigt.

ROBERT SCHUMANN

ZWICKAU, Nov. 24, 1834.

6.

TO JOSEF FISCHOF, AT VIENNA.

ZWICKAU, SAXONY, Dec. 14, 1834.

HIGHLY HONORED SIR, — Our Ludwig Schunke is dead; or rather, let me say, has gently passed away. I thought it right to inform you, of whom he spoke so often and so affectionately. A friend of the glorious youth will forgive his junior if he says no more of this loss to art and the world. Should you hope to find in me, the survivor, aught to compensate for his loss, let me first extend to you my hand in token of the alliance formed and hallowed by our departed friend.

My first prayer is this: I should like to have some memorial of our Ludwig in our Journal; and, if it breaks my heart, I'll do it if I can, so that it shall not be unworthy him. Will you tell me, as soon as possible, all you know of his life, especially while with Counsellor S. of Vienna?

Then I entreat, I hardly need say what, that you will mention his death in Haslinger's Advertiser. He died on the 7th of December. Among the works he left behind him are an excellent piano concerto (his last labor), and twelve waltzes, in which, spite of their freshness, some little hint of death intrudes.

I begin our friendship with petitions, and am bold enough to add a third to the foregoing. You may consider the young work, our Journal, which our friend so joyfully and zealously supported, worthy your aid. I have motives, which I will explain later, for begging you *most urgently* either for letters or reviews. We could not have chosen a worse publisher. A change is to be made; if not at Christmas, certainly at Easter, 1835. We have been sufficiently annoyed to justify us in taking the Journal from Hartmann. He will resist, and matters may become complicated. But, meanwhile, a Journal which enjoys such favor must not cease to circulate. I will answer for your prompt payment for future work, and hope soon to be able to offer you the best of terms. Be so kind as to send all contributions to my address, care " Mlle. Dumas, No. 1246 Inergasse, Leipsic." The editors will be extremely obliged if you will consent to become an assistant, and will then explain to you the purposes of the Journal. Seyfried has promised to contribute; but Kiesewetter has refused.

Will the Haslinger Advertiser be continued? I prefer it to any other sheet of the size. Do you know my kind critic, " No. 76 " ? He gives me fresh zest for work, and bright ideas. I will send Intermezzi (in two numbers) and an Allegro for your criticism. If you will promise to review them, receive my hearty thanks: art cannot exist without encouragement. A Mozart or a Raphael would have been mere tillers of the soil on the favorite solitary island in a peaceful sea.

Pardon my hieroglyphics. I anxiously await an answer.

ROBERT SCHUMANN.

We have received nothing from you since last October. Can it be that Hartmann has withheld or returned your letters? Pray let me know at once.

7.

TO IGNAZ MOSCHELES, AT LONDON.

LEIPSIC, Feb. 26, 1835.

MOST HONORED OF MEN, — Spite of all our efforts, we have not yet succeeded in obtaining any musical news from the capital you inhabit Wherever we applied, promises were plenty, but labor scarce.

We are, therefore, in some degree, excusable, if we now apply to the man who, we know, has never ceased to take an interest in the aims and efforts of German musicians. Our question and request is, whether you chance to know a musician — that is, a careful, clever, if possible a German musician — who would write us a certain style of letters from London on the events of the day, English musical life in general, and the musicians there; not mere facts, but elaborate pictures of the musical condition of England. To be sure, we do not know if you consider our Journal worthy your commendation, but think ourselves not wholly wrong in saying that the general idea, tone, and spirit would gain your approbation. At any rate, your gracious intercession would be a favor, which, though we may never be able to repay, we shall never forget.

The requisitions could easily be explained to any correspondent you might recommend. For the present, permit us to say that we should be glad to pay twenty thalers per printed sheet. It is our earnest wish, which we utter so humbly that you may never hear it, to receive an occasional contribution to our Journal from the illustrious master to whom these lines are addressed, under any title whatsoever (perhaps an extract from your contemplated piano-method). And so we trust to you to fill up in thought what we have but hinted.

We printed a preliminary notice of your fine Septet in No. 18; since we have hitherto had neither the score, nor an opportunity to hear the whole. When may we hope for the publication of your piano-method and your Concerto Fantastique? A certain Miss Schmiedel, of Dresden, played your "Irish Recollections" at the Gewandhaus concert to-day.

Finally, we beg you will inform us how we shall send you our Journal, which enjoys uncommon and universal favor. Our publisher has weekly communication with London.

Your indulgence and pardon for these lines, dictated by interest and enthusiasm for music. With heartfelt esteem, I part for the present from the man whose bright and intellectual eyes have so often glanced at and blessed me.

In the name of the editors of the "Neue Zeitschrift für Musik."

ROBERT SCHUMANN.

8.

TO THERESA SCHUMANN, AT ZWICKAU.

L(EIPSIC), ⅔, 1836.

Edward and I have just left the Hotel de Bavière, where we dined with Mendelssohn. The post goes in half an hour: so I shall only tell vou, first, that I love you from the bottom of my heart; then, that Edward will arrive early the day after to-morrow; and, finally, that I'm very well, since I've talked with him for some minutes, and have yet much to do for you and for myself. . . . Clara is in Breslau. My stars are wonderfully unpropitious. God grant all may end well!

A cordial farewell for to-day.

Remember me to your sister Natalie.

Yours,   R.

9.

TO IGNAZ MOSCHELES.

LEIPSIC, March 8, 1836.

MOST HONORED SIR AND DEAR MASTER,— Would I could offer something more worthy your attention than a letter full of unintelligible characters! But if you can decipher enough to see that I think with great joy of those October days,* when I was permitted to hear you and ·to talk to you, and that I have written a sonata in memory of them, — to which, with your consent, I will prefix your name, — then the chief purpose of these lines will be fulfilled. Perhaps you will set my mind at rest by one word.

I refresh myself daily with your Concerto Fantastique, and the Handel duo, that accords so quickly, but echoes all the longer. The Jungfrau overture is rather reserved, but grows in breadth and charm with every hour. You will find more on the subject in "The Journal;" though I may not reveal the author. . . . This brings me to something disagreeable. The resident commissioner from . . . [illegible], &c., refuses to send any thing more to London: so that I fear you have not received "The Journal" since New-Year's Day. Wouldn't it do if I sent you three copies regularly through Mr. Emden of Hamburg, which you could distribute as you saw fit? I know no means of sending to Edinburgh. I have also two librettos for Mr. Thomson which he wished to possess. A hint from you as to how I can forward them will be gratefully received.

I consider it as a rare mark of kindness that you have gained my paper a new correspondent in Mr. Hogarth. The London article has been missing for three months; so that I should like to hear as soon as possible. If he wants a special invitation, he shall have it forthwith. Excuse my many questions and petitions. I wrote to Mr. Thomson last January, but have received no answer. Perhaps the letter was too late

* I. Moscheles was in Leipsic the preceding October.

to find him in London. Clara Wieck has gone on a grand concert tour. My sonata (the first) is not in print: the publishers won't listen to me; nor have I much hope in Haslinger. . . . Mendelssohn wishes to be kindly remembered. He has finished his oratorio, and will direct it himself at the Düsseldorf Musical Festival. Perhaps I shall go there: Chopin may go too. We have written him on the subject. May we ask you to consider whether a steamboat will not leave London some time between May 20 and June 1, which will bring the master whom we all esteem so highly?

With most cordial respect, yours,   R. SCHUMANN.

10.

TO THERESA SCHUMANN.

LEIPSIC, April 1, 1836.

MY BELOVED THERESA, — I have thought so often and so earnestly of you during the past weeks, that I frequently imagined that I grasped your hand. I am more than sure and safe in your love, and you know not how happy it makes me. That is because you have a brave heart, and can endure, comfort, and support. If I leave this place, it will only be because I have more favorable prospects. Edward was only jesting about Vienna: those hopes are but a dream at present. In no case shall I leave before Christmas. Consider what I leave behind! First and foremost, my home, — may my heart ne'er grow cold and indifferent to it! — then my relations, — you, whom I can see and talk to in two hours; then Leipsic itself, where all is bright and prosperous; then Clara, Mendelssohn, who is to return this winter; and a hundred others. If a change of residence would *assure* my future, I should not hesitate an instant; but I shall do nothing rashly. That would bring me back what I never could go after. So you shall have me, and keep me, and I you, for a year; and we'll spend that year happily, and serve one another. I shall visit you in January, at any rate; but, of course, you must come to me first. If we only could settle it all nicely! Listen: Mendelssohn and I want to go to the festival in Düsseldorf; then I should leave about the 18th of May. But if any thing prevents, or I foresee obstacles, I shall only go to Frankfort with M. in three or four weeks. I wish I were certain when you would come; for it all depends upon you. Edward must. Why do you hesitate? I shall not fail to be in Leipsic between May 14 and 18. So arrange your visit for that time.

You would be much pleased with my present behavior. As I always like to be odd . . . [illegible], I, once the most inveterate smoker and beer-drinker, have become just the reverse. At most, only four cigars a day, and *no beer at all* for two months. But all is well, and I'm getting quite conceited about it. So don't praise me; for I praise myself all day.

I look up to Mendelssohn as to some lofty mountain. He is a true divinity, and you ought to know him. I am also intimate with David (the concertmeister) and a Dr. Schlemmer (tutor to young Rothschild), and also with the latter. You may yet meet these three in Leipsic. The doctor would just suit you, — a man of the world from top to toe. Dr. Reuter and Ulex are, of course, my friends, as ever. We'll talk of Wieck and Clara when we meet. I am in a critical condition, and lack the calm and clear sight requisite to get out of it. Matters are such, that I must break with her forever, or she must be mine at once. You shall know all when you come, and shall claim my best.

Thanks for all you do for me: you have my consent to all in advance. I should like fine sleeves to the shirts. The best will in the world to make my washing clear to you is of no avail. A woman must see to such things with her own eyes, and not hesitate between the wholly and the half ragged, as we men do. So come soon, and be a right good sister to me: I have, indeed, no other woman to help me. This thought would kill me if you did not aid me in every thing.

Edward meets with great opposition. Encourage him! ah, do!

Write to me soon, my beloved Theresa. Farewell! I kiss you, brow and eyes.   Yours,   ROBERT.

11.

TO IGNAZ MOSCHELES.

LEIPSIC, July 30, 1836.

MOST HIGHLY-HONORED SIR, — Mr. Mendelssohn has told you that I have not approached an inch nearer you during my silence — physically; for I busy myself daily with you and your compositions. I had to give up Düsseldorf: so I've worked all the harder, both in music and literature. I have also extended your permission to dedicate a sonata to you, to a concerto for the piano *only,* which I have just sent to Vienna, where it will be published by Haslinger. In about a month it will be in your hands; and then you can wonder at the foolish fancies men may have.

We long for news of you, the concerto pathétique, the études, and the piano-method. Do not forget to write us when you have leisure.

My best thanks for your last letter, enclosing one from Thomson, who would greatly oblige me by frequent news from Edinburgh. Since I received no further accounts of your May concert, I patched up what I could from the notice in "The Atlas," which you sent to Mendelssohn, and he to me, and made a letter, whose spuriousness you doubtless detected. "The Globe" is now the only source whence I take a notice; although I don't think it adequate. Mendelssohn wrote me in glowing terms of Mr. Klingemann, secretary of legation. Do you think he would write, now and then, at my express request and your recommendation?

I now send the Journal to Mr. Emden of Hamburg. I should like to know how many numbers you have, what you like or dislike in them, &c. I am more interested in it than ever, and you will readily recognize my articles.

One thing more, which just occurs to me. More than a month ago I sent you, through your father-in-law, the sonata which you heard Clara Wieck play. Since I consider myself a link in the great chain, it should be briefly introduced to the readers of my Journal. An auto-criticism has naught in its favor, and is quite as difficult as thankless. So won't you send me your opinion of the work in as few words as possible, and permit me to publish it with your name? The sonata does not bear my name, but those of "Florestan and Eusebius," as authors; so that they alone appeal to you. I should then introduce your words as follows: "On account of the fraternity of authors (Florestan and Euseb.), the editors felt obliged to seek the opinion of a third party, in regard to this sonata, Prof. Moscheles being kind enough to send us the following lines."

Should you, my dear sir, have any open or secret reasons for refusing my request, I should of course withdraw it at once; but if you have none, and consider the composition worthy that high form of art in which it is clothed, and, on account of the aspiration by which I am sure it is marked, deserving commendation, you may believe me deeply grateful: your words would have great influence in increasing the circulation of the Journal, which would much delight Mr. Kistner, the publisher This is the prosaic side of the matter. But did you know how I hope to reach the topmost branches of the tree of heaven, and how I seem to hear in my lonely hours songs from above, which I shall yet reveal to my beloved fellow-men, you could not refuse me the encouraging word essential to every artist.

With most heartfelt and reverent greetings, believe me, yours very truly,

R. Schumann

12.

TO EDWARD AND THERESA SCHUMANN.

LEIPSIC, Aug. 28, 1836.

DEAR EDWARD AND THERESA, — Alas! I cannot get away, much as I should like to. Still it doesn't seem necessary. I can trust Oberländer to do what he thinks for my advantage; only let me have the proper dividend.

How is it with you, my much-loved rose? Every night I lie down with the firm resolve, "To-morrow you shall write;" and when morning dawns I'm as cold and gloomy as ever. And so it's been hitherto. I've just written to Chopin, who's said to be at the Marienbad, to know if he be really there. I shall visit you in the autumn, at any rate. But if Chopin answers at once, I shall start earlier, and go by Carlsbad to Marienbad. Theresa, how would you like that? You must go with me. Read Chopin's answer, and then we'll make our plans.

You must have seen by the Journal how busy I am; but the ground burns beneath my feet, and I would fain away. I expect a decisive letter from Haslinger directly. Dr. Schlemmer is in London, and will remain there with young Rothschild. I've worn my black dress-coat one whole day. And David, hark you, is to be married, in a few weeks, to a Baroness von Liphardt of Dorpat. . . . He told me so himself yesterday. Would we too were in port! Mendelssohn will be here in a month. I visit Voigt often. Dine there to-day with David. Goethe's birthday.

Farewell! dear ones; keep busy. Think of me sometimes, Theresa. So, — Regards to Natalie.

R. S.

13.

TO HEINRICH DORN, AT RIGA.

LEIPSIC, Sept. 14, 1836.

MY DEAREST SIR, — I had just received your letter day before yesterday, and prepared to answer it, when who should walk in but — Chopin! There was great rejoicing. We spent a delightful day, which I celebrated again yesterday. But to-day I have seated myself, determined to discharge my old debt as well as I can in so limited a space. So, first, I think of you almost daily, often sadly that I was so irregular, though so grateful a scholar, for I learned more than you think. You know somewhat of my life and its changes in those days. The rest I will keep until we meet, as I doubt not we shall yet do, however remote the time may be.

Thanks for your many proofs of interest in our effort. Much is yet undone; but we are young, and time does good to all. Special thanks for mentioning the Journal, and gaining it friends. I enclose a few lines to Mr. Weitzmann. The Davidsbund is merely a literary and romantic society, as you have long known. Mozart was as great a Bündler as Berlioz now is; so are you, though you never received a titulary diploma. Florestan and Eusebius are my double, whom, like Raro, I would gladly melt into a man. The other pseudonymes are *partly* imaginary; many, too, are taken from the history of the real Davidsbündler. I could write quires, but you must be content with this little . . . [illegible]: 1 [The 1 above has no 2, as I just noticed.] . . . Your annual report has been missing from No. 13. I am most anxious to hear of the musical festival.

This extract from the Iris is (with all respect) just fit for the Iris; very dull and stiff. If you feel like sending us a few honest reviews, especially in regard to musical festivals, and how to make them instrumental for the culture of the people, and on the music of the future, recent dissensions and discords, &c., pray do so. A comparison between Breitkopf's Journal and ours would be interesting; but of course it must be in a third paper (the Journal of Elegance, the Comet, or the Evening Journal.) Won't you think of it?

2.) Of course I'm very much pleased with the fantasie. I should be delighted to assist you in any way. I have come to consider Haslinger very honest. I will bide my time, and tell you more soon. For the rest, you may well believe, that, if the publishers didn't fear the critics, the world would know nothing of me. Perhaps it would be well for the world, although I am far too well pleased with the black thoughts that have been printed. I would also draw your attention to my sonata in F-sharp minor, and more especially to a concerto without an orchestra, just published by Haslinger. I should be glad to learn your opinion of them.

I have a new ballad by Chopin. I think it his most charming (not his best) work. I told him that it was my favorite. After a long and thoughtful pause, he said, with great emphasis, "I am glad: it's my favorite also." He also played me a number of new studies, nocturnes, and mazurkas, all incomparable. It is touching to see him at the piano. You would love him dearly. But Clara is a magnificent *performer*, and gives even more expression to his compositions than he does. Imagine the perfection of a skill which seems ignorant of its own power! We shall lead a glorious life this winter. Mendelssohn, David (a genius), Lipinski, *Liszt*, Clara; two series of concerts, two musical papers, twelve quartets; fine church-music; Stegmayer (alas! very lazy); Banck (a good song-composer); many others, who don't please me equally well. In short, they're wrong.

Write me soon, and as encouragingly as before. I need it. With cordial friendship, yours,

R. SCHUMANN.

14.

TO THERESA SCHUMANN.

L(EIPSIC), Nov. 15, 1836.

MY BELOVED THERESA, — How often I see you sitting in your wonted place at the window, your head on your hand, softly humming a song, perhaps doubting whether a certain R. deserves all the love bestowed on him! Of course you wonder why I neither came nor wrote. First, Chopin, Lipinski, Mendelssohn, the Carl,* Ludwig Berger, and a hundred other reasons. They came in rapid succession. If you were here, how much I'd show you! how many people you should see and know, very different from those of Zwickau! A young "Stamaty" has just arrived, who seems as if dropped from the clouds for my special benefit; a bright, remarkably handsome, cultivated, and thoroughly good fellow; born in Rome, of Greek parents, educated in Paris, and now completing his musical studies with Mendelssohn. You would like him much: we fully intended to come to Z. for the festival, but had to give it up. But he will be here till spring. So, if you don't see him at the fair, we will pay you a visit. German is very hard for him, which is all the better for my French. Then there is a young Englishman, William Bennett, in daily intercourse with us, thoroughly English, a splendid musician, and a poetic and beautiful spirit: perhaps I'll bring him too. Mendelssohn is betrothed; so is very much occupied, but great and good as ever. No day passes in which he does not utter at least two thoughts worthy to be graven in gold. His betrothed is called Cecilia Jeanrenaud, daughter of a Calvinist clergyman, and cousin of Dr. Schlemmer. He goes to Frankfort, at Christmas, to visit her. Dr. Schlemmer has at last — just think! — received a decoration from the Elector of Hesse. It's a good thing for him: I've long foreseen that he would not die undecorated. He is in Heidelberg, with Rothschild. David is to be married this week. . . . Besides these men, a rich and talented young fellow, Frank of Breslau, and young Goethe, grandson of the old one, but as yet insignifi cant, dine at our table.

* A charming singer of the day.

Here you have a faint picture of my life. I spent many pleasant hours with Lipinski. I think he loves me like a son: he has a lovely daughter of sixteen, a Pole. You can imagine how she looks. So one succeeds another. As for the Carl, who is now here, she's not much of an artist, and the newspaper gossip is intolerable. However, I like her: she's not a flatterer, speaks her mind, is perfectly well aware of her defects, has the old prima-donna manner, which doesn't become her ill, &c. But now for business and the prosaic part of my letter. My life for the last two months has re-acted so strongly on my purse, that I am obliged to ask a loan of Carl and Edward; and you must be my left hand, and help me. I shall require fifty thalers until the end of November, and fifty more till the end of December. Write, or let Edward write, this week if possible, whether he or Carl can send the hundred thalers or a bill of exchange. I might borrow elsewhere; of David, for example, — he placed his purse at my disposal; — but I shouldn't like to take it, except as a last resource, as you may imagine. So think of me! I hoped Edward would come, so that I might ask him myself; but he really has staid away a long time. Write and tell me how all progresses, — the dictionary, Carl, your new home, the sale of the business, &c.

I enclose a letter from Moscheles; please keep it carefully for me. I think of you daily with joy and emotion; I often feel as if I leaned on you, and felt your life.

Your truly loving   ROBERT.

(FOR YOU ONLY.)

C. loves me as warmly as ever; but I'm fully resigned. I often go to Voigt's. That's a matter of course. A wonderful thing, this life!

15.

TO THERESA SCHUMANN.

LEIPSIC, close of 1836.

What have I done to deserve such love, my Theresa? I danced round the Christmas-tree like a child as I saw one thing after another — and then the hair-chain! How good you are! and how thoughtless I am! Believe me, I haven't felt capable of writing to thank you. The whole day long I've been nailed to my study-table, and had a hundred things to do, many of which were very prosaic. Finally, I resolved to write to you, so that my good wishes should reach you on New-Year's Day. May they indeed be such, and sound as if from a loving brother! How much this year may bring! I often feel anxious. To stand upon the heights of time and vision, to assist others, to struggle, to be independent, — not to mention all the mental and secret relations, it often makes me feel faint and sick. Yet I receive so much love from mankind, that I can never hope to repay it. From you too: ah! remain my friend. In the torturing heartache which sometimes attacks me, I have none but you to shelter and support me. Farewell!

Your   ROBERT.

16.

TO IGNAZ MOSCHELES, AT FLOTBECK, NEAR HAMBURG.

LEIPSIC, Aug. 23, 1837.

You will receive herewith, most honored sir, two new and very different compositions. It will be child's play for you to decipher the Masquerade; and I hardly need assure you that the grouping and titles were written long after the music was composed. I hand you the Studies with more confidence. Some of them are still dear to me (they are almost three years old). You know how I value your opinion. Say a few words for my ear only.

I was as pleased as a child at Christmas with your Studies; but I have not yet heard any thing of the Sonata Pathétique.

Now a request, for music as much as myself. My urgent entreaties have at last moved the publisher of my "Journal" to insert some good composition every four months. I shall put all sorts of fine ideas into it, and it will make a stir among the musicians. Songs are also to be written, and the most interesting published in a volume, one or two bad ones with the rest, to give the critics some work, and make the reader follow, notes in hand. The manuscripts of talented and unknown composers will be preferred: your name would break the ice (the Journal has about five hundred readers, who would all receive the compositions gratis). From time to time we shall give old music, extant only in manuscript, such as Scarlatti's fugues and the score of a Bach concerto. I should be grateful to my friends for a set of lesser compositions: one might begin, the next examine piece and add another, and so on; the whole thus having that power which albums so generally lack. In short, I intend to do a great deal.

My next plan is to get *four Etudes by different masters*, the first of which will be ready by New-Year's Day, 1838. I am far too much interested in all your doings, honored sir, to fail to hope that you will give one of the studies from your second volume, to the Journal, before

Kistner publishes them. Such a name would induce confidence in the work, and the first step would be to victory. Chopin has promised me something. I already possess a study by A. Henselt, a most promising young composer, who would *truly* delight you. As to the fourth, I'm still in doubt as to whether it will be by Mendelssohn or by some one else.

Be so kind as to send me a favorable reply from the Continent; and, if you like my idea, perhaps you will send me one or more *études*. You would increase my debt, but my thanks as well.

I have just heard that Mendelssohn has engaged an English prima donna for our concerts. Can you tell me her name? perhaps Miss Clara Novello?

I should like exact information in regard to the missing numbers of "The Journal."

Hoping for a favorable answer,

I am, with true esteem, yours most truly,

ROBERT SCHUMANN.

17.

TO THE SAME, AT FLOTBECK, NEAR HAMBURG.

LEIPSIC, Sept. 22, 1837.

MY DEAR AND HONORED SIR, — May the knowledge that you have given a young artist, who often thinks himself alone on his rough road, fresh courage for work, reward you for so kindly hearing my requests! Your letter contains three words in regard to the character of my compositions, which never sounded half so sweet as when uttered by you.

You must overlook much in my style of notation. I really knew no other way of writing the three A-flats over one another: —

For  or

produces a very different effect. The high A-flat should echo very gently: so I knew nothing but

All that you said on the subject inspired me with the greatest joy. The Carnival was mostly written for a special occasion; and all but three or four movements are based on the notes A, S, C, H, which form the name of a little town in Bohemia, where I had a musical friend, and which, curiously enough, are the only musical letters in my name. I added the title afterwards. Don't you think the music speaks for itself? Estrella is such a name as one adds to a portrait, to hold it faster; Reconnaissance, the recognition; L'Aveu, love's confession; Promenade, a promenade, as at a German ball, arm in arm with your partner. The work lacks artistic merit: the various soul-states alone seem interesting to me. . . .

Let me heartily thank you for your kindness in sending a Study as supplement to the *Neue Leitschüft*. Dr. Kistner will by this time have written you that your twelve new Studies will be published before Christmas; and that the supplements, if they excite interest, will contain nothing previously published. Perhaps you would send me one of your minor compositions — an Etude, Impromptu, &c., three or four pages in length — from Hamburg. *It would appear before the new year, when the first compositions are to be given with "The Journal," and must be entirely new.* You will soon see a full account of the plan in the Journal. I need not repeat that it would be a very great favor.

I am also obliged to you for the reviews of last season. I shall certainly use them soon for the Journal.

You already know Mr. A. Gerke, the bearer of these lines. His modesty and sensibility endear him to all who know him.

Think of me, as very gratefully yours,

ROBERT SCHUMANN.

18.

TO THERESA SCHUMANN.

LEIPSIC, March 25, 1838.

MY DEAR AND FAITHFUL THERESA, — Had you read my last letter to Clara, you would have seen how hard it is for me to leave this place. Well, 'tis the will of Heaven, which will provide for the future. However, I think you'll accompany us to the wedding in Vienna; and then we'll spend a couple of weeks, in which we'll enjoy a year and more in happy memories. Besides, the separation is but comparatively great. Have we ever met more than once a year? and I hope still to visit you annually, especially as Clara's parents are to remain in Leipsic for the present. So be of good cheer — and, what we cannot say to one another, we will write.

Clara wished to write to you herself, — I told her she might call you sister, — to which she answered: "I would gladly call her sister; but sister needs one little word more, — that little word which brought us so close together, which made me so happy." She hasn't had time to write, having very little to bestow on me: so don't be offended with her. But she will certainly spend a few hours with you on her return from Munich. I will set the day another time. Then receive the noble girl as she deserves, for my sake; for, Theresa, I cannot tell you what a creature she is, — how she unites all qualities, and how unworthy of her I am. But I will make her happy. I can't speak of it: my feelings are too deep for words.

Call her sister when you see her, and think of me!

Now comes an important matter, in which I desire your aid and advice. Clara has won quite high rank by her fine performance of chamber-music. I, too, am honorably known, though not in equal degree.

For my own part, I'd be glad to die a musician, and know no superior but my art; but, for my parents' sake, I would fain become great. You know Hartenstein well;[*] and must write either to him or to Ida,[†] as follows: —

That I (you can give my name, or not, as you like and *think fit*) am betrothed to a certain maiden by the consent of her parents; and that they would be much pleased by a "Dr." before my name, which would speed me on my way. Now, I should like to learn, through Hartenstein's goodness, if many formalities would be requisite to obtain a degree from the philosophic faculty. I could not spare much time, being pressed by various professional duties. He would then tell you what steps must first be taken. I desire merely a title, and should then leave Leipsic. But there's no great hurry. If I only knew his opinion, I would apply in person for further information. Finally, ask if the Leipsic University ever gives the title of doctor of music. Earnestly entreat him or Ida to preserve the strictest secrecy, as it is to be a surprise. You women can do any thing. Whisper to Ida that she can thus serve an old acquaintance.

Yours truly,   R. SCHUMANN.

---

[*] Professor of the Leipsic University.
[†] His wife.

20.

TO JOSEF FISCHHOF.

LEIPSIC, April 16, 1838.

MOST HONORED FRIEND, — The form of your diary pleases me as much as it will its readers. Be so kind as to continue sending me news, especially in this way, even if I do not ask it every time I write: I depend upon it.

It's from selfishness again that I answer so quickly. In extraordinary cases I must also beg for extraordinary letters. This is on account of Liszt, of whom I expect speedy news from you.

Did I, indeed, invite myself so earnestly to your house for Vienna's sake? It can't be done so hastily; 'twould cost me much labor, both before and afterwards. Still the gods may grant it. I sometimes long for something new. I've been a fixture for eight years. My best thanks for your cordial invitation to visit you. I can hardly accept it· You would soon learn to know me, and be glad to get rid of me.

Then I shall receive your review in about three weeks. I'm much pleased with all the rest. I confess it's rather hard to express the idea of " musical transposition " clearly. I'll talk to Härtel. To-day is an Easter holiday, and all the shops are shut. What is the name of Palestrina's novelist? Did you really promise him admission into the Journal? I didn't want him.

I hear that Emminger has painted a life-size picture of Clara W. Is it the one from which the lithograph is taken, that is such a striking likeness? Pray answer this question; and also tell me, if you know, whether Haslinger is coming to our Easter fair *in person!*

Liszt knows but very few of my works. Show him some, with my regards, and ask him to answer the letter I wrote him at Milan. How much I should like to be with you!

Now a cordial farewell! A new work will be ready in a few days, "Kreisleriana." There's food for thought in it.

With thanks and friendship, yours truly,

R. SCHUMANN.

22.

TO J. FISCHHOF.

LEIPSIC, May 8, 1838.

DEAR SIR AND FRIEND, — My " Kreisleriana " are ready, and I hope soon to see them in print. Will you help me? It would take too long if I gave them to Härtel, who has published four large works this year. So I would offer them to Haslinger, through your kind mediation. The title is "Kreisleriana: Fantasies for the Piano. Dedicated to Miss Clara Wieck.* Op. —." And it would make eight or nine printed sheets; the price the same as for the Etudes Symphoniques; to be ready by Michaelmas (a chief condition; for, if not, I shall go to Breitkopf, who pays better).

I beg this favor as a friend. Do it at once, if possible, because I'll give the composition to Schott, if Haslinger hasn't time.

Most cordial thanks for your prompt reports. Liszt wrote to me himself. Has he gone?

Pauline Garcia and Beriot arrived yesterday: you will soon have them in Vienna.

Of many other important and interesting subjects, next time.

Don't forget to continue your diary; the form and concise opinions just suit me.

I hear Thalberg is among you again. Write and tell me if it's true. Would it do send him a copy of the Davidsbündler Dances or the Fantasies? I never saw him. How do you stand with him?

Hoping for prolonged friendship, I am with cordial regard, yours,

R. SCHUMANN.

Don't forget to note down your outlays for me (for music for Liszt). Don't you know any thing of Clara Wieck? We have lost all trace of her since she left Vienna. Farewell! dear friend.

23.

TO HEINRICH DORN.

LEIPSIC, Sept. 5, 1839.

MY DEAR AND HONORED FRIEND, — Your long-expected letter came quite late: I only got it ten or twelve days ago. It must have lain in Königsberg some time. I shall miss your letters to the Journal this year, and yet I see it can't be helped. Nor do I see how I can ask for more, after so many proofs of good-will and sympathy. If I do but gaze at your writing long enough, the old times rise up before me, and with them the admonishing, never-smiling, well-known face of my teacher; and then I know how I dare to ask so much.

I should be very much pleased if you could put me into your gallery,

* The printed edition of "Kreisleriana" is dedicated to Chopin.

for the world really knows nothing of me. You know why. Some-times a man imagines he can do without the world; but I rather agree with Jean Paul, when he says, "Air and admiration are the only things which man can and must unceasingly swallow." Yet I would not complain. I'm *really* happy in my art, and hope to labor *long*. Then there is one by my side to praise and to encourage — Clara; I may call her my betrothed. . . . I feel rather confused, as you may easily imagine; still I could conceal it from you no longer, since Clara has long known and loved me, as is well known to all. I feel sure of your sincere congratulations: the girl is one of a thousand, *and extremely good*. My music must bear many marks of the battles Clara has cost me: you must have understood them. The concerto, the sonatas, the Davidsbündler dances, the Kreisleriana, and the Novelettes were inspired by her alone. I scarcely ever saw any thing more awkward and shallow than Rellstab's review of the "Scenes of Childhood." He thinks, forsooth, that I set up a sobbing child, and sought for music in its tears. It's just the reverse. Still I do not deny that I had a few childish heads in my eye while composing; but the titles, of course, did not occur to me till afterwards, and are merely hints for the execution and conception of the music. But Rellstab can't always look beyond A, B, C: he wants nothing but accords. So, too, I am far from con-sidering B. Klein a great musician; L. Berger was far more creative in his little sphere. Set my mind at rest on the merits of the case by a couple of words.

I don't know whether it's proper to have any thing about myself in my own paper. It depends a great deal upon how it is done: people must know that I have the best of reasons for saying nothing on such a subject, &c. But I trust to your judgment and insight.

I always regard the essay on Novello with a sort of pang. I like it so much, it contains so many truths! — and yet you must know that the Novello is engaged to a dear friend of mine, — Dr. W., — who would never forgive me if I printed it. What do you say to that? Don't blame me.

Isn't your "Judgment of Paris" to be performed in Germany? Didn't you to send it to Ringelhardt? * Is it not to appear in print? Lortzing's opera is a success, almost inconceivable to me. Aren't you coming to Germany yourself? Leipsic has altered greatly for the better, through Mendelssohn's influence. The theatre begins to revive. Stegmayer has retired from the stage, and is in Bremen: his place is filled by an M. D. Bach, his opposite in every thing, — a man who never composed a bar of music. The old one is my daily Bible. Lühe is a

---

* Then manager of the Stadt theatre.

bookseller in Adorf, as perhaps you know. Harrwig has disappeared in Heligoland. In a word, nothing is as it was; still all is satisfactory. I must now write to Clara, who is in Berlin with her mother.

Send me soon a few sympathetic words.

As ever, yours truly,   R. SCHUMANN.

24.

TO JOSEF FISCHHOF.

LEIPSIC, Sept. 5, 1839.

MY DEAR FRIEND, — 'Tis hard to-day to begin, 'twill be harder yet to end; for where shall I begin and end, when I have so much to tell, — all that has happened since we parted? You always take such interest, that I'd like to tell you every thing, being sure of a kind and appreciative hearer. But I lack the time and quiet requisite for a detailed account, and so, accept these few lines in friendship.

You know the one thought that fills my heart and soul. What I have long feared and foreboded has come to pass. . . .

Clara has returned from P., and we're progressing. We shall be married by Christmas, at latest. Then my peace and happiness will return. I tell this to *you only;* and will you tell it to your dear mother and sister, of whom I always think with great affection?

I did not find my brother alive, as perhaps you already know. This loss entails much labor, the business being left without a head. But we found every thing in the best condition.

There's been almost nothing new in the musical world since April. Clara, who has been here for a few days, and went to Berlin day before yesterday with her mother, played to me much and wonderfully. That was a great joy, after so long a separation. I've composed nothing but trifles. In the Mozart album, which Conductor Pott is to publish, you will find a short Fughetta which pleased me much. I suppose you have the Mechetti matters and the Novelettes; my second Sonata will appear in a few days.

Now, favor me with one word soon, that is, one thousand; tell me how you do, and if you ever think of me. I am very grateful to you, and shall not forget it.

Have you heard nothing of . . . [illegible], and of Rössle, the Bohemian? What is the lady from Pesth doing? Where did you spend the summer vacation? What and whom are we to expect next winter? Will Liszt return?

Now, a trouble, and your frank opinion. Vienna has long been neglected in the Journal. I now know what life is there, especially with
you, and how hard it would be for you to find time for me. But I
must have a regular correspondent, and thought, — of course with your
consent, — of asking Carlo C. . . . [illegible], who seems to have plenty
of time, if he will undertake the office of regular correspondent rather
than mere reporter. If you don't approve, just tell me so. Perhaps
we might engage Carlo, and you would help me *too*, as much as your
time allowed. Write me your real, honest opinion.

One thing more: would Lenau consent to write a couple of introductory verses for the Mozart album? I think he would do it.

How does Walter von Goethe? If you see him, give him my regards
and thanks for his letter. I shall answer it soon.

Give my regards to Lickl . . . [illegible], Sulzer, *Hauser*, Streicher,
&c. . . . But enough; I hope for speedy news of you, and greet you in
cordial affection.

Yours,   R. SCHUMANN.

25.

TO KEFERSTEIN, AT JENA.

LEIPSIC, Jan. 31, 1840.

MOST HONORED SIR AND FRIEND, — I received your friendly letter
and its interesting enclosures this morning. I have only been able to
glance at the latter; the former I will answer at once, with a few grateful lines.

A long pause lies between this and my last letter, as also much joy
and sorrow, musical and mortal. When the editor has a holiday, the
composer takes his turn; and circumstances of a most agitating nature
have claimed much of my time and strength. So you must excuse my
long silence. I have often — dare I confess it? — doubted if you took the
same interest in the efforts of the junior portion of the musical world that I
once remarked. A remark recently made by you in a Stuttgart paper
confirms my suspicion. You said, " From Bach and Kuhnau we first
learn the source of Mozart and Haydn's music, but not where the new
generation get theirs." Such, at least, was the idea.* But I don't
quite agree with you. Mozart and Haydn knew Bach but partially, on

* Dr. Keferstein says that Schumann mistook his meaning.

single sides; and it is by no means clear how a more intimate knowledge of him would have affected their productions. But the deep combinations, poetry, and humor of the new school of music draws its inspiration largely from Bach. Mendelssohn, Bennett, Chopin, Hiller, and
all the romanticists (I mean the Germans) approach Bach much more
nearly than Mozart; for they all are thoroughly acquainted with
him. I myself bow daily before this lofty spirit, aspiring to purify and
strengthen myself through him. Then Kuhnau, honorable and delightful as he may be, should not be ranked with Bach. Even had Kuhnau
written the Well-tempered Clavichord, he would be but the hundredth
part of Bach. In my estimation, Bach is incomparable, incommen-
surable. No one (Marx excepted) has written of Bach so well as my
old Zelter: * he, usually so gruff, grows gentle as a coaxing child when
he speaks of Bach. But enough: pardon my writing to you what
would better befit my " Journal." You are right about the Berlin man:
he was very saucy. Still, if you knew his music, you'd judge him more
mildly. He is one of the most dauntless geniuses I ever knew. Didn't
you say Beethoven's theory of counterpoint was compared with Bach's
in that review? I don't exactly remember.

I am sorry you receive "The Journal" so late. It contains a great
deal that ought to be read and profited by at once. I should like
another contribution from you. The honorarium is two louis-d'or per
printed page. Becket, the organist, tells me that you wrote him "that
the Journal was to be given up." That will never be until the force
of circumstances obliges me to resign the post of editor. On the contrary, the Journal gains influence every year, and has such a position, that the loss of one hundred subscribers would not affect it at
all.

And now one private prayer: I know no one more kind or better
informed than you, to whom I may apply. But promise me, most
honored friend, that you will tell no third party.

Perhaps you know that Clara is my betrothed . . . Clara's illustrious
position as a musician often makes me think how petty mine is; and although she is not ambitious, and loves me simply as a man and musician,
still I think it would please her could I attain higher rank, in a municipal sense of the word. Permit me to ask: Is it difficult to become a
doctor in Jena? Should I have to pass an examination? and in what?
To whom ought I apply? Would not my position as editor of a paper
(which has been established for seven years), my position as a composer, and my constant effort after truth, assist me to obtain this title?

* Herman Hirschbach.

Tell me your *candid* opinion, and grant my request to observe strict silence on the matter.

. . . .

Feel ever kindly towards me, and gladden me with a speedy answer. Yours most truly,

R. Schumann.

Perhaps you haven't seen my new compositions, — " Kreisleriana," a second sonata, Novellettes, " Childish Scenes " ? I'll send them to you if you'll write me.

———

26.

TO KEFERSTEIN.

Leipsic, Feb. 8, 1840.

Most honored Sir and Friend, — Did not the season forbid, I should be charmed to burst in upon you in reply to your friendly lines, to receive the old care, to tell you this and that, and all the events of my troubled life. The tale would be both joyful and sorrowful, as I hinted in my last letter. Clara delights me both by what she now is, and what she is yet to be to me. . . .

The academic dignity of doctor is only desirable under one of two conditions; namely, that I become worthy of it through some future work, or that the diploma be granted me as an author and composer. The former would be the more difficult, the second the more useful and pleasurable to me. Give me some good advice. I know but little Latin; but feel fully capable of a good German disquisition. I am now preparing an article on Shakspeare's relations with music, his judgment, opinion, the way in which he introduces music into his plays, &c., &c.; a most rich and beautiful theme, whose elaboration will, of course, require some time, as I shall have to read all his works. But, if you consider such a task unnecessary and unsuitable, ask, for Clara's sake if not for mine, if the diploma cannot be given as a reward of my earlier efforts. I take the liberty of sending you, for this purpose, a series of essays by me and by others on me,* such as I have been able to collect hastily. I also enclose a few diplomas, and will send later, if required, a certificate of good character from the authorities, as well as the *curriculum vitœ*, and the customary fees of which you spoke. Will you go to the dean once more, and say a good word for me; per haps tell him of my position in the musical world, and, for it is r.ɟ

———

* I do not own that in Schilling's Lexicon : perhaps you can add it.

longer a secret, my relation to Clara, . . . and that this title would be of great service to me just now, when the public talk so much and so confusedly about us. In a word, to conclude, I wish, not only that people should say I have become so and so, but a reason must be given in the diploma. I heard that an eminent divine of this place was recently given a degree in your city in a similar way, merely by paying the fees. Is this so?

And now comes the question, in case I win the diploma by an essay or otherwise, would it make me a doctor of music? I sLould, of course, prefer it. Give me, if you please, some information as to the manner in which the diploma, however gained, would be drawn up. Rest assured of Clara's and my thanks, which we hope soon to be able to express in person, if you do not visit us in our new home previously.

Clara, to whom I have just sent your last letter (she is in Hamburg with her mother), will certainly answer it, and thank you for the kind way in which you spoke of her. She is just what you depict her, a rare creature, who embraces many fine qualities.

I hope to refresh your memories of me in some slight degree by the enclosure. Examine the picture with a friendly eye. It is not a perfect likeness, though drawn by a master of his art; a proof that even a master may fail. Still, I think he has caught my characteristics. Hang me up, but not near the criticising D.D.'s of this place and Stuttgart, — rather by Sebast. Bach, whom I should so like to have heard play the organ. Well, I'm beginning to dream.

Most hearty greetings from yours truly,

R. SCHUMANN.

On other subjects of your letter soon. The fees for the Journa are my affair. Perhaps you'll draw up a contract, which I will sign and seal.

Send me something for the paper soon.

27.

TO KEFERSTEIN.

LEIPSIC, Feb. 29, 1840.

MOST HONORED FRIEND, — Every thing conspired to fill my cup of joy. The eulogy was so glorious that I never can thank you enough for it. It has given me and my friends the deepest satisfaction. The first thing I did was, of course, to send a copy to my maiden in the North, who is still a perfect child, and will jump with joy at the idea of

15

being a doctor s bride. She will write, and thank you herself, but will send picture and letter from Berlin, where all her things now are. She will probably give up the journey to Copenhagen, in which I was to join, because she has a horror of the sea. Still we may go yet. At any rate, I shall see you soon, and what hours those shall be! — dreaming at the piano with you; but I need not tell you this.

Let me again thank you for your intercession, trouble, and speed. Friendship has wings, too, as I now learn, and hope you will trust to mine, if you ever wish to try them. I shall write a few lines to Counsellor Reinhold myself; the letter he enclosed with the diploma was most friendly.

I enclose a contract with "The Journal." I look forward with delight to an article from you. As you have read Becker's "Household Music," pray oblige us by a short notice of it, — say one column in length. I wish it to be short: first, because Becker is a regular correspondent; and, second, because a great part of the book has been printed in the paper. I have not spoken to him for some time: I will send him your review as soon as I receive it. I hope to be able to show you some of my songs soon: Breitkopf and Härtel have just published a number. It is too contemptible of Fink never to have mentioned a single one of my compositions for nine years,* although they have always made such an impression that it was almost impossible to overlook them. It does not trouble me for my own sake, but on account of their influence, which I know to be that of the music of the future. There's much good in the New Romanticist; but the composition is most feeble. . . . You can easily obtain the second part. The author † would be glad to send you the whole book if you would favor him with a brief notice in "The Journal of Literature." Be so kind as to tell me what number of that paper contains the account of the doctorate, as I do not read it regularly.

. . . .

Cannot you tell me something more definite about the plan of the academy at Weimar? This is the first I have heard of it. Is it connected with Lobe's Institute?

Write to me soon, and believe me, yours truly, who for the first time signs himself,

DR. R. SCHUMANN

---

* The nine years were really seven, as is proved by " Allgemeine Musikalische Zeitschrift," then edited by Fink; but this is long enough, and quite inconceivable.

† Julius Becker.

29.

TO KEFERSTEIN.

LEIPSIC, Aug. 24, 1840.

MY DEAR FRIEND,— Many thanks for your encouraging report, and your kindness in allowing me to enjoy it. I have constantly hoped to visit Jena this summer, but was obliged to change my plans. Clara has gone from Weimar to Bad Liebenstein, near Eisenach, to visit her friend, Emilie List, who unexpectedly wrote her thence. She will remain there for some weeks, until our marriage, but will stop nowhere on her return; so I shall not go to meet her in Weimar, passing through Jena. Nothing (thanks to a higher power) now prevents our marriage, as you feared. Our banns were published yesterday for the second time, and I listened in silent ecstasy. Clara is also perfectly happy, as you may imagine. All our trials now seem trifles. She wrote me with great pleasure of her visit in Jena at your house: the honors you paid her deeply delighted me. Your article is a new proof of your friendly feeling. Some things in it, particularly in regard to myself, seem to me (don't take it amiss) too enthusiastic. If the article bore the signature of its kind author (which I could not expect of you in your situation), I should have no scruples. But the public are rather suspicious of anonymous enthusiasm, and imagine there's some good friend in the case; and if this is so, for you are a dear and valued friend, the public require the name, that they may be able to trust and believe. However that may be, *your* sympathy gladdens my heart: I hope my future works may, at least, not lessen it. If you wished to bestow public praise upon Clara and me, the Frankfort Journal would be a good place. Still, I fear the editors take too little interest in strangers. Try them, dear friend. If they won't take your article, I would propose "The Evening Journal," or, still better, "The Journal of Elegance."

I am, to tell the truth, too proud to wish to influence Fink through Härtel, especially as I hate any quickening of public opinion by the artist himself. Any one who is really meritorious will succeed. Do not think I am deaf to solid, skilful criticism, but an artist should not trust to himself for it. Clara agrees with me, much as encouragement pleases her, and she *really needs* it. She often has inexplicable attacks of melancholy, for which I have to scold her well.

But enough. Let me assure you, as I hardly need do, that I am most happy in the present, as well as in my hopes of a blissful future. I had to praise the journey to St. Petersburg in glowing terms to Clara; or else she declared she would go alone. I believe she'd be capable of it, in her disregard of appearances, where our welfare is concerned.

You must excuse me from telling you how *unwilling* I am to leave my quiet home. I can't think of it without distress, but dare not let Claia know it. However, 'twill be good for her: tender as she is, she is strong, and can endure as much as any man.

Farewell, then, my dear friend. Write to me soon again. I will tell you speedily the day of our marriage.

With cordial greetings, yours, ROBERT SCHUMANN.

30.

TO CARL KOSZMALY.*

LEIPSIC, Jan. 8, 1842.

Enclosed, most honored friend, you will find the fee for your contributions to the last (15th) volume. If possible, that for the "Marschner" shall soon follow. I received *that* and your letter punctually. The general observations make the article peculiarly interesting. I can't quite agree with your opinion of Marschner. Still, your reputation will defend it. Marschner deserves respect; and, for my part, I'm glad to give it to him. Perhaps he's preparing for new labors. Let me ask one favor: I'm going away shortly for two months, in consequence of our invitation to a philharmonic concert in Hamburg, at which my symphony will be given, and of course my wife goes with me. Thence we shall go to Bremen, and, perhaps, farther north. So I must collect as much manuscript as possible; and beg you will send me whatever you have, this month. Franz Schubert deserves a friendly word. Doesn't that attract you? To be sure, his greatest works are unpublished. Still, his songs and piano compositions form an attractive picture. Think it over. Do you know his Symphony in C? A glorious work, rather long, but remarkably spirited, and *entirely novel* in character Try to become familiar with it.

I am very glad you wish to perform my Symphony. It does not exist in score, but the first violin part contains pretty nearly the course of the whole. I reserve a few hints until later. The two orchestral works, a second Symphony and an "Overture, Scherzo, and Finale," which were performed at our last concerts, were not as successful as the first. It was really too much for one time, I think, and then they missed Mendelssohn's direction. But it's no matter. I know they are not at all inferior to the first, and must succeed sooner or later. I am much pleased to hear that you are coming here this summer. I shall certainly

* Now living, and working as director at Stettin.

be here. Bring some new compositions. I *surely think* Mendelssohn will return to Leipsic this winter. Dear friend, he is the best musician the world now has. Don't you think so? An extraordinary man, or, as Santini said at Rome, a *monstrum sine vitio.*

Now I have chattered enough, and have much to do to-day. So, *addio!* for the present. Be cheerful and courageous, and believe in the regard of your friends, among whom you must not forget to reckon me.

ROBERT SCHUMANN.

34.

TO CARL KOSZMALY.

LEIPSIC, Sept. 1, 1842.

DEAR FRIEND, — Your letter came late, but was as ever welcome. Much in it pleased me much, especially that you should take my remarks so kindly. Many lovely thoughts lie buried in you, worthy to be spoken or sung; may they not sleep too long in head and heart!

I hope the future, when I mean to do more than ever, may confirm your opinion of me. Much in my past career gives me cause to rejoice; but there's nothing there, to compare with the prospects which open before me in happy hours. Do you know my morning and evening musical prayer? It is for *German opera.* There is work for you. But the symphonies must not be neglected.

I have read most of your diary, and was pleased to see that a good, practical artist always peeped from behind the philosopher, and *vice versâ.* You are perfectly right about the "Opposition Party." Unfortunately the article is not adapted to my paper, since Christern's would have to be printed too, which would be laid to the score of vanity. You said something about receiving offers from Schmidt of Vienna. If you like, I'll send the review to him, and will try to get the article from "The Telegraph," and enclose it. Write me what you wish. This brings me to a petition. We (my wife and I) made an excursion, a short time ago, to Bohemia, and among other places to Königswart, where Prince Metternich was. He received us most graciously, and promised his protection in a very friendly manner, if we should visit Vienna. This quite pleased me. Now, I should like to have the people there know somewhat of my compositions, and should specially like my first symphony, and perhaps one other, performed. The Viennese are ignorant people, and, on the whole, don't know much which goes on outside of their own city. However, they are well known in the musical world, and a favorable reception there would be most advantageous to me. Will you not introduce me and my symphonies by an article in Schmidt's paper. In that case, I will send you the piano score à *quatre mains*, and, if you wish, the whole score. The review must be published by October, because if we go we must start in November. Write me a friendly yes, if possible, and let me thank you in advance for it. We parted with gloomy shadows, which have often made me laugh since. Now bright ideas and images have returned, and your letter confirms them. I hope mine will do the same. I would like to stand before you as often and as clearly as you do before me; pray take your pen in hand, and tell me you wish it too.

Your truly loving,   R. Sch.

35.

TO CARL KOSZMALY.

Leipsic, May 5, 1843.

My dear Friend, — There won't be much in this letter: an itinerant band is blowing and howling beneath my window, and there's much confusion in the house; to-morrow there's to be a christening (our second girl), and still I must write to you, because you always think so kindly of me. Thanks for your lovely songs. I won't tell you my opinion until I can do so in "The Journal," which will be soon. Do have some more printed, and come to Leipsic yourself. Nobody knows any thing decided about the changes at the theatre. I hear that Dr. Schmidt is to be director; I know him slightly, and will certainly mention you to him in due time.

The period during which we have not met has been most fertile. Couldn't you have the three quartettes I have just published performed in Detmold? I wish you could. I shall soon publish a quintette for piano, &c., a similar quartette, and many other things. At present I'm busied with a great work, the greatest I ever undertook. It is not an opera: I really think it's something entirely new to the concert-room. I shall put all my strength into it, and hope to complete it in the course of the year.

With some timidity I enclose a parcel of my old compositions. You will easily perceive how immature and incomplete they are. They are mostly reflections of my agitated youth, the man and musician in me strove for simultaneous expression. It is so, even now that I have learned to command my music and myself better. How much joy and sorrow are buried in this little pile of notes! Your sympathetic heart will soon discover them.

I'm sorry I can't find a copy of the piano compositions, which I consider my best. They are, "Kreisleriana," six Fantasias, Novelettes in four parts, and Romanzas in one part. These four are my last piano compositions (1838): still the earlier ones will give you a picture of my character and my struggles; for the germ of the future often lies in such attempts. So judge them kindly with all their faults. I can say no more.

These things are but little known, for simple reasons: first, from their innate difficulty of form and contents; second, because I am no performer, so could not play them in public; third, because I edit one journal, so *cannot* mention them there; fourth, because Fink edits the other, and *will* not mention them. But things have altered. The public, I hear, now take greater interest in my works; and the later works — the "Kinderscenen" and fantasias, which I'm sorry I can't send you—have been most successful. Times have altered in other ways also. Once I was indifferent whether people cared for me or not; but, when a man has a wife and children, it's another affair. Then he has to think of the future, — wants to see the *fruits* of his labors, not the artistic, but the prosaic, matter-of-fact fruits, which can be brought and increased only by fame.

Now, don't call me vain, if I send you these old things, which I outgrew long ago, and thankfully accept your kind offer to say a few words about them. I always despised an artist who sent his trash fresh from the press to all the editors, as fast as the post could carry it. But why say all this? You know and understand me.

My works, I think, give food for reflection; and it will be easy for you to write a couple of columns on them. As Härtel published most of them, he would be much gratified by a brief notice in your journal. As these early works are to be brought before the public, perhaps it will be vell to state that none but the first four have been alluded to in any paper br ten years. I think it would do to write your article independently, ind not in the usual style of reviews; but do as you like, dear friend. When you have waded through this first heap, I'll send you, if you wish, a second (my lyric period), and perhaps the symphonies, and my last chamber-music.

Let me say once more, that the compositions in the two bound volumes and the rest are arranged in the order in which they were written, — the Variations and Papillons, 1830, up to the Concerto, 1836. Those not bound are as follows: Fantasies, 1836; Davidsbündler dances, 1837; second sonata, 1835–38; Kinderscenen, 1838; the rest, 1839.

Here you have my confession. You will discover without my aid that Bach and Jean Paul exercised a marked influence over me in my younger days. Now I am more independent.

I send this parcel with my best wishes. Please accept, as a remembrance from me, whatever pleases you among the single pieces.

Write to me soon. Yours,

R. SCHUMANN

36.

TO HEINRICH DORN, AT COLOGNE.

DRESDEN, Dec. 1, 1845.

MINE HONORED FRIEND, — Verhulst tells me that you spoke to him with interest of my "Peri," and perhaps thought of performing it in Cologne. I need hardly tell you how much pleased I should be to hear my music echo through your venerable city and under your wings. "The Peri" is to be performed at Elberfeld, near here, Dec. 6; and they want the orchestral parts that I sent you. Perhaps you may want to use them yourself; and *in that case* I beg you to write a few words to Mr. F. W. Arnold of Elberfeld, telling him whether he shall send you the vocal parts or not; *if not*, please return the rest to me, through Mr. Arnold.

If you would also write a few lines to me, I should esteem it a mark of friendship. As I have been ailing for almost a year, it would be doubly welcome to me.

With ever-increasing attachment, yours,

ROBERT SCHUMANN

37.

TO FERDINAND HILLER, AT DRESDEN.

[Undated. LEIPSIC, Jan. 2, 1846.]

DEAR HILLER, — We are all well and happy, and wished you could have been here yesterday. All went well. But we hardly see our various acquaintances yet: we must keep perfectly quiet for some days Clara needs rest. We hope to be back in D. by Tuesday at latest You'll let my wife off from playing at your concerts for the present won't you? You know how glad she'd be to gratify you; but it would be too much for her just now; even yesterday quite knocked her up.

I'll tell you every thing when we meet. The life and people here interested us as much as ever. Sooner or later, I really think we shall return here to live.

David will come to the fifth concert. Has he written to you? I have not yet inquired about the Mayer,* but will do so to-day.

---

* Then prima donna at the Leipsic Stadt Theatre.

Pardon my bad writing, but I've had little rest to-day.

Farewell! Remember us to your wife and cousin, and think of us often.

R. SCHUMANN.

Härtel is to publish the concerto; Kistner, the overture, &c.

38.

TO HEINRICH DORN.

DRESDEN, Jan. 7, 1846.

MOST HONORED FRIEND, — I've just returned from Leipsic, where I spent a fortnight, and found your kind letter on my table. The orchestral parts of "The Peri" will be sent you from Elberfeld, if your offer to perform it in Cologne in the course of the winter is favorably received. If not, be so kind as to inform Mr. Arnold of Elberfeld, so that he may return the score to me.

You cannot imagine how much we want to hear your symphony here; but our concerts are but the germ of a goodly tree. We have only six this winter, three of which are past, and not a Mozartian nor any new symphony at them. At the last three we are to have, as previously decided, Mozart's C-major, the "Weihe der Töne," and Gade's symphony. So, even with the best intentions, 'twould be vain to propose any thing else to the directors.

I wish you could hear Wagner's "Tannhäuser." It is deep, original, and a hundred times better than his earlier operas, although there's much trivial music in it. On the whole, a great thing may be made of it on the stage; and I know he has plenty of courage. I consider the execution and instrumentation remarkable, — incomparably finer than any thing he ever did. He has another libretto ready, "Lohengrin."

Hiller gives a great concert to-morrow for the Weber Memorial. He was very busy all summer.

My wife has just published a set of fugues. I should like you to see them, as well as my Pedal Studies. I hope you won't find them quite unworthy your pupil. You will soon hear of many new things by me.

Our cordial regards. May you ever think of us kindly!

Yours truly, ROBERT SCHUMANN.

39.

TO CARL REINECKE, AT LELÆ &

DRESDEN . . . 22, 1846.

DEAR MR. REINECKE, — I lacked time to send you a letter yesterday, so write a few lines to-day. I read your compositions with great
interest, and liked much in them, — the rare cleverness and the noble
aims revealed in them. But you must not deceive yourself into thinking that you can produce any thing perfectly new, or avoid the frequent
repetition of recollections and prefigurations. At your youthful age
all creation must needs be mere reproduction; just as the ore must un-
dergo many cleansing processes before becoming pure metal.

The best culture for an individual melodious mind is to write a great
deal for the voice, for an independent chorus, and, above all, to conceive
and shape mentally as far as possible.

Look forward with joy to your future, but do not forget the pianist.
Skilful execution is a great thing when it is the means of representing
truly artistic work.

Continue to take an interest in me and my compositions. I feel real
pleasure in your . . . [illegible] musical conception, and your fiery and
energetic execution; also in those of your friend and comrade. Don't
forget to remember me kindly to Mr. Grabau, Königslöw, and Wasie-
lewsky.* I hope to see you again soon.

                        Yours truly,   R. SCHUMANN.

40.

TO FERDINAND HILLER.

[Undated. About the middle of 1847.]

DEAR HILLER, — To our sorrow, you left so suddenly that we had not
time even to say farewell; but I will, at least, send it after you. You will
be sure to return from the baths well and strong. We and all your
friends were disturbed that you had to go alone; still, it will restore that
healthy self-reliance, which is the best physician.

We are not very well. Clara is still very weak, as I often am also.
Perhaps the little journey which we're planning will restore our health
and strength.

---

* They gave a concert in Leipsic during Schumann's stay there, at which
among other things, they played the master's three string quartetts, Op. 41.

The text for the opera is progressing slowly but surely. A good, kind man is our R., but frightfully sentimental; and he has a most powerful model of his subject in Hebbel (you know we chose Geneviève). For the rest, I'm charmed with my subject, and think you will approve.

I have also just finished a trio, which I consider very good. You shall hear it when you return, with another composed a few years ago, and one by my Clara.

If any thing occurs in regard to your opera which would interest you, I will write. Only arrange to be present at the rehearsals, and write to us if it won't be too great an effort.

Clara will add a few lines, so accept my hearty good wishes, regards, and thanks for your friendly interest.

Yours truly,   R. Sch.

41.

TO FRIEDRICH HEBBEL, AT VIENNA.*

Dresden, May 14, 1847.

Highly honored Sir, — Pardon the liberty which an utter stranger takes in introducing himself to you, with a request whose fulfilment depends on you alone, and would be a great pleasure to the petitioner.

After reading your Geneviève (I am a musician), I was struck, not only by the poem, but by the thought that it would be a splendid subject for music. The oftener I read your tragedy, which is unrivalled, — I can say no more, — the more vivid and musical did the poetry seem. At last I consulted a gifted poet resident here, and, surprised by the extraordinary merit of the poem, he at once consented, at my request, to alter it into a libretto, to the best of his ability.

Two acts now lie before me: the last two I shall soon receive. But, good as my assistant's intentions may be, I am ill content with the result: it lacks power, and the ordinary style of librettos is repulsive to me; I cannot and will not provide music for such tirades.

Finally, in a fit of despair, it occurred to me that the straight road was best, — that I had better apply to the poet, and beg him for aid. But do not misinterpret me, honored sir. I could not expect you to re-write, as an opera, what you have already seen in its deepest and inmost sense, and converted into a masterpiece; but that you should look it over

---

* Schumann's letters to Hebbel were published in "The New Journal of Music," in 1859, vol. 50, p. 254.

give me your opinion of it, and merely give a touch to it here and there
— such is my heart-felt prayer.

Is it vain? Is it not your own child who begs your aid? And, if it
comes to you robed in music at some future time, I could wish you to
say, " Thus, too, do I love thee." I also read " Judith." The world is
not so wicked, after all. When such poems as " Judith " and " Geneviève " are written, we are far from ruin.

An answer, if you will deign to honor me with one, will find me here.
If it brings a yes, I will thank you to the best of my power; if not, at
least you can reckon me among your most sincere admirers, and grant
me an opportunity to prove it.

> Believe me, dear sir, most truly yours,
>
> ROBERT SCHUMANN.

42.

TO FRIEDRICH HEBBEL, AT VIENNA.

DRESDEN, June 28, 1847.

HONORED SIR, — The completion of the libretto has been somewhat
protracted. We have stumbled upon difficulties which we did not foresee. Now it will hardly be ready before your arrival (the end of July,
you said). On the whole, perhaps, it's better so: we can arrange matters more speedily when we meet. Will you be so kind as to notify me,
directly you arrive, that I may visit you; and, if you need a guide in
this strange city, pray take me. Also allow me, if your wife accompa-
nies you, the pleasure of presenting to you my wife, who remembers
her in Hamburg. My doubt that I was unknown to you as a composer
was a fancy with which I punished myself for never knowing you until
this year, and your " Judith " and " Geneviève " have existed for years,
— bright stars which should be familiar to all, — and I am comparatively
new.

But now, if I have the pleasure of seeing you, we shall be strangers
no more; and " The Diamond " will have done its work. That, too, for
contemplative comedy and natural freshness is unique in German
poetry.

Pardon me if I say something not becoming; i.e., something very
flattering of your poetry: but many hands are ready to award you the
crown for the loveliest, loftiest work; so let the musician also add a leaf.

> Yours most truly,   R. SCHUMANN.

43.

TO GUSTAV NOTTEBOHM, AT VIENNA.

DRESDEN, July 29, 1847.

DEAR NOTTEBOHM, — My writing may not be quite unknown to you. 'Tis long since we met; but I've thought of you often, and hope you've done the same by me.

First, in all brevity, the cause of my letter: I see by the papers that there is a vacancy in the directorial staff at the Conservatory. The place is one which I should much like. I feel my strength suffices, and long for active life. But I would not seriously sue for it until I know all the duties, so you must lend me a helping hand; and I know you will, for I well remember your former interest in me.

The chief thing, therefore, is that you mention *my name* to no one, but give me all possible information respecting the re-occupation of the post. I should also like to know why Preyer resigned, who will decide at the election, whether a committee of the association, and who compose that committee; also to know who has already petitioned for the place, and what is the common opinion, and that of the musicians, in regard to it. In your inquiries, however, as I said before, please keep my name a secret.

You can obtain information on all these points from Fischhof, A. Fuchs, or Likl. I should have written Fischhof myself; but I think he generally goes on a journey at this season, so I feared he would receive my letter too late. But, if he is in Vienna, don't tell him I have written to you. I will await your reply.

Be so kind, dear Nottebohm, as to take an interest in the matter, and write to me soon; for, as the post must be filled by the first of October, there's no time to lose.

This is all for to-day, and egotistic enough, nothing else. More soon. I wish and hope that these lines may find you well and happy.

Yours,   R. SCH.

44.

TO HILLER, AT DÜSSELDORF.

DRESDEN, Jan. 1, 1848.

DEAR HILLER, — You shall receive the first letter of the year, and also the first petition for pardon for my long silence to your friendly lines. But since you went away I've had and done much work; but of that hereafter.

There's little news to tell. There are to be three subscription-concerts in the opera-house, but the pangs seem fearful. Wagner wants to bring out a short time ago: he doesn't look well, but will soon return to "Lohengrin."

We went to Bendemann's for the Christmas holidays: they were all well but Hübner, who has been ill for some time. We often think of you, especially at the "Liedertafel;" which gives me pleasure, and urges me on to work. Mr. Bartheldes sent me your "War Lyric:" we have not sung it yet. I, too, shall soon publish three patriotic songs; look them up.

The chorus-club, too, is becoming a reality: the 5th of January is the first meeting. There are now a hundred and seventeen members; that is, fifty-seven active ones, and the rest passive. All this keeps me very busy. My strength increases with my work,—I see it clearly; and, if I can't keep myself perfectly well, still it's not so bad as a close inspection of trifles often leads me to suppose.

Then, I've been very busy musically: I can't tell you how, until I see my labors are drawing to a successful end. Would you could feel quite at ease in your sphere of action! You will not lack pleasure and praise for your work.

You will soon receive the music of "The Peri." I was very much amused to hear that it was to be performed in New York.

. . . .

Receive the dear child, whose growth you have watched, kindly Have you asked about your opera in Berlin? and aren't you thinking of a new oratorio? Write to me soon again. My wife will add a few words.

Remember us to your family, and think sometimes of yours truly,

R. SCHUMANN.

45.

TO CARL REINECKE AT HAMBURG.

DRESDEN, June 30, 1848.

DEAR MR. REINECKE,—I was very glad to hear from you again, and that you are again in our neighborhood. Let me hasten to say that I was very much pleased with the notes; and, did I not know that you liked many of my compositions, I must have learned it from your remarks. On the whole, I am, as you may suppose, no friend to song-transcriptions; and Liszt's are, for the most part, abominable. But I felt quite easy in your hands, dear Mr. Reinecke, because you understand in as but few do: you only pour the music into another vessel, without peppering and spicing it, *à la* Liszt. So I like your work, and thank you heartily for it.

To come to particulars: "The Lake," excellent; so is "The Lotus-flower." More hints for the execution, and use of the pedal, you will, of course, add later, as in the solo songs. "Liebesbote" pleased me much, as far as the passages marked with a red cross: I should like them simpler. The "Serenade" sounds very lovely. At the cross, I think the harmony should be on G: $\frac{7}{4}$ The variations on the last page seem too hard. "Am Rhein" pleases me from beginning to end. But "Sonnenschein" is not simple enough to suit me, nor do I like the *finale*, if you will excuse my saying so. I think the close of the melody in the dominant should be kept up throughout. The succeeding passage is excellent again. You must re-write "When first I saw thee." It has not taken root in my heart. For the sake of completeness I would fain see that done.

Of the songs for four voices, I prefer "The Minstrel" and "Frühlingglocke." What do you mean to call them? Settle all securely with Mr. Sch., for if not we may be surprised in some way!

I'd like to have a look at the proof-sheets, and set to work at revising them immediately.

I prefer the four-part songs altered into duets (for female voices) rather than solos; but then there must be some transpositions. I enclose a letter from my wife to Miss Parish. Give my special regards to that amiable lady.

About a fortnight ago I sent you a new trio, through Whistling. Did you get it? It would please me to know that it harmonized with your feelings. I almost think the first movement will.

We had the closing scene from "Faust," with an orchestra, last Sunday, for the first time here. It was given to a very small audience. I thought I should never finish it, especially the concluding chorus; but I've enjoyed it greatly. I'd like to have it performed in Leipsic next winter, and perhaps you will be there then.

I'm sorry to say that I have read nothing but the announcements of your new compositions: the music-dealers here never keep any thing good on hand. Write me soon of your works and plans. Rest assured of my deep sympathy.

Yours truly,   R. SCHUMANN.

46.

TO GUSTAV NOTTEBOHM, AT VIENNA.

DRESDEN, July 3, 1848.

DEAR FRIEND, — I've thought often of you of late, and that these exciting events might alter your plans for the future: Vienna and Berlin, as you yourself say, are no homes for a musician now. Here all is externally quiet; but even Dresden, seemingly so indifferent to politics, cannot long resist this universal commotion. Of course you will leave Vienna while you can; it looks dark for a good musician, unless he be an impostor or a millionnaire. Would there were also a revolution in your musical maws; but the "Neue Zeitschrift" sets a bad example, and the papers are always full of anecdotes of mediocre performers, never saying a word about the workers. It's truly pitiful.

I'm glad to hear from you of your labors. I, dear Nottebohm, have been awfully busy. A week ago we gave the scenes from "Faust," to my great pleasure. I think the general impression more powerful than that of "The Peri." Of course, that's owing to the poem. I have also published the trio of which I wrote you. Then the score of my string quartette, a birthday present from Härtel, delighted me. At last I can say that my opera makes rapid progress, and that, with Heaven's help, I hope to finish it this year.

My wife and children are well. So I have every cause for content and gratitude.

Write to me soon, and tell me your decision, and be ever assured of my cordial sympathy.

Yours truly,   R. SCHUMANN

47.

TO FRANZ BRENDEL, AT LEIPSIC.*

DRESDEN, July 3, 1848.

DEAR FRIEND, — Being pressed for time, I borrowed an introduction for the last scene in "Faust" from Deyk's book. Do you approve? The performance went off excellently well (in private); the general impression struck me as good, superior to "The Peri," the natural result of a better poem, which challenged me to greater exertion.

---

* Schumann's letters to F. Brendel were published in the "Neue Zeitschrift für Musik," in 1858 (vol. xlviii. p. 184), and are inserted here by the permission of the recipient.

I shall be very glad to perform the music to my friends in Leipsic, and earnestly hope to do so early in the winter. My most ardent wish is to be told that the music explains the poem. For I fear the reproach, "Why write music to such consummate poetry?" At other times I felt, since studying these scenes, that they needed music's gracious aid. Well, you'll soon be able to judge for yourself. Consider the above confidential, and say nothing about it in "The Journal."

I owe you many thanks for the music you sent me, especially "Palestrina." It often sounds like the music of the spheres; and, then, what art! I think he's the greatest musical genius Italy ever produced.

My clubs give me great pleasure, especially the Choral Club. We are now singing Beethoven's "Missa Solemnis," *prima vista.* Thus we shall, at least, become clever; and I like to have them follow through thick and thin. But we study when necessary, as in Gade's "Comala." Dear Brendel, I think the Leipsic people rated this work too cheaply. It certainly is the most important of recent creations, — the only one worthy of laurels. How's "The Journal"? I'm glad it still holds its own in the foremost ranks. Who is the Magdeburger (?) of whom I read in the last number? Franz is very nicely characterized, as he has many good and beautiful traits. I would question the accounts of Meyerbeer and Gade: the one is too much honored, the other too little. However that may be, the author shows knowledge, rare power of intuition, and true and warm interest in the condition of art. Who is he? And who is Dörffel? I read his article on the symphony with great pleasure, only I thought he was too much impressed by the Leipsic performance of the *finale.* If he heard it now, I surely think he'd be better satisfied. With many kind remembrances,   R. Sch.

48.

TO CARL REINECKE.

DRESDEN, Oct. 4, 1848.

DEAR MR. REINECKE, — But two lines to-day, and a full reply to your letter, received to-day, with proofs, as soon as possible.

"The Album," especially from No. 8 onward, will, I think, win many a smile from you. I don't know when I felt so in the mood for music. It fairly gushed forth.

Now a confidential communication: I asked Schuberth fifty louis-d'ors. If you think it too high for his means, tell me so candidly. But, if Sch. himself don't think so, so much the better.

My wife, as well as I, beg you will hurry matters as much as possible, since Christmas is very near.   Yours,   R. Sch.

49.

TO CARL REINECKE.

DRESDEN, Oct. 6, 1848.

DEAR MR. REINECKE, — I did not receive yours of Sept. 19 until Oct. 4. So you see how difficult communication is. Write me, please, how I shall send the songs and proofs; through Mr. Schuberth's publishing-house, in Leipsic? or as before? I found but very few mistakes, and liked "Sonnenschein" far better. I think we might class it among the songs for male voices, transcribed for the piano (as in "The Minstrel").

The songs for male voices couldn't have been transcribed better for two sopranos. I've only altered a note here and there. I think "Die Fraümende See" would sound best in soprano (transposed to F-major). Perhaps you'll do it.

Accept many thanks for the trouble and labor bestowed on these elder children of mine. The younger, too, — born day before yesterday, — plead for your sympathy. Really one always loves the youngest best; but these are peculiarly dear to my heart, and truly belong to family life. The first thing in "The Album" was written for our eldest child's birthday; and in this way one after another was called forth. It seemed as if I were beginning my life as a composer anew, and you'll see traces of the old humor. They're decidedly different from the "Kinderscenen." Those are retrospective glances by a parent and for grown folks; while "The Christmas Album" contains foreshadowings, presentiments, and peeps into futurity, for the young.

But why tell you all this? — you who dive so deeply and sympathetically into my music. You will understand the meaning of these little things better than any one else, and get on their right side.

I applied to Mr. Schuberth to publish them, because haste is necessary, and because I think that he always succeeds when he likes. And I will answer for it that this won't be a bad bargain; for I think these will be the most popular of all my compositions. "The Album" must have a handsome exterior. Tell Mr. Schuberth, that as soon as he decides to publish it, and has chosen an engraver in Leipsic, he must tell me the latter's name, so that I can arrange with him in person, as I shall be in Leipsic next week for a few days.

At first, I thought of having an illustration to each *morceau;* but, as I said before, Christmas is too close at hand for that. We must have a handsome titlepage, at any rate. I think the engraving must be small, as in "the Kinderscenen," and edged round with neat arabesques, not all round, but in each corner.

Tell Mr. Schuberth my ideas, as far as you see fit; and beg him, if ne does not accept my manuscript, to return it *by post*, as soon as possible, so that I may find another publisher without delay.

When are you coming to Leipsic? I shall be very glad to spend a few weeks with you there, as I expect to be there for some time in January to settle about my opera. Then we'll make music to our hearts' content, and play your symphony and concerto, I hope.

Remember us to Mme. Peterson, and accept our hearty good wishes for yourself.

Please let me know, by return of post, if you receive "The Album" all right, and what luck you have with Schuberth.

Yours,   R. SCH.

50.

TO C. REINECKE.

DRESDEN, April 9, 1849.

DEAR MR. REINECKE, —I return the manuscript with many thanks. "The Saraband " * is an old favorite of mine, which I've played dozens of times. But let me tell you one thing: I always thought the execution should be *forte* (marked and forcible); and the character of the other Sarabands strengthened this opinion. Ask some musician. It's clear you wrote the variations for the love of it. You are particularly easy and happy in the twists and turns of the canon. But the general impression is by no means satisfactory, on account of the brevity, and, if you won't be offended, the commotion of the *finale.*† It would also be well if the theme were broader. Think it over. The chief *motif* must, of course, remain; but the 4-2 time must, in any case, be altered to *alla breve* C.

Many passages are not full and round, but that can't be helped.

The third variation looks rather curiously, especially in the first measure, which really belongs to the second variation. Wouldn't you rather begin the 2-4 measure with

I advise you to put the variations away for a couple of months, and then give them a finishing touch.

---

* A Bach Saraband, on which C. Reinecke wrote variations, published as Op. 24.

† It was changed as Schumann wished.

Of the Myrtles, I particularly like, —

1. " Widmung."
2. " The Lotus-flower."
3. " Du bist wie line Blume."

In which I can find nothing to change.

'The Nut-Tree" also pleases me as far as the place marked with a red cross, which would sound better an octave lower.

" The Bridal Songs" are very effective; only I'd like to get rid of the prelude in the 2d. I don't like the transposition of the melody to a lower octave in the song from the " Orient Roses; " and you must make " The Highland Lullaby" perfectly simple. It will be much more effective.

The two " Venetian Songs" are, I think, the least suited to the piano. They are too short; in fine, not worth the trouble they'd give the pianist (between ourselves, it's the composer's fault).

Here you have my candid opinion, and mustn't be offended at it. You know how precious I esteem your interest in my compositions.

Now, we must try to string the songs together in the prettiest order, being specially careful not to change the key too quickly and curiously. I shall ask Mr. Senff to revise them when the time comes, as you may tell Mr. Schuberth. Many disagreeable things still remain to be done.

Pardon these hasty lines. I'm just going off on an excursion.

With hearty regard,   R. Sch

51.

TO FRANZ BRENDEL, AT LEIPSIC.

[Easter, 1849.]

DEAR BRENDEL, — Young Mr. von Bülow asks for a couple of lines to you, which I gladly give; for he is a very good pianist, and also a cultivated man, who improves on closer acquaintance. I beg you will receive him kindly. My opera, or rather its performance, is to be put off as long as possible by the intrigues of the resident musicians. So some one wrote me; but I don't believe it. Even if it's true, it'll be all the better in the end. Honesty is the best policy; and, you know, I mean honestly and uprightly by music.

These few hasty lines are all to-day. Sooner or later, I hope we shall meet.

Yours,   R. Sch.

I liked your article on public taste very much, and also the arrangement of my symphony; only I was sorry Gade was forgotten.

51.

TO FERDINAND HILLER.

DRESDEN, April 10, 1849.

DEAR HILLER, — It's long since you heard from us, and I can no longer delay sending you a greeting.

We hear of you occasionally through Reinecke, that you and your wife have been well, and that you're always happy and busy. The same is true of us, dear Hiller, with but few exceptions. Both of us have worked and composed all winter to the best of our ability.

My Choral Club (60–70 members) gives me much pleasure. I can have what music I like performed. I've given up the male Choral Club. I found too little real musical effort among them, and I thought I wasn't suited to such fine folks as they were. M. D. Otto has resumed the direction.

I think I've helped young Ritter's progress. His nature is decidedly musical, though as yet undeveloped. I don't know whether he'll do something great, or vanish without a trace. He needs incessant guidance.

Now I've told you of all your friends here, for whom I must again thank you. The "Leidertafel" especially has restored my sense of directive ability, which, in my nervous hypochondria, I thought was lost for ever. I feel quite at home.

I hear most favorable accounts of your symphony from all quarters. Unfortunately, there's no hope of having any thing new here. You know how it is. The sloth is greater than ever.

Reinecke also told me that you played one of my symphonies. Isn't it the second? I'd like to hear what you think of it. If your opinion is printed, an exchange of ideas is always beneficial to the future.

I have been very busy for a long time: this has been my most productive year, — as if the external storms drove men to greater mental action. I found it nought but a counterweight to the frightful war without.

Of course you know my "Album of Youth." Don't you like it? The publisher says it found speedy circulation. I shall soon publish a church composition for chorus and orchestra (from Rückert's text); a set of songs in canon for male voices; two sets of compositions à quatre mains; a set of fantasias for piano and clarionet; an Adagio and Allegro for horn and piano; a couple of sets of ballads for chorus singing, which sound very well; and a little while ago I wrote a concerted piece for four horns, with full orchestral accompaniment, which I consider one of my best works; then, I finished my opera last year, and hear it is to be brought out in Leipsic after the fair. In short, I can but be grateful that I have had such strength for work in these terrible times.

But enough for to-day. May these lines find you safe and sound. Remembrances to your wife, and let us hear from you soon.

Your friend,　　　　　R. SCHUMANN

52.

TO FRANZ BRENDEL, AT LEIPSIC.

DRESDEN, Sept. 18, 1849.

DEAR FRIEND, — All that I've read on "Faust" from your pen has given me the utmost pleasure. The external result was evident to me before the performance. I never expected any thing else. I knew very well that the music would meet certain wants. I was not satisfied with the closing chorus as you heard it; the second arrangement is, as you know, far preferable. But I chose it because the second arrangement was not written out. If it were repeated in L., I should, of course, prefer the latter. I shall certainly write something more from the first part of "Faust."

You are wrong about ——. He is an honest artist. I have proofs in plenty. He has always shown the greatest interest in my efforts; and he would not be what he is if he did not. For an artist who refuses to recognize the struggles of his best contemporaries may be considered good for nothing: —— is the only exception to this rule.

I don't understand the want of recognition, from which I'm said to suffer. The opposite is more true. Your "Journal" gives many proofs of it. Then I have proofs, which, though prosaic, are very convincing such as the publishers' eagerness to buy my works, and the high value they set on them. I don't like to talk of such things; but I may as well tell you in confidence how, for example, "The Album of Youth" has found a better market than almost any recent work: I have this from the publisher himself; and the same is true of many of my songs. And what composer is there, all whose works spread with equal rapidity? How excellent Mendelssohn's "Variations in D-minor" are! Yet I think they're not a quarter as well known as his "Songs without Words." What composer is admired by all? What *sacro sanctitas* of a work is acknowledged by all, even the greatest? Indeed I have worked, tooth and nail, for twenty years, regardless of praise or blame, to earn the name of a true servant of art, striving for the highest aim. But is it not a satisfaction to see one's works mentioned, as you and others often mention mine? And, as

I said, I am quite satisfied with the recognition hitherto bestowed on me in abundance. Shallow, mediocre men always talk in a way unworthy notice. Don't do any thing about the opera just yet. I am most grateful to you for your kind intention.

You can have your music at any time. Write me whether I shall send it to you, or keep it till you come. Doesn't Mr. Kistner send you his publications? Then I will. I have not yet, I think, written any thing else in the style of " The Spanish Vaudeville." I was very happy while I worked on that. I wish you could hear it sung by four lovely voices, as we hear it here.

Friendly regards from yours truly,

R. SCHUMANN.

53.

TO MORITZ HORN, AT CHEMNITZ.

DÜSSELDORF, April 21, 1851.

HONORED SIR, — From the press of business, I have been unable to answer your letter until to-day. The poem * is most certainly suited to music, and I've already thought of a host of melodies for it. But it must be greatly curtailed, and made much more dramatic. But this is only as regards the music; for I am far from criticising the poem, as a poem.

I have taken the liberty to note down a few alterations, such as I considered necessary, on the enclosed slip of paper. Up to the words, —

> " And offers up a friendly prayer
> For shelter," . . .

it is all fit for musical adaptation. From there onwards the action must be developed more briskly and dramatically.

If you conclude to alter a few things for the sake of the music, I shall take great pleasure in setting your poem to music. It is so fresh in my memory, that the sooner you begin these alterations the better. If you choose to print the poem, the present form could be retained, and these words be added to the composition: " *After* a poem by," &c.

Let me recommend this to your kind consideration. I should like to begin at once.

Will you be so good as to give Mr. —— my best thanks for his letter? and accept many yourself for making me familiar with this charming poem.

Yours most respectfully and truly, R. SCHUMANN.

* The poem is " The Pilgrimage of the Rose."

54.

TO M. HORN.

DÜSSELDORF, May 3, 1851.

HONORED SIR, — With many thanks for your present, I make the following suggestions. It would be well to dramatize No. 4 of the Second Part into a terzette or quartette, perhaps as follows: —

> *Grave-digger.* Upon this linden bench, &c.,
> My child, thou shalt be glad.
>
> > [Four lines.]
>
> SOLO. *Rosa (alone).* The long-awaited bliss
> Of knowing some true heart, at last I find, &c.
>
> > [Four to eight lines.]
>
> TERZETTE OR QUARTETTE.
>
> *Grave-digger (calls from the house).* Come in, little girl!
>
> *(Greeting from the people of the mill, and joy over the pretty child, with a short relapse into sorrow for their lost daughter.* ROSE *is taken as foster-child.)*
>
> > [Twelve to sixteen lines.]

After this, No. 5, as in the original. Let me also say that short sentences (verses of one line) are best adapted to the quartette.

And one remark about the closing song: "O Spring! so fair, with welcome bare," &c. I understand it perfectly as a poem, and that it outshines the whole; but the *finale* is ill suited to music, as it now stands. It is best to close with a chorus. Couldn't you bring in something inspiring?

If you could send me the mill-scene first, I should like it. There's no hurry about the closing chorus. I meant to do a part of the work this month, and much is already completed.

Pardon these hasty lines.

> Yours truly,　　　　R. SCHUMANN.

55.

TO M. HORN.

DÜSSELDORF, June 9, 1851.

To-day, honored sir, I am at last able to answer your last friendly letter. I have been very busy with "The Rose." It has made great progress. I shall yet make many claims to your aid, especially in regard to the end. How would it be to introduce an angelic chorus after Rosa's death? Rosa is not changed to a rose again, but to an angel.

> "Not to thy blossom bright,
> But up to higher light
> Thou soar'st aloft," &c.

The gradation — rose, maiden, angel — is very poetic, and hints at that doctrine of transmutation of being to a higher state, which we all cling to so fondly. This would destroy those barren reflections which I so disliked at the end. I would we could talk this over. Perhaps you will understand what I mean. The whole idea could be given in twelve lines.

. . . .

I hope you won't take my criticisms ill, and will soon send some sign of your interest in

Yours truly,   ROBERT SCHUMANN.

POSTSCRIPT. — Something has just occurred to me. Many parts of "The Rose" have received a lyric form in composition; so they would gain much if it could be *repeated* (at least in part). It would be a good excuse for singing the same words over twice; but it would be very hard for you to find new verses for such peculiar pieces. Still, perhaps, you'll feel disposed to try. These parts are, "The Elfin Chorus," —

> "Little sister, in the human heart,"

as well as the whole of —

> "Hast thou wandered in the wood?"

and "The Wedding Song," —

> "In the miller's house, let shouts resound."

Not only the size of the verse, but, if I may say so, the *punctuation* also, must be the same as that of the first verses; so that the repetition may agree with the music. Finally, I require for the song, "Midst verdant trees, wavy curls and snowy breast," another verse of four lines, in which the description of the idyllic mill must be elaborated.

The verse, "But in the house," must be omitted, and the new stanza immediately ensue, "By the gray-haired man conducted," &c. I would particularly like this latter stanza: there's plenty of time for the repetition of the longer parts.

SECOND POSTSCRIPT. — One more question and request. We shall probably visit London in July: and I should very much like to have

"The Rose" performed here *previously* to a small audience. If you cannot complete the alterations and additions in time, of course we must do
as well as we can without them.   Now the other question, — couldn't
you come to Düsseldorf for this performance?   I will let you know the
date, and we should be glad to have you stand godfather to the charming child.

Perhaps you can come.   Yours truly,   R. Sch.

57.

TO MORITZ HORN.

Düsseldorf, Sept. 29, 1851.

Honored Sir, — You will think me very ungrateful.   Your "Rose"
was performed some months ago, and you will be surprised that I did
not tell you at the time.   It came to pass thus.   We have no good tenor
here, so I had to ask a gentleman of Cologne * to take that part.   He
did not give me a decisive answer until two days before the performance, so that it was not possible to send you word.   To be sure, I might
have written after the performance, — might have told you of the favorable impression which the piece produced.   But we went shortly after
to Switzerland for a long visit, and afterwards for a few weeks to Bel-
gium, so that the summer passed away, and my debt was still undis
charged.   I hope all this will excuse me in some measure.

As for the composition, it went off very well.   I originally composed
nothing but a piano accompaniment, which I thought perfectly adequate
to the fanciful subject; but I have been urged by friends and acquaintances to arrange the piece for instrumentation.   Undeniably, the composition would thus be made available to larger circles.   But this instrumentation would be quite a task, and I could hardly do it in less
than two months; added to which, my time is at present taken up by
a multitude of things.   In fine, I hardly think I can prepare it for the
press in less than a year.   For this reason, I have made no arrangements with a publisher; but this must not deter you from giving your
"Rose" to the public as soon as possible.

As it seems of the utmost importance to me, that you should become
acquainted with the text as arranged for my composition, I have had it
copied, and enclose it.   I have no doubt, that, in an independent edition of
your poem, you would, for the most part, remain true to the original

* Ernst Koch, a well-known tenor of Cologne.

text. At any rate, I shall be interested in seeing the poem, as prepared for the press by you, before its publication.

Please be kind enough to return the enclosed copy at your convenience. It is not yet quite correct. But more on the subject, another time.

Sha'n't you have some new poem to send me soon? It would please me much.

Hoping for friendly remembrance,   R. SCHUMANN.

58.

TO M. HORN.

DÜSSELDORF, Nov. 21, 1851.

HONORED SIR, — Being overwhelmed with work, I can only say briefly that I am busily arranging "The Rose" for instrumental performance, and hope it will be performed with an orchestra by the end of January. I've enjoyed the task much, although rather doubtful about it at first. You shall certainly know the date of performance in time to be present, as I earnestly hope you will be.

"Hermann and Dorothea" * is an old favorite of mine: hold it fast. Please let me know when you're ready to begin, that I may tell you my ideas in detail.

I would like you to return the text I sent you, that I may complete and polish it; since it seems advisable, taking your permission for granted, to have the words printed, so that the audience may follow the performers.

Pardon the haste of these lines: I have a great deal to do to-day.

I hope to hear from you soon on the subject of "Hermann and Dorothea."

Yours truly,   R. SCHUMANN.

---

* M. Horn some time previously imparted to Schumann his plan of altering Goethe's poem into an opera. Schumann was delighted, and wrote to Mr. Horn, Dec. 8, 1851, as follows: "I've had no time to collect my ideas about H. and D., but hope you will reflect whether it can be so treated as to fill up a whole evening. I doubt it. There can be no talking in an opera, of course, you know. It must be treated in music as in poetry, in a simple, national, German style I hope you'll stick to your plan."

59.

TO M. HORN.

DÜSSELDORF, Dec. 21, 1851.

MOST HONORED SIR, — "You came late — but you came." A tedious nervous attack unfortunately caused my long delay in answering. For the first time in many weeks, I feel better. Accept kindly "The Rose," which I suppose you received long ago. The titlepage is a masterly design.* I like it very much.

It would give me great pleasure to convert "Hermann and Dorothea" into a concert-oratorio. Tell me something more about it.

I have just finished an overture, as I believe I wrote you.

Has "The Rose" been performed in Chemnitz? Be so kind as to write me soon of your new poetic labors.

Yours truly,   R. SCHUMANN.

60.

TO DEBROIS VAN BRUYCK, AT VIENNA.

DÜSSELDORF, May 10, 1852.

HONORED SIR, — Accept my sincere thanks for your very gratifying letter. It gave me double pleasure, as coming from a region where my efforts have taken little root. I only feel that you extolled my early works too highly; as, for instance, the sonatas, whose defects are but too clear to me. My later and longer works, such as symphonies and choral compositions, are more worthy such kind recognition. It would please me to have you hear the labors of my riper years, and confirm my opinion.

Your remarks on Vienna I know to be true from personal experience. Yet, I'm always attracted thither, as if the spirits of the great departed masters were still visible, — as if it were the special *habitat* of music in Germany. It is not impossible that we may revisit Vienna. I should be charmed to do so; but some time must elapse ere it can happen, and perhaps you may, meanwhile, carry out your plan for exploring the Rhine, where there's plenty of good wine, and, if I may say so, plenty of lovers of good music.

I should prefer to speak with you of the musical works of which you wrote me, — writing is always so clumsy. Accustom yourself — suppos-

---

* By Theodore Wintrop of Düsseldorf.

ing you have been otherwise accustomed — to think out music freely in your mind, without the aid of a piano. In this way only will the mental fountains flow, and gush with ever-increasing clearness and purity. You must write, as I said, but little. The most important thing is, for the musician to refine his inner ear.

I hope you will keep me posted as to your musical plans, present and future, and rest assured of my sympathy for your efforts.

Yours truly,   ROBERT SCHUMANN.

APPENDIX.

APPENDIX

APPENDIX.

COMMUNICATIONS

BY DR. RICHARZ OF ENDENICH, NEAR BONN, CONCERNING ROBERT SCHUMANN'S ILLNESS AND DEATH.*

I GLADLY consent, at your request, to tell what I know of Robert Schumann's illness and death. I shall begin with the results of the post-mortem examination as a fixed, objective basis; give a brief account of the chief symptoms of his last illness, and an explanation of its character and course. I shall speak of no abnormities but those of the brain; all others being unimportant, and irrelevant to your purpose. It may be interesting to know that the transverse folds marking the edge of the fourth cavity of the brain (the roots of the auditory nerves) were numerous, and finely fashioned. The following abnormities were revealed, in an ascending scale of importance, according to their genetic consequence: —

1. Distended blood-vessels, especially at the base of the brain.

2. Ossification of the base of the brain, and abnormal development of the normal projections, as a new formation of irregular masses of bone, which partially pierced the external (hard) covering of the brain with their sharp points.

3. Concretion and degeneration of the two inner (soft) coverings of the brain, and unnatural growth of the innermost (vascular) covering and the rear portion of the cerebrum.

4. A considerable consumption (atrophy) of the whole brain,

---

* Contributed to the biography at my express request.

which weighed almost seven ounces (Prussian troy-weight) less than is usual in a man of Schumann's age.

These four points stand in close connection with his physical condition for many years: as a whole, they indicate serious disease, which first took root in early youth, gradually increasing with the growth of the man, and not resulting in madness for a long time. The course of this disease is clearly marked throughout his life, especially by the difficulty of enunciation apparent for some years before his death, which is usually one of the first consequences of this condition of the brain. One of the chief external causes of this disease is excessive mental exertion; we might call it intellectual extravagance, — a danger to which all artists, particularly musicians, are very liable. There is no doubt that Schumann induced this disease by over-work. The brain, like any other organ, when over-taxed, is at once distended by a rush of blood proportionate to the excess of labor, for a certain time, and to a certain degree. But this produces swelled blood-vessels, impoverished blood (causing ossification), concretion and degeneration of the tissues: further results, over-growth of the innermost (vascular) tissue and brain, incapacity of this tissue to fulfil its function of blood-conveyer to the brain, diminution of nutriment for the brain, and final consumption thereof.

In this organic disease of the brain there is always more or less appearance of idiocy or gradual decay of the intellectual powers, which in Schumann's case was not developed for some time. The spirits, *as a rule*, are light, although occasional fits of depression may intervene.

Not so with our great tone-artist: his organization was such, that his mental infirmity was stamped by intense melancholy, such as is seldom witnessed in similar cases. Instead of the strange gayety, idle self-satisfaction, and shallow optimism, which usually bless and delude the patient in such diseases, the innate fervor, peculiar reserve, and contemplative nature, which were his in health, became the key-note of his mental discord, changing to melancholy, depression, sad forebodings, secret delusions, depreciation of his claims and merits, refusal of the homage due him, and final infection of his whole frame.

This melancholy, which never abated during his illness, must have been the product of a great fund of primitive mental power, as it existed when the opposite condition generally occurs. Quiet and persistent melancholy in this disease is the expression of a struggle against that faintness which presages idiocy. But the poetic aroma of holy melancholy floats like a breath from the past around every great and glorious exemplar in art and in the world. Think of Beethoven!

Melancholy preserves in the sick man a higher knowledge of himself, but often of his illness also : it disfigures the primitive personality less, but entails a mood less congenial to disease than gayety, which robs the patient of all consciousness of disease, even when his corporal and mental powers are but too evidently declining; also investing him with a mood in horrid contrast to reality, deeply painful to an observer, because it is often but a mere caricature of the former man.

This melancholy also rendered possible the apparent improvement of Schumann's health in the spring of 1855, which, however, could not deceive an adept as to the continuation of the worst symptoms, and the true value of this favorable change in outward aspect; for, before the catastrophe at Düsseldorf, he was, seemingly, as well as ever.

This melancholy is also closely akin to the hallucinations which were at first almost solely confined to the ear (such as the hearing of voices, words, and set forms of speech, whose importance was in proportion to their illusory nature), but finally extended to the organs of smell and taste on increasing weakness, and, towards the end of his life, reached the highest degree in *these* organs, being long over in the ear.

Finally, melancholy, although a mark of rare powers, hastened the death of this honored master : for while excitement in this disease, in spite of the rapid decline of the higher organic powers, disturbs their vegetative side but little, the case was here so far reversed, that the mind, and all the instincts, tastes, and habits connected with it, held out in a comparatively great degree until his death, although constantly sinking; but the common physical organs struggled vainly and laboriously against the burden of melancholy imposed upon the nervous system, and failed rapidly from lack of nutriment, thus producing death by extreme emaciation.

A.

BIOGRAPHICAL NOTICE OF CLARA WIECK.

CLARA JOSEPHINE SCHUMANN, *née* WIECK, was born in Leipsic, Sept. 13, 1819. The first years of her life flowed quietly by, without revealing her great talent, which in later years, when fully cultivated, won her a European fame. At first, indeed, it seems that she was not considered to be especially endowed by Nature, since it was very hard for her to learn to talk, which, difficult though it may be in a certain degree, never checks the growth of artistic talent. In her fifth year she began to study the piano, whose unequalled mistress she was yet to become. She was taught by her father's judicious method; not progressing head over heels like some wonderful children, but developing quietly, gradually, and thus all the more surely. After the lapse of four years, she had so far advanced as to assist for the first time at a public concert. This occurred Oct. 20, 1828, at a concert given by a pianist by the name of Perthaler, from Graetz, with whom she played four-hand variations by Kalkbrenner. In the musical society of her father's house, which was a rendezvous for all the distinguished native and foreign artists, Clara found the desired opportunity to form and increase the talent so happily developed. In this respect we must especially notice the lasting influence which Paganini's presence in Leipsic, in October, 1829, exercised upon her.

Besides piano-playing, Clara soon tried her hand at compo

sition. In her eleventh year, she stepped before the public as a concert performer. Her father took her upon a small concert tour, thus preparing her for the longer journey which she soon made to Paris. In Paris she gave several concerts,* also playing in large private companies, where she acquired the fame which decided her fate, receiving equal applause wherever she played ; while in Germany, especially in her native city of Leipsic, her talents had met with but slight recognition. Her sojourn in Paris, although it lasted for several weeks, was cut short by the sudden appearance and fearful increase of cholera. She then returned with her father to Leipsic, and resumed her musical studies with the utmost zeal, not only studying technique under her father, but also theory, which she began at the age of eleven under Cantor Weinlig, continued with M. D. Rupsch, and completed under H. Dorn's instructions. She was not contented with the study of harmony and counterpoint; but she worked industriously at the art of instrumentation, and reading from score. She even studied for some time violin-playing under the direction of Prinz, then a well-known violinist, and afterwards singing, under the celebrated and lately deceased Mieksch of Dresden, in order to acquire as much general knowledge as possible, — both at her father's request. She made other concert tours in company with her father, in 1836–38, to Berlin, Breslau, Dresden, Hamburg, and Weimar, when she introduced Chopin's works to the German people, and everywhere achieved the most extraordinary triumphs by her admirable efforts. In January, 1839, she went alone, by Nuremburg, Stuttgart, and Carlsruhe, to Paris, returning to Germany in August of the same year. The following winter, she gave concerts in several cities of North Germany

---

* J. J. Fétis contradicts this statement in his " Biographie Universelle." He says that he can find no notice of these concerts, either in the " Revue Musicale " or the " Universal Journal of Music." He therefore assumes that I have confounded two different occasions. This notice of Clara Schumann is from her father's dictation, — a source, which, in this particular case, is probably more reliable than the journals quoted by M. Fétis.

with equal success. With this she closed her early-begun and illustrious career as Clara Wieck, to re-appear with Robert Schumann, whom she married in September, 1840.

B.

FRANZ LISZT ON R. SCHUMANN'S IMPROMPTU (OP. 5), SONATA (OP. 11, F-SHARP MINOR), AND CONCERTO WITHOUT ORCHESTRAL ACCOMPANIMENT (OP. 14).

From the Gazette Musicale for Nov. 12, 1837.

No. 46.

FRANZ LISZT wrote as follows in a letter respecting his motive for writing this review: —

. . . "After the interest and excitement occasioned by my review of Thalberg in the Parisian 'Gazette Musicale' (whose meaning, by the way, has been entirely misrepresented), which was echoed in the German journals and parlors, Maurice Schlesinger, then owner of 'The Gazette Musicale,' visited me, requesting that I should write a very eulogistic review of any recent musical phenomenon for his paper. For months, Schlesinger sent me for this purpose all sorts of novelties; among which, however, I was unable to find any thing praiseworthy, until at last Schumann's Impromptu in C-major (properly speaking, variations), his 'Sonata' (Op. 11), and the 'Concert sans Orchestre' (afterwards published in the second edition under the more appropriate title of 'Sonata in F-minor'), fell into my hands while at Lake Como. On playing these pieces through, I at once perceived what musical merit they contained; and although I had never before heard of Schumann, nor did I know how and where he lived (since I had never been in Germany, and he was quite unknown in France and Italy), I wrote the review, which appeared late in 1837 in 'The Gazette Musicale,' and was shown to Schumann. Soon after, when I gave my first concerts in Weimar (April and May, 1838), he wrote to me, and sent me a manuscript called ' Germany's Welcome to Franz Liszt.' " *

PIANO COMPOSITIONS BY MR. ROBERT SCHUMANN.

Works of art may be divided into three different classes, — three styles in some degree opposed, corresponding to the three ideas of *éclat*, extent, and duration, whose re-union forms complete celebrity. There are some which the breath of popularity takes up, whose expansion it protects, and which colors them with most vivid hues; but like April flowers blossoming at morn, whose frail petals are crushed at eve by the north wind, these works, too much caressed, fall and die at the first sign of justice from a contemporaneous posterity. There are others long hidden in the shade, whose veiled beauties are only visible to the watchful eye of him who seeks lovingly and perseveringly, but which the fickle and absent crowd pass coldly by. Others again, happy privileged, at once lay hold of the sympathy of the masses and the admiration of the critics. In respect to these, criticism is almost useless. It is superfluous to record beauties universally felt: it is almost seditious to seek out faults, which, after all, are nought but the imperfections inseparable from human handiwork.

The musical compositions we are about to speak of belong to the second class. They do not strike us as destined for great success; but, to make amends for this, no cultivated mind could fail to perceive at a glance their superior merit and rare beauty. Without stopping to consider whether Schumann belongs to the *new school* or the *old school*,—to that *just starting* or to that whose *work is over;* without pretending to classify and number his artistic worth as species and specimens are classed in a museum of natural history, — we shall merely say that the works of which we propose to make a hasty analysis entitle their author to rank high among the composers, or pretended com

* No. 2 of the Novelettes.

posers, who swarm at the present day. We accord to few men
the honor of considering them as founders of schools, or inventors
of systems; and we regard the present use of great words and
phrases in relation to small things and people a *deplorable abuse*.
Therefore, without giving Mr. Schumann the *brevet of inventor*,
which he would be the first to discard, we would draw the attention of musicians to the works of this young pianist, which,
of all the recent compositions known to us (Chopin's music
alone excepted), are the most remarkable for individuality,
novelty, and knowledge. When Chopin's second collection of
studies is published, we shall take occasion to examine his
works as a whole, and show the great progress which he has
made. At present, we will confine our remarks to three of Mr.
Schumann's works, — "Impromptu upon a Romance, by Clara
Wieck" (Op. 5); "Sonata" (Op. 11); "Concerto without Orchestral Accompaniment" (Op. 14), — the only ones we have
thus far been able to procure.

Jean-Jacques said that he could write excellent impromptus
at his leisure. Mr. Schumann's could not have been written
otherwise than very leisurely. It abounds in new, harmonious,
and rhythmic combinations : we refer especially to pages 4, 8,
9, 10, and 19. As a whole, the impromptu up to a certain
point may be considered as belonging to the same family as
Beethoven's variations in E-flat major upon a theme of his
heroic symphony, and his thirty-three variations upon a theme
by Diabelli, itself a work which proceeded from thirty-three
variations in G, by J. S. Bach. The last work by Beethoven
would hardly be popular now : it owed its birth to a caprice
of this man of genius, to whom Diabelli, his publisher, one day
handed a theme, requesting him to be kind enough to add his
variation to those given him by most of the celebrities of the
day, — H. Herz, Czerny, Pixis, and others. Beethoven, as we
all know, was not of a prepossessing disposition : his austerity
was hardly redeemed by his natural shyness. Taking the book
from the hand of Diabelli, — who was already covered with confusion at his severe glance, — "You don't suppose," said he, " you

cannot think, that I would join my name with those of all these scribblers;" and, with these words, he turned his back on him. A few days after, the music-dealer's door was opened suddenly: a thin hand cast a huge manuscript upon the desk; and Beethoven's voice uttered in a more terrible tone than usual, "You asked for a variation; here are thirty-three: but, for Heaven's sake, leave me in peace for the future."

The title of the Sonata (Op. 11) is wrapped in a mystery, which might seem affected in France, where poetry and eccentricity are too often confounded in the same reprobation. In Germany, the case is different: the public does not take umbrage at an artist's fancies. It knows that we must not cavil at him who produces, and that, if the work is fine, we should respect the sentiment or caprice which inspired it. The beginning of this sonata is solemn, simple, and sad. We should say, were not the comparison rather ambitious, that it resembled those Pronaos borrowed from the Greek which the first Christian architects built before their basilicas, and which prepare us for entrance into the temple, as meditation prepares us for prayer. The first *allegro* which follows is written in a powerful style: its logical ideas are concise, inexorable. These qualities are the distinctive stamp of Mr. Schumann's works. Let us hasten to say, that they not only do not exclude originality, but in a fashion provoke it, and cause it to stand out more boldly. The aria on pages 14 and 15 is one of the most perfect things we know. Although the author wrote on the margin, "Senza Passione," it is characterized by the most impassioned *abandon*. Passion is in truth revealed there indirectly and disguisedly: it is rather betrayed than blazed forth. But it is true and deep, appealing to our inmost sensibilities. Let us remark here, that Mr. Schumann's music is more especially addressed to meditative minds, — to those serious souls who are never contented with a superficial view, who dive to the lowest depths to seek the hidden pearl. The more intimately we understand his thoughts, the more force and life we find; the more we study, the more we are struck by the wealth and

fecundity which at first escaped us. The "Scherzo" is a fragment exceedingly remarkable for rhythm and harmonic effects.
The song in *A* (page 16, lines three and four) is ravishing.
The interlude in *re lento a la burla* (page 18), followed by a
recitative for the left hand, surprises and astonishes us: it is an
artistic feat, to give a new sense to a vulgar phrase, trivial in
itself, by the arrangement of the preceding parts. The secret
of this is only known to those who have learnt by hard labor
to handle form. Yet we would not have the delicious song in
A disappear forever after once hearing it. It is an error to
consider repetition a sign of poverty. From the public point
of view, it is indispensable to intelligence; from an artistic point
of view even, it is almost an essential condition of perspicuity,
order, and effect. Beethoven, whose creative skill and wealth
will hardly be contested, was a composer who made large use
of this style. The *scherzo* of the trios in *B* and *E*, and that of
the symphony in *A*, are among those which are repeated three
times in all.

The finale is grandly original. However tragical the course
of the original ideas may be, and in spite of the overpowering
fervor of the peroration, the general effect of this fragment is
often broken and interrupted. The length of the develop-
ments may have contributed to the uncertainty of the whole.
Perhaps, too, the poetic idea should have been indicated. The
musical idea, although complete in itself, does not suffice, in
our opinion, to explain all the details. Here the great question comes up, of poetic and picturesque music with or without programme, which, though often agitated, has rarely been
handled wisely and in good faith. It has always been inferred
that the so-called *picturesque* music laid claims to rivalry with
the pencil; that it aspired to *paint* the aspect of forests, the
undulations of the mountains, or the winding course of a stream-
et through the meadow. But it is a gratuitous absurdity. It is
very evident that things generally objective are by no means
amenable to music, and that the most ignorant landscape-
painter could reproduce a scene by a stroke of his pencil more

easily than the most accomplished musician with all the re-
sources of the most skilful orchestra. But have not these very
things, affecting the soul in a certain manner, these subjective
things, if I may so express myself, when changed into reverie,
meditation, and rapture, a singular affinity for music ? and
should not Music be able to translate them into her mysterious
tongue ? Should we conclude, from the imitation of the quail
and cuckoo in the Pastoral Symphony (at the risk of being
taxed with puerility), that Beethoven was wrong to try to
move the soul as does the sight of a smiling landscape, a fertile
country, or a village feast suddenly disturbed by an unex-
pected storm ? Does not Berlioz, in his " Harold " symphony,
strongly recall to the mind mountain-scenes .and the religious
effect of the bells, whose echo dies away in the twists and turns
of the steep path ? As for poetic music, does anybody think
that it would be indispensable to him to express the human
passions, such as love, despair, rage, to aid some stupid refrain
of romance, or some declamatory libretto ?

But it would take too much time to develop here a subject
which has more than one connection with the famous quarrel
between the classic and the romantic, — a quarrel in which the
field for discussion has never been closely marked out. Besides, our friend Berlioz has treated the question in the columns of the " Gazette Musicale ; " and we could only repeat
less effectively what he has said so well. But let us repeat
once more, for the sake of the critics, the fact that nobody
dreams of writing music as ridiculous as that which is called
picturesque. What is intended, what great men always have
intended, and always will intend to do, is to tincture music
more and more with poetry, and to render it the organ of that
part of the soul, which, if we are to believe all those who have
felt, loved, and suffered severely, is inaccessible to analysis,
and resists precise and definite expression in human speech.

We will permit ourselves to cavil in some degree with the
Concerto sans orchestre. In the first place, we consider the
title illogical; since *concerto* means a re-union of concerted in

struments. To call it a concerto without orchestra is almost the same as calling it a group of a single figure. Besides this, the title *concerto* has always been applied exclusively to pieces intended for public performance, and which, for this very reason, exact certain conditions of effect which Mr. Schumann does not seem to have considered. His work, from the shape and severity of the style, belongs rather to the class " sonata " than to that of concerto. In establishing this distinction, we do not intend to assign a special, invariable shape to each class of composition. In old times, a concerto was divided into three parts : the first with three solos, interspersed with the orchestra; the adagio; then the rondo. Field, in his last concerto, has given the adagio by way of a second solo. Moscheles' " concerto fantastique " united the three parts in a single one. Weber first, and Mendelssohn afterwards, to say nothing of Mr. Herz in second concerto, tried a similar shape. In fine, liberties from all sides have extended and diversified the form, which is surely progress, though not in the direction of our observations. But in music, as in literature, there are two grand divisions, — things written or composed for public representation or execution; that is, things clear in sense, brilliant in expression, and grand in style: and then secret works from mere solitary inspiration, where fancy rules, which are of a nature to be appreciated but by few. Mr. Schumann's concerto belongs wholly to this latter class. Therefore it is wrong, in our opinion, to give it a name which seems to call for a large audience, and promises a splendor which we seek in vain. But our criticism shall be confined to this German error ; for the work in itself, considered as a sonata, is rich and powerful. The beginning and the melody of the first allegro are magnificent: in their treatment we find the same qualities of style which we have already admired elsewhere. The finale especially, a sort of toccata in $\frac{6}{16}$, is extremely interesting from its harmonic combinations, whose novelty might shock the ear were it not for the great rapidity of the movement. We will close this inadequate sketch with the hope that Mr. Schumann

will soon make known to France such of his productions as
have hitherto been confined to Germany. Young pianists will
be strengthened by his example, in a system of composition
which has met with much opposition among us, but which is,
ever, the only one of the present time which contains germs of
duration. Those who love art will rejoice in this new hope
for the future, and will turn still more confidently to the country which has given us, in these latter days, such men as Weber, Schubert, and Meyerbeer.   LISZT.

C.

EXTRACT FROM A LETTER BY FRANZ LISZT.

. . . " I enjoyed daily and hourly intercourse with Schumann
while in Leipsic (especially at the beginning of 1840); and my
knowledge of his works thus became still more intimate and
deep.   Since first becoming acquainted with his compositions, I had played several of them in private circles of Milan,
Vienna, &c., but without being able to win any attention. They
were, happily, too far beyond the absolutely erroneous, vapid
taste of that time, to be brought into the haughty empire of
applause. They did not suit the public, and few pianists understood them.   Even in Leipsic, where I performed ' The Carnival' at my second concert in the Gewandhaus, I did not succeed in gaining my customary applause.   The musicians there,
who considered themselves connoisseurs, had (with few exceptions) too dull ears to comprehend this charming, tasteful
'Carnival,' so full of harmonious and artistic fancy. I do not
doubt that the time will come when this work will be unanimously awarded a place by the side of the thirty-three variations on Diabelli's waltzes by Beethoven (which, in my opinion, it surpasses in melodic invention and pregnancy). The
repeated failure of my performances of Schumann's compositions, both in private and in public, discouraged me from en

tering them on the programmes for my concerts, which followed in rapid succession, and which I but seldom planned myself, partly from want of time, partly from negligence and weariness when at the height of my fame, — committing this duty now to this person, now to that one, according to the whim of the moment. This was an error which I afterwards recognized, and indeed regretted, when I learned, that, for an artist who would deserve the name, it is far better to displease the public than to let himself be moved by its caprice; and every practising artist will be especially exposed to this danger if he does not decide at once to answer for his convictions seriously and consistently, and to perform those things he considers the best, whether people like it or not.

" So too, no matter how excusable my cowardice in respect to Schumann's compositions may have been, I have unintentionally set a *bad example*, which I can hardly repair. The current of custom, and the slavery of artists, who, for the preservation and improvement of their life and fame, are swayed by popular opinion and applause, is so subduing, that it is exceedingly difficult even for the boldest and best-disposed (among whom I am vain enough to class myself) to defend their better self against all the greedy, confused crowd, who are unworthy to be called musicians."

LIST OF ROBERT SCHUMANN'S PUBLISHED WORKS.

I. — PIANO COMPOSITIONS.

1. — *For Piano (two hands).*

Album for Youth (Op. 68)
Album Leaves (Op. 124)
Allegro (Op. 8)
Arabesque (Op. 18)
Flower Pieces (Op. 19)
Bunte Blätter (Op. 99)
Carnival (Scènes Mignonnes) (Op. 9)
Piano Sonatas, three (Op. 118)
Piano Compositions, seven, in fughetta form (Op. 126)
Davidsbündler Dances (Op. 6)
Etudes de Concert (6), from Paganini's Capriccios (Op. 10)
Fantasia (Op. 17)
Fantasies, three (Op. 111)
Fantasies (2 numbers) (Op. 12)
Carnival Pranks in Vienna (Op. 26)
Morning Songs (Op. 133)
Humoresque (Op. 20)
Impromptu on a theme by Clara Wieck (Op. 5)
Interludes (2 numbers) (Op. 4)
Kinderscenen (Op. 15)
Kreisleriana (Op. 16)
Night Scenes (Op. 23)
Novelettes (4 parts) (Op. 21)
Papillons (Op. 2)
Romanzas, three (Op. 28)
Scherzo, Jig, Romanza, and Finale (Op. 32)
Sketches for the Pedal-Piano (Op. 58)
Sonata (F-minor) (Op. 14)
Sonata (F-sharp-minor) (Op. 11)

271

Sonata (G-minor) (Op. 22)
Studies for the Pedal-Piano (Op. 56)
Studies from Paganini's Capriccios (Op. 3)
Thème sur le Nom Abegg (Op. 1)
Toccata (Op. 7)
Four Fugues (Op. 72)
Four Marches (1849) (Op. 76)
Waldscenen (Op. 82)

2.— For Piano (four hands)

Ball Scenen (Op. 109)
Pictures from the East (Op. 66)
Piano Compositions, twelve (Op. 85)
Kinder Ball, six easy dances (Op. 130)

3.— For Two Pianos.

Andante and Variations (Op. 46)

4.— For Piano, with Accompaniment of different Instruments.

Adagio and Allegro with Horn (Op. 70)
Fantasias with Clarionet (Op. 73)
Fantasias with Violin and Violoncello (Op. 88)
Legendary Pictures with Bass-Viol (Op. 113)
Legendary Tales with Clarionet and Bass-Viol (Op. 132)
Quartette with Violin, Bass-Viol, and Clarionet (Op. 47)
Quintette with two Violins, Viola, and Violoncello (Op. 44)
Romanza with Oboe (Op. 94)
Sonata with Violin (A-minor) (Op. 105)
Sonata with Violin (D-minor) (Op. 121)
Popular Pieces for Violoncello (Op. 102)
Trio with Violin and Violoncello (D-minor) (Op. 63)
Trio with Violin and Violoncello (F-major) (Op. 80)
Trio with Violin and Violoncello (G-minor) (Op. 110)

II.— PIANO COMPOSITIONS, WITH ORCHESTRAL ACCOMPANIMENT.

Piano Concerto (A-minor) (Op. 54)
Concert Allegro with Introduction (Op. 134)
Introduction and Allegro appassionato (Op. 92)

III. — COMPOSITIONS FOR STRINGED INSTRUMENTS.

Three String Quartettes for two Violins, Viola, and Violoncello (Op. 41)

IV. — Concert Pieces for Different Instruments with Orchestra.

Concerto for Violoncello (Op. 129)
Concert-Stück for four Horns (Op. 86)
Fantasia for Violin (Op. 131)

V. — Orchestral Compositions.

Festal Overture on the Rhine-Wine Song (Op. 123)
Overture to Geneviève (Op. 81)
Overture to Manfred (Op. 115)
Overture to the Bride of Messina (Op. 100)
Overture to Julius Cæsar (Op. 128)
Overture to Hermann and Dorothea (Op. 136)
Overture, Scherzo, and Finale (Op. 52)
Symphony (B-flat-major) (Op. 38)
Symphony (C-major) (Op. 61)
Symphony (E-flat-major) (Op. 97)
Symphony (D-minor) (Op. 120)

VI. — Organ Compositions.

Six fugues on the name of Bach (Op. 60)

VII. — Vocal Compositions.

1. — *Vocal Compositions for one voice with Piano Accompaniment*

Belshazzar, a ballad (Op. 57)
The Glove, a ballad (Op. 87)
Poet Love, a cycle of song (Op. 48)
Three Songs (Op. 31)
Three Songs (Op. 83)
Three Songs (Op. 95)
Three Lyrics (Op. 30)
Three Lyrics (Op. 119)
Woman's Love and Life (Op. 42)
Five Merry Songs (Op. 125)
Five Songs (Op. 40)
Poems of Queen Mary Stuart (Op. 135)
Album of Songs for the Young (Op. 79)
A Song-Wreath from Heine (Op. 24)
A Song-Wreath from Eichendorf (Op. 39)
A Series of Songs from J. Kerner (Op. 35)
Lyrics and Songs (4 numbers) (Op. 27; Op. 51; Op. 77; Op. 96)
Lyrics and Songs, from Wilhelm Meister (Op. 98a)

17

Lyrics and Songs (Op. 127)
Myrtles (4 numbers) (Op. 25)
Romanzas and Ballads (4 parts) (Op. 45; Op. 49; Op. 53; Op. 64)
Six Lyrics by Lenau (Op. 90)
Six Songs (Op. 89)
Six Songs (Op. 107)
Six Songs (Op. 36)
Six Lyrics (Girlish Songs) (Op. 304)
Four Songs (Op. 142) (missing in Schumann's list*)
Four Hussar Songs (Op. 117)
Twelve Songs from Rückert's "Love's Spring" (2 parts) (Op. 37)

2. — Vocal Compositions for two or more voices with Piano Accompaniment.

Three Songs for two Voices (Op. 43)
Three Songs for three Female Voices (Op. 114) (missing in Schumann's
    list †)
Three Songs for Chorus Singing (Op. 29)
Girlish Songs for two Sopranos (Op. 103)
Minnespiel by Rückert (Op. 101)
Requiem for Mignon, from "Wilhelm Meister" (Op. 98b)
Romanzas for Female Voices (2 parts) (Op. 69; Op. 91)
Spanish Love-Songs (Op. 138)
Spanish Vaudeville (Op. 74)
Four Duets for Soprano and Tenor (Op. 34)
Four Duets for Soprano and Tenor (Op. 78)

*3. — Vocal Compositions, with Instrumental or full Orchestral Accom-
paniment.*

Advent Song by Rückert (Op. 71)
To be sung on Parting (Op. 84)
The Luck of Edenhall, a ballad (Op. 143)
Paradise and the Peri (Op. 50)
The King's Son (Op. 116)
The Pilgrimage of the Rose (Op. 112)
The Minstrel's Curse (Op. 139)
Five Songs for four Male Voices and four Horns (Op. 137)
Geneviève, an opera (Op. 81)
Mass in C-major (Op. 147)
Motet by Rückert (Op. 93)
Music to Byron's "Manfred" (Op. 115)
Night Song by Hebbel (Op. 108)
New-Year's Song by Rückert (Op. 144)
Requiem (Op. 148)
Requiem for Mignon, from "Wilhelm Meister" (Op. 98b)
The Page and the Princess (4 ballads) (Op. 140)

* These Songs were composed in 1852
† These Songs were written in 1853.

4. — Vocal Compositions for Male Chorus without Accompaniment.

Three Songs (Op. 62)
Ritornella (Op. 65)
Six Songs (Op. 33)

5. — Vocal Compositions for Mixed Chorus without Accompaniment.

Five Songs (Op. 55)
Romanzas and Ballads (4 parts) (Op. 67; Op. 75; Op. 145; Op. 146)
    (missing in Schumann's list *)
Four Double Chorus Songs (Op. 141)
Four Songs (Op. 59)

VIII. — COMPOSITIONS FOR DECLAMATION.

The Ballad of the Shepherd Boy (Op. 122. No. 1)
The Fugitives, a ballad (Op. 122. No. 2.)
Fair Hedwig, a ballad (Op. 106)

IX. — UNNUMBERED COMPOSITIONS.

Three Songs for a single voice with Piano Accompaniment.
Patriotic Song for one voice with Chorus and Piano Accompaniment, (missing in Schumann's list †).
The same Song arranged for Male Chorus without Accompaniment.
Scenes from Faust, for Solo, Chorus, and Orchestral Accompaniment.
National Airs for one voice with Piano Accompaniment.

* These Songs contained in Op. 145 and 146 were composed in 1849.
† Written in 1842.